AMERICAN WAR STORIES

A Volume in the Series
VETERANS

Edited by
Brian Matthew Jordan and J. Ross Dancy

AMERICAN WAR STORIES

Veteran-Writers
and the Politics
of Memoir

MYRA MENDIBLE

University of Massachusetts Press
Amherst and Boston

ISBN 978-1-62534-631-5 (paper); 630-8 (hardcover)

Designed by Deste Roosa
Set in Cormorant Garamond, Alternate Gothic No 1 D, and American Typewriter
Printed and bound by Books International, Inc.

Cover design by Frank Gutbrod
Cover photo by Pixabay.

Library of Congress Cataloging-in-Publication Data

Names: Mendible, Myra, 1954–author.
Title: American war stories : veteran-writers and the politics of memoir /
    Myra Mendible.
Description: Amherst : University of Massachusetts Press, [2021] | Series:
    Veterans | Includes bibliographical references and index.
Identifiers: LCCN 2021017189 (print) | LCCN 2021017190 (ebook) | ISBN
    9781625346308 (hardcover) | ISBN 9781625346315 (paperback) | ISBN
    9781613769065 (ebook) | ISBN 9781613769072 (ebook)
Subjects: LCSH: Veterans' writings, American—History and criticism. |
    American literature—20th century—History and criticism. | American
    literature—21st century—History and criticism. | Politics and
    literature—United States—History—20th century. | Politics and
    literature—United States—History—20th century. | Veterans in
    literature.
Classification: LCC PS153.V48 M36 2021 (print) | LCC PS153.V48 (ebook) |
    DDC 810.9/3526970904—dc23
LC record available at https://lccn.loc.gov/2021017189
LC ebook record available at https://lccn.loc.gov/2021017190

British Library Cataloguing-in-Publication Data
A catalog record for this book is available from the British Library.

An earlier version of chapter 2 was previously published as "Saving Face: Humiliation,
Shame, and the Affective Economy of War," in *War, Literature, and the Arts* 28 (2016). An
earlier version of chapter 5 was previously published as "Silence Amid the Din of War:
Sound and Vision in Brian Turner's *My Life as a Foreign Country*," in *War, Literature and
the Arts* 32 (2020).

TO MY BELOVEDS:
Jennie, Ray, Ben, Vivi, Jonathan,
Angelina, and Amanda.

"When we love, we always strive
to become better than we are."

Wars are nothing, in the end, but stories.

—Frederick Busch, *The Night Inspector*

But this too is true: stories can save us.

—Tim O'Brien, *The Things They Carried*

CONTENTS

PREFACE

We tell ourselves stories in order to live. . . . We look for
the sermon in the suicide, for the social or moral lesson
in the murder of five.
—Joan Didion, *The White Album*

Stories are always born from endings. It is from endings that we forge new meanings, seek direction, encounter and remake ourselves. Endings—even happy ones—reek of finality and stagnation, anathema to anything that lives. Thus when wars end, war stories follow. What did it mean? Was there a purpose? Is there a moral? This need to find bits of meaning amid remnants of a former self turns warriors into storytellers. Iraq war veteran-writer Matt Gallagher says it best: memory has "a nasty habit of rescuing the worthy fragments from the garbage disposal of the mind" (*Kaboom* 292). Gallagher's service in the army ended in 2009, but his "worthy fragments" begat new stories: the war lives on in his memoir and novels, but also in workshops he leads for New York University's "Words After War" program. Like Gallagher, the veteran-writers featured in this book understand that war stories use the past to imagine the possibility of a future, that stories are means without end.

I hope this book helps rescue some "worthy fragments." I hope it gives rise to new stories: the ones critics may tell about its merits or flaws, the ones readers will share with their friends about these veterans' "rescued" memories, the ones that will be written by other veterans who will talk back to these stories with their own salvaged remnants of experience. Wars end, but stories never can. "Stories are for eternity, when memory is erased, when there is nothing to remember except the story," Tim O'Brien writes in his brilliant *The Things They Carried.* A veteran of the Vietnam War and among the finest writers of his generation, O'Brien understands that through stories, the dead can "smile and sit up and return to the world" (36, 213).

A story, pieced together from scraps of memory and from other stories, led me to this book, and while the story ended in death, it would live on in my teaching, in my writing, and in the veterans' stories that inspired this study. The story began in the summer of 2005, when, driven to understand the war that shaped my generation, I participated with a handful of scholars in a National Endowment for the Humanities seminar on the Vietnam War. Among the participants was Bob Topmiller, who at nineteen served as a navy medic in Vietnam during the siege at Khe Sanh. "Doc," as he was called, had seen firsthand what war does to the human body, and it haunted him four decades later. The war ended, and Bob came home, earned a PhD in history, authored a book on the Buddhist rebellion, founded a school for orphans in Vietnam, and wrote a powerful memoir (*Red Clay on My Boots: Encounters with Khe Sanh*). But throughout the seminar, it was clear that Bob still grieved and raged at what he saw as the unnecessary deaths and suffering of so many Americans and Vietnamese.

Bob knew that endings demand something from us: he chose history as his calling, in that way ensuring that stories about the Vietnam War—its lessons, tragedies, warnings—would not end. Bob traveled to Vietnam fourteen times, listened to stories told by victims of the My Lai massacre, witnessed the legacy of Agent Orange on the bodies and minds of children at the School of the Beloved in Hue. As historian George C. Herring notes, "Doc's efforts to come to terms with Vietnam represented a journey that never ended" (*Binding Their Wounds*, x). In 2008, a seminar colleague notified me that Bob had taken his life. This devastating news—this tragic ending to a good man's life—demanded something of me. The genesis of this book lies in that ending.

Bob mourned the "the shattered lives, broken hearts, ruined minds, and wrecked families brought on by the conflict" (Topmiller 11). His memoir, he tells us, "is their story as well as mine" (11). It reflects his effort "to make sense" of the past, but like most war stories, it was fueled by a concern for the future. Bob did not relish the "misguided admiration that suddenly surrounded [veterans]." Noting that "many young Americans in the twenty-first century admired Vietnam vets" and looked up to him (10), he asks, "Was it just as bad to idealize us as it was to demonize us?" (11). While "better than the loser image we carried after the conflict," he writes, it was no more accurate (11). I believe he understood that the stories we tell about war matter, that they shape the present in continuing cycles of remembering, revising, and reconstructing. As William Faulkner famously quipped, "The past is never dead. It isn't even past."

The story of "Vietnam" has been told in countless ways, each generation of Americans adapting it to meet the needs or sensibilities of the moment. These stories inform how a new generation of soldiers interpret their own wars, how politicians spin justifications for new wars, and how Americans respond to present conflicts. This is the political force that fuels war stories—the impetus toward a future that a past makes possible. "That's what stories are for," O'Brien tells us. "Stories are for joining the past to the future. Stories are for those late hours in the night when you can't remember how you got from where you were to where you are" (O'Brien, *Things They Carried*).

As he watched his country slipping into "a new, confusing struggle in Iraq that would create another generation of bitter, disillusioned vets and cynical chicken hawks" (11), Bob must have felt this connection between then and now, between how war stories end and others begin. Like most of the veteran-authors featured in this book, Bob never ran for political office. He served his country—and his humanity—in ways that did not fit neatly into boxes labeled "liberal" or "conservative." Bob didn't have answers to the questions that plague those who survive war; the best war memoirs do not provide answers. Answers are endings. They are definitive. Instead, war stories raise questions that it is up to each of us to mull over. Because of this ability to provoke and invoke, war stories can do more to change hearts and minds than any political spinmeister ever could.

I believe that writing is an act of hope, and all of the veteran-writers featured in this study—no matter how cynical or disillusioned they may seem—express hope by sharing their stories. "Stories are," Frederick Busch reminds us, "about ending and about endings," but they are "also the heart-felt prayer, the valiant promise, that what we have loved might live forever" (166). They carry the hope that there will always be someone to read them, that some "worthy fragments" will find their way into the stories we tell ourselves in order to live.

ACKNOWLEDGMENTS

With this book I acknowledge, along with the contributions Bob Topmiller made to the ongoing story of war, the many soldiers and veterans whose wars have not ended. I also wish to acknowledge another Bob—my friend Robert L. Hilliard, who as a young Jewish GI during World War II had the courage to expose the criminal neglect and anti-Semitism shaping American policy in occupied Europe. His refusal to remain silent saved lives and helped bring about critical reforms. Bob's powerful memoir *Surviving the Americans: The Continued Struggle of the Jews After Liberation,* along with his lifelong advocacy and undaunted concern for others, continue to impassion and inspire positive change.

I wish to express my gratitude to my friend and colleague Delphine Gras, who so generously read drafts and lovingly urged me to keep going when I thought I'd reached dead ends. To Matt Becker, my editor, thank you for believing in this work. I am also indebted to my students, past and present, who give me hope, and thus inspire me to be a better storyteller, and more importantly, storylistener. Last but always first, I am grateful to my husband, Ernesto, whom I met, many chapters ago, in a college short story class.

Myra Mendible, March 2021

AUTHOR'S NOTE

While race is a social construct with no meaningful biological significance, it has real-world consequences, some of which I highlight here. I use the labels "White" and "Black" throughout this book not to reduce a diverse range of individuals and cultures to an identity defined by skin color, but to reflect the fact that such categorizations has shaped and continue to shape the experiences of racialized people in the United States, specifically the treatment of veterans and soldiers. I use "Black" to refer to individuals who self-identify or are identified by others as persons of African descent. Similarly, I use the pan-ethnic label "Latino/a" to refer to people of Latin American, Spanish, and Spanish Caribbean ancestry, understanding that it homogenizes peoples whose histories, language usage, and citizenship status differ. My aim is to show that despite their differences, those identified as "Black" or "Latino/a" have experienced group-based discrimination and cultural exclusion within a racialized social order.

AMERICAN WAR STORIES

Introduction

PLAUSIBLE DENIABILITY
Real Soldiers, True Fictions

Whenever you find a doctrine of "nonpolitical"
esthetics affirmed with fervor, look for its politics.

—Kenneth Burke, *Rhetoric of Motives*

"This book does not pretend to be history," Philip Caputo writes in the opening lines of his award-winning Vietnam War memoir *Rumor of War*. "It has
nothing to do with politics, power, strategy, influence . . . or foreign policy"
but is "simply a story about war" (xiii). With this disclaimer, Caputo both
denies and affirms the validity of his account. After all, soldier memoirists
are neither bound to the historian's claims to accuracy nor tainted by the
politician's self-serving inauthenticity. This ability to have it both ways—to
be "simply a story" and credible firsthand account, gives war memoirs their
intrinsic political power. As stories, they help shape our perceptions of reality
and history. They substantiate, through the particulars of individual characters
and experiences, elusive concepts such as heroism, courage, honor, and duty,
concepts that are instrumental in the figurative construction, legitimation,
and commemoration of war. As memoirs, they bid for our trust as earnestly
as any politician. This mirrors a contradiction veteran-author Samuel Hynes
points to when he notes that "the man-who-was-there asserts his authority as
the only true witness of his war; but the truth that he claims to tell is compromised by the very nature of memory and language" (25). As figments of
memory, war memoirs are both factually dishonest and emotionally true. Yet
their epistemic uncertainty makes them no less consequential: the primacy of
firsthand experience endures, the sense that we have been privy to something
that "feels" authentic. The affective and cognitive responses memoirs evoke
are inherently political, shaping judgments about the efficacy or failure of
American power, strategy, and foreign policy.

    American War Stories explores the complex relationship between memory
and politics in the context of postmodern war, focusing on memoirs written

by veterans of the Vietnam, Iraq, and Afghanistan conflicts. It argues that soldiers' shared memories play an important, though underexamined, *political* function, informing how Americans remember their wars and reinforcing or subverting the legitimacy of American power.[1] Ask most civilians what they know about the Vietnam or Iraq Wars and most will draw from books they have read and movies they have seen. Few will cite history textbooks as their source, and fewer still will recall factual details (the date of a battle, the exact number of casualties). Representation and remembrance are always politically situated, always contingent on social relations of power and privilege—on the lens through which events are seen and interpreted. As Stuart Hall reminds us, "Representation is a vastly different notion from that of reflection. It implies the active work of selecting and presenting, of structuring and shaping; not merely the transmitting of an already existing meaning, but the more active labor of making things mean" (64). These choices matter precisely because they have political effects—the power to inspire and mobilize, to shape interests and identities, to inform constructions of "Americanness." My interdisciplinary approach draws on historical, political, literary, ethnographic, and critical military studies research. I aim to show how veterans' war stories are both derivative and representative of our political beliefs and culture, an expression of and at times a rebuttal to the nation's stated values and objectives. As one aspect of war's many "meaning-making" functions, soldiers' accounts contribute to public narratives and debates about war; respond to prevailing attitudes toward government, patriotism, shame, and honor; and reflect the nation's broader postmodern crisis of truth and authority.

  This book's primary concerns are animated by three founding claims. First, that veterans retain a stake in the decision making, judgments, outcomes, and politicizing forces of war making, a return of sorts on the investment that their service entails. This view implicitly rejects the disclaimer, made by both memoirists themselves and their critics, that soldiers "aren't political."[2] Second, that the memoir's ambivalent relationship with "truth" is politically expedient, as the form's generic and epistemological instability masks its politics and facilitates "the interplay of disclosure and disguise."[3] This literary sleight of hand gives the genre a built-in alibi: the plausible deniability provided by memory's lapses and imperfections. Building on this claim, I treat the memoirs examined in this study as "true fictions": "true" because their perceived credibility and authenticity stem from their source ("real soldiers") and "fictions" because they are stories born of memory (representations). A final founding claim underlying this study is that the convergence of credibility and marketability make the military memoir a persuasive form of political communication in post-9/11 US society. Americans increasingly distrust their own government and media institutions, but service members today return to the most proveteran homeland in decades. This translates into cultural and symbolic capital, turning the warrior into a trusted brand and lending their memoirs credibility and moral authority at a time when both are in short supply. While this promilitary disposition privileges veterans' perspectives, the memoir's popular appeal further amplifies their voices.[4] Some critics contend that the genre "now rivals fiction in popularity and critical esteem and exceeds it in cultural currency" (Couser 3).[5] Military memoirs are capitalizing on this trend: once the purview of a specialized, mostly male readership, the genre now attracts diverse audiences. Their reach extends beyond consumption to production, as today's war stories are just as likely to feature grunts as generals, and women have moved from the periphery to the very centers of military life.[6] This combination of factors gives veteran-memoirists an influential platform and makes this study's focus timely, especially in light of America's casual militarism and the military's increasing politicization—cultural trends I take up in this study.

The claim that veterans remain deeply vested in their civic identity is perhaps a risky one to make in an environment marked by cynicism and disengagement. Many Americans express frustration and even disdain for political institutions and doubt their ability to effect substantive positive changes in their lives. Motivated by pragmatic concerns (economic needs and personal security), the citizenry seems increasingly detached from what they perceive as the machinations of Washington elites and far too politically polarized to put much stock in the prosocial attitudes and solidarity that are hallmarks of civic duty. This attitudinal move away from an idealistic civic engagement might also inform how some soldiers and veterans perceive their own role in political processes. Some scholars contend that today's all-volunteer military no longer sustains a citizen-soldier tradition, an ideal that gave veterans a privileged role in the nation's political arena and affirmed their status and responsibility as civic actors. Ronald Krebs explains that this tradition suggests a force that is "representative of society at large; soldiers whose service is motivated by a sense of duty to the nation; and soldiers whose primary identity is that of citizens, temporarily in uniform" (155). In the absence of a draft, critics assert, citizenship is less about obligation and duty to country than it is about "a culture of rights in which civic virtue is not prized, obligations are hardly acknowledged, and market-based solutions have proliferated" (158). With the links between military service and citizen-ship presumably severed, the soldier's service is no longer seen as an integral component of national belonging and shared commitment but simply as a career choice. Thus, Elliot Abrams and Andrew Bacevich proclaim that "the mythic tradition of the citizen-soldier is dead" (19). In this view, the citizen-soldier has been replaced by homo economicus, a being "motivated by the skills, salary, and educational benefits that military service bequeaths, rather than by patriotism or obligation" (Moskos 3). This suggests that military service members are a kind of contractual labor force whose only incentive is "getting the job done."

But whatever their motives for enlisting, soldiers' service to what stands as a pivotal institution in America implies membership in its political commu-nity, a community that shares an interest in the defense of territory as well as personal rights. As R. Claire Snyder points out, "Situating military service within a broad array of civic practices should remind us that a democratic society has a military not just to defend its borders but also to defend its democratic principles," including participatory citizenship (9). We should note, for example, that America's 22.7 million military veterans tend to vote at higher rates than nonveterans (Teigen). The identity of the soldier is bound up in concepts that cannot be reduced to tangible rewards (money for college or access to technical training). While many will cite such reasons as motives, self-interest is compromised by the experience of war, the bonds it forges, and the moral obligations it imposes. As Gulf War veteran and author Anthony Swofford puts it in his memoir *Jarhead*, "The men who go to war and live are spared for the single purpose of spreading bad news when they return, the bad news about the way the war is fought and why, and by whom for whom" (253). Even when not "spreading bad news" soldiers invariably invoke the language of sacrifice, fraternity, and duty in their representations. Their memoirs suggest that they differentiate themselves from private contractors or mercenaries, even when they have difficulty articulating why they are different or what that difference demands of them. Iraq War veteran and author Phil Klay admits, "When I try to trace the precise lines of responsibility of a civilian versus a veteran, I get all tangled up." Years after his enlistment and service, he still wonders "what obligations I incurred as a result of that choice, and what obligations I share with the rest of my country toward our wars and to the men and women who fight them." Yet he adamantly defies the "notion of a military filled with ne'er-do-wells who are in it only for the money" not only because it is insulting and false but, more importantly, because "it takes the decision to put one's life at risk for one's country and transforms it, as if by magic, into a self-interested act." He insists that "people join the military to be a part of something greater than themselves, and ultimately it's deeply important for service members to be able to feel their sacrifices had a purpose." Despite the frustration that veterans may feel over the execution of the war or its outcomes, Klay argues that many see their political engagement as an extension of their role as soldiers and citizens:

> I've met veterans who, horrified by the human cost of our wars overseas, have joined groups like the International Refugee Assistance Project or the International Rescue Committee. I've met veterans who've gone into public service. . . . I've met veterans who've lobbied Congress, worked to fight military sexual assault, established literary non-profits, or worked to make public service—military or otherwise—an expectation within American society. A recent analysis of Census data shows that, compared with their peers, veterans volunteer more, give more to charity, vote more often, and are more likely to attend community meetings and join civic groups. This is the kind of civic engagement necessary for the functioning of a democracy. ("Citizen-Soldier")

Similarly, Iraq War vet and writer Matt Gallagher reminds us that after 9/11, men and women joined the military precisely because of that altruistic impulse: "The people I knew who joined the military then weren't stereotypes: We didn't want to kill. We wanted to serve. We weren't losers. We were idealists. We sought to do something bigger than ourselves. We sought to do something just" ("Father's Impossible Promise").

Beyond parroting the obligatory "thanks for your service" or referring to all service members as "heroes," most Americans know little about their soldiers. This disconnect between civilian and military life leads civilians to make all kinds of assumptions about what motivates men and women to enlist, about their "patriotism," even about who they vote for. As Jack Dempsey points out, we "fill gaps in our understanding of others with stereotypes and assumptions. The American army is especially susceptible to this dynamic, as few Americans have direct experience with military service. Because of this . . . soldiers can become a blank slate upon which we might imagine the best, or worst, of America" (xv). Not all soldiers are heroes—nor are they mindless tools of the state or underachievers with no other career options. Such characterizations disregard empirical evidence and are themselves politically situated, filtered through personal biases or through a postpolitical lens in which "the market" reigns as sole arbiter of value and self-interest trumps broader concerns. They are also ahistorical, for as I show in the first chapter, these assumptions ignore a long history of veteran activism and civic participation.

POLITICS BY OTHER MEANS

Politics is not simply about elections, campaigns, or organized movements. Writing itself can be a political act. In "Why I Write," George Orwell identifies what he sees as the four primary motives for writing. Along with egotism, and aesthetic and historical aims, he proposes that in varying degrees, all writers are motivated by a political purpose: "Desire to push the world in a certain direction, to alter other peoples' idea of the kind of society that they should strive after." In his view, "no book is genuinely free from political bias" and, in fact, "the opinion that art should have nothing to do with politics is itself a political attitude" (5). I agree, and hope to show that as writers, veterans and soldiers convey attitudes that reflect political subjectivities—for instance, attitudes toward authority or the obligations and limits of patriotism. They also implicitly contribute to something beyond their own egos or personal gain. The act of writing sparks connections between the personal experience of war and broader questions about America's exercise of military force. Veterans' stated motives for sharing their stories vary, that is, to advocate change, help others, or help themselves. Some seek cathartic relief, others see writing as a way to memorialize, inform, or warn. But in choosing memoir rather than fiction as the vehicle for their stories, they expose themselves to public scrutiny and judgment, unable to hide behind imaginary events and characters to disavow their own opinions or actions. As "unsurrogated narrator," to use Vivian Gornick's apt term, memoirists pick through scraps left behind by personal experience—sorting, discarding, revising, judging, and assembling to create a story (7). They engage in a personal process of self-creation as writing gives shape to otherwise inchoate or unintelligible dispositions. Writing can spark the emergence of an individual's political consciousness, forging connections between the articulation of memories and their implications for questions of power, authority, and the legitimacy of the state. At the same time, authors must navigate competing interests— between what their editor wants, the public expects, the uniform dictates, and their conscience demands. As a result, soldier-memoirists step onto another battlefield, now wielding the proverbial pen in a symbolic, but no less consequential, battle for hearts and minds. The act of "representing" is, after all, an exercise of power, a way of "standing in" and "speaking for" (presenting another's point of view, telling their story) or influencing how an event is remembered, understood, articulated, or contested. Representations of reality help produce political culture and, more importantly, "can also transform it" (Krebs 170). The reflective and transformative potential inherent in the memoir as a literary form suggests that what begins as a personal journey can ultimately breach gaps between the personal and the political in ways that writers may not have intended or anticipated.

Implicit in the choice to share one's personal story with the outside world is a desire for recognition—not in terms of status or achievement but as acknowledgment that one's experiences have value, that they are part of a group's or nation's larger story. By contributing to a story of war that is personal but ultimately public—veterans' memoirs entail a social gesture, a way of straddling the "I" that recalls and the "we" that commemorates. As Nancy Miller argues, memoirs use personal experience not as an end but as a means to connect with a broader community. Similarly, Julie Rak suggests that memoirs "explore—and upset—the balance between public and private, personal and political" and help articulate an individual's "imagined relationship with others in a public sphere" (211–12). This movement from private to public is why memoir has the potential to shape social action. Soldier-writers acknowledge that they are always walking a fine line "between romance and vision, between reality and imagination, between propaganda and what you lean on to survive" (Scranton and Gallagher xiii). They must traverse the distance that differentiates witnessing from testifying, the event and its representation; this is the realm of politics, where compromises and choices are made, where the critical differences between remembering and memorializing are negotiated, and where certain points of view are privileged. Their published memoirs reflect not only the outcome of this personal journey but also a kind of negotiated settlement, a truce that aligns economic forces ("selling" the manuscript to potential presses, "branding" themselves for readers, navigating the marketing and publicity circuit); aesthetic demands (forging a compelling "literary" work while remaining true to the "real" story); and political currents (the public's prevailing attitudes toward a particular war, the level of vitriol or patriotic rhetoric feeding those attitudes). Veterans "are key protagonists in the negotiation of relations between geopolitics, the state, the

military, and society" (Bulmer and Eichler 162). Their memoirs offer readers a
look behind the wall that separates civilian from military life, and while this
glance is partial and short-lived, it can deepen Americans' relationship with
the service members they claim to support. Veterans' accounts also express
broader cultural vicissitudes and power struggles over who is authorized to
speak, whose "truths" we trust, and what stories shape public memory.

Reading countless military memoirs in preparation for this book, I encoun-
tered views and perspectives across a wide ideological spectrum. Most are
not reducible to a party line or a sound bite, despite the stereotype, often
exploited by the Right in American politics, of service members as gung-ho
patriots. But how these authors interpret their actions, the tone and attitudes
they convey, and the narrative choices they make are inherently political,
as these express judgments about the ways that America wages its wars,
for better or worse. Some may rail against incompetent leaders or question
America's benevolent motives for war, while others draw on a wellspring of
patriotic themes to shape their experiences into redemptive stories; in most
cases, however, critiques and affirmations of America's strategies or policies
are implicit—to be inferred by readers in their encounter with the story and
its characters. While most veterans claim unit cohesion and camaraderie as
primary factors in combat motivation (as opposed to patriotism or fighting
for a cause), soldiers also cite ideological reasons as important incentives
(liberation, freedom, democracy). Many are neither indifferent nor uninformed politically. In fact, studies suggest that today's professional American
soldier is often "politically savvy," "amazingly in touch with the pressing issues
of the day," and aware of key "policy debates" (Wong et al. 19–21). Veteran
memoirists can expose the negative outcomes of leadership decisions or the
discrepancies between what the public is told and what they witnessed ("we
are winning the war" or "we will be greeted as liberators"). Their stories map
the intriguing intersection where national politics, personal memory, and
collective history interact and often collide.

Yet in the course of my research, I was surprised to discover a dearth of
academic books focused on contemporary American military memoirs, and
fewer still concerned with their politics.[7] Most monographs that are available blend war films, blogs, poetry, and fiction into their analyses. Others
tend to read soldiers' memoirs as trauma narratives rather than as literary
works that reflect the writer's aesthetic choices and political agency. As Iraq
War veteran-author Benjamin Schrader acknowledges, "Many examinations
of veterans fail to fully recognize the ways in which veterans are subjects

(political agents fighting to reshape the lives of themselves and others) rather than objects (waiting for medical/administrative attention)" (65). I made the decision early on to focus exclusively on war memoirs, excluding "milblogs" (military blogs). While these give soldiers ready access to an online readership and expand their reach, the aims, form, and effects of blogging differ significantly from published memoirs and merit discrete analyses. Blogs offer soldiers a less filtered and more spontaneous platform to air their views, an almost "real time" broadcast of events perceived through the fog of war rather than the haze of memory. Although there are certainly important political repercussions related to milblogs, my interest is in the ways that memoirs negotiate the ever-shifting lines between fiction and nonfiction, history and memory. Memoir is the most intimate form of storytelling, one born out of a dramatic event and its aftermath; this is a tricky terrain for storytelling, one with wide latitude for veering off the factual or descriptive and into the interpretive. Unlike milblogs, the published memoir is the culmination, at its best, of months or years of self-reflection and self-evaluation, an intensely personal search for understanding and meaning. Soldier-authors are also something of a breed apart: they are far more likely to write about their experiences if they are deployed individually rather than with their own unit (Kleinreesink). Their "outsider" position can foster a certain critical distance and a motivation to share their perspective.[8]

WHOSE MEMORIES ARE THESE, ANYWAY?

The Vietnam, Iraq, and Afghanistan Wars have done what wars have always done—generate great poetry and fiction.[9] For those who have never stepped foot on a battlefield, war stories are not simply popular entertainment but ways of knowing; they provide a basis for forming judgments about the nation's leadership, the consequences of certain choices and actions, and the effects of war on its participants. They transport viewers and readers into the subjective experience of war, and while contingent on the whims of selectivity and perspective, contribute to public memory. This slide from individual subjectivity to collective memory is more likely when individual experiences resonate with historically significant national events. Since this book focuses on what is arguably a most historically significant kind of national event, the experience of war, it is less concerned with soldiers' memoirs as chronicles of personal experience than as distillations of cultural history—stories produced, circulated, and sometimes incorporated into a citizenry's repertoire of collective myths and ideological struggles. When a war is turned into a site of memory—whether through historical texts, fictions, movies, or memoirs—what is known about it refers not so much to the "actual event" but to "a canon of existent medial constructions, to the narratives and images circulating in a media culture" (Erll and Nünning 392). This suggests that the line dividing history and fiction becomes, in public memory, mutable and even irrelevant in shaping how wars are remembered. Similarly, critics increasingly question the boundaries between memory, fiction, and history, for as historian Yuval Harari posits, soldiers' memoirs are among the "most influential historical texts ever to be written" and probably shape the public's image of war more than any other source (19). Memoir's basis in "reality" aligns it with history, while its emotional pull borrows fiction's persuasive power. Images and stories about war are always poised at this intersection between self and nation, a point of encounter that shapes how we imagine our history and cultural identity.

This is, of course, a dialogical and coproductive process. While I suggest that veterans' stories feed into the discourses of nation, they also draw from them. The stories that individuals and cultures tell about their past are always aligned with "culture-specific configurations" (Neumann). Preexisting cultural narratives frame how wars are interpreted and remembered, as well as what meanings we may ascribe to our experiences of war. The most pervasive and persuasive representations of war in both political discourses and literary texts are those that activate these schemas of war remembrance, drawing from the images, myths, and tropes that a culture uses to apprehend past wars. These act as templates through which later wars are understood and function at the political level to intensify responses and mobilize citizens during present conflicts (Ashplant et al. 34). For example, veteran and author David Buchanan argues that critics should "examine war literature according to the symbolic scapegoats it creates" (7). He identifies the "savage Indian" stereotype as one template that informs Americans' perceptions of war to this day (8). Drawing from cultural images and tropes related to the frontier wars, both civilians and service members superimpose these on current conflicts, framing how they respond to events in the present. Soldiers overlay this template on "their own war experiences because they have become a subconscious part of their national identity" (7). Buchanan points to Vietnam soldiers' use of the term "Indian Country" when referring to Viet Cong–controlled areas, to the military's use of Native nomenclature for the machinery and weaponry of war (i.e., Tomahawk missiles, Apache and Black Hawk helicopters), and to the name given the mission to kill Osama bin Laden: Geronimo. But this template also frames political rhetoric when leaders want to "circle the wagons" or "rouse the cavalry"—as when Donald Rumsfeld gave a speech at an army base in 2003 equating US soldiers with nineteenth-century Indian fighters.[10] The politics of such a vernacular is obscured by its familiarity; such tropes are so ubiquitous that few Americans take notice of them, despite their evocative power.

These cultural tropes and images rile us to sympathize with a hero or to despise an enemy; they enact metaphysical conflicts of good versus evil and evoke a range of moral and ethical judgments. Mediated tales of Arab men as uncivilized, irrational, and sexist, for example, have long fed our cultural imaginary and fueled the politics of war.[11] John Esposito argues that media-driven phobia of the "Green Menace" (the color of Islam) "has profoundly affected American perceptions of Islam and the Middle East" (203). As Iraq War veteran Mike Prysner testified during the 2008 "Winter Soldier" hearings, racism is "a more important weapon than a rifle, a tank, a bomber, or a battleship. . . . More destructive than an artillery shell or a bunker buster, or a tomahawk missile" (IVAW). Stripped of causality or context, racist "templates" function at both the political and personal levels; in the former, leaders can activate the psychic charge embedded in these meanings to gain support for anti-Muslim policies or Middle East invasions—while in the latter they inform how the individual soldier-author interprets and recounts their war experiences. These cultural assignations do not reproduce a preexisting "reality." Rather, they help define and constitute it. As some of the memoirs examined in this book suggest, they form the basis of predispositions toward the enemy, frame readers' expectations about what is "true" or "realistic," and affect soldiers' behavior in the field.

Granted access to the warrior's unique perspective, readers may also be initiated into a way of seeing and interpreting the world. But this is never an "innocent" or simple exchange. As Stanley Fish argues, "It is interpretive communities, rather than either the text or reader, that produce meanings" (465). That is, readers are situated in time and space; we bring to our reading of war stories certain interpretive strategies and expectations. Truth in this sense is a matter of convention—a way of telling that conforms to civilians' sensibilities and mythic conceptions of war. How readers identify and situate themselves within a political and social genealogy plays a pivotal role in their narrative expectations and, more importantly, their foreign policy opinions. In particular, gender and political affiliation are significant predictors of attitudes toward the Afghanistan and Iraq Wars. A study of male and female West Point cadets, for example, found that male conservatives expressed the most favorable attitudes toward sending troops to both Afghanistan and Iraq; including gender and political party into advanced statistical models explained most or all the effects of military affiliation on support for both wars (Rohall et al. 74). As I argue in chapter 3, veteran-writers navigate the benefits and perils of credibility in diverse ways, but gender further complicates how authority is granted and evaluated.

When soldiers' stories do not conform to prescribed generic conventions or are not easily refracted through our mythic lens, their legitimacy is called into question. Female soldiers face a double bind in this regard: their narrative authority is subject to gendered assumptions and cultural predispositions. The "Green Menace" is not just a set of negative stereotypes about our Others; it is also a lens through which we see ourselves. Through this cultural lens, "our" women enjoy equality and freedom; "theirs" are subjugated, veiled, or victimized. Female veterans' memoirs can paint a more complex picture, for while male soldiers have limited access to Afghan and Iraqi women, female service members may often interact with them on a personal level. Sarah M. Jackson, who served as army operations officer in charge of a seven-hundred-person-unit Afghan military base, recounts the warm friendships she developed with some Afghan women who, despite extreme poverty and hardship, showed immense courage and resilience. Jackson's memoir *The Devil Dealt the Cards: One Female Soldier's Account of Combined Action in Afghanistan* also provides a more nuanced view of the Afghan soldiers she oversaw, noting that while some treated her with resentment or hostility, others "were extremely respectful and went to great lengths not to offend me" (79). Some kindly welcomed her and shared meals and stories about their families. Jackson explains that the "degree of restrictions placed on Afghan women depended on how strictly or loosely [the local *mullahs*] interpreted the Koran" (77). "Overall," Jackson writes, "most of the Afghans worked well with our females, some begrudgingly at first but eventually warming to the idea" (80). Her descriptions of Sahil, for example, a young male interpreter with whom she "developed a respectful but affectionate friendship," counters stereotypes; Sahil "was thoughtful, smart, kind, and devoted" (80). Upon her departure, Colonel Durrani, a battle-seasoned Afghan warrior with whom she worked at the base, presents Jackson with "a beautiful set of light blue prayer beads," assuring her that "instead of reciting prayers to Allah with each bead" she could repeat, "Jesus, Jesus, Jesus" (172). Like many other veteran-writers, Jackson insists that she does "not promote any political angle" (10). But her complex rendering of Afghans defies cultural expectations, fostering the kind of receptivity and mutual acceptance that can influence foreign policy views.

Clearly, factors unrelated to content coproduce a text's meanings and help warrant its claims. In America, the war stories we expect to read—and the ones likely to be published and turned into Hollywood movies—tend to be redemptive and rehabilitative. This frame imposes a burden on soldier-writers, a duty to enlighten readers with their "truths" and moral lessons, to bestow a knowledge that they alone possess. But that "knowledge" is validated only when it conforms to the reader's preconceptions and generic conventions. Veteran-author Roy Scranton, for example, challenges what he calls the popular "trauma hero myth" that "informs our politics, shapes our news reports, and underwrites our history." This myth dominates academic interpretations of war literature and "affects whom we vote for" ("Trauma Hero"). Most important here is Scranton's insistence that "understanding the problem of American political violence demands recognizing soldiers as agents of national power and understanding what kind of work the trauma hero is doing when he comes bearing witness in his bloody fatigues." While these "trauma heroes" are certainly inspirational models of personal strength and resilience, the political work they perform is significant. In *Words of Hurt: Reading the Literature of Trauma*, Kali Tal shows how memories of individual psychic traumas, through their telling and retelling, "enter the vocabulary of the larger culture where they become tools for the construction of national myths" (6). Tal argues that the cultural representation of traumatic experience is always political. In my view, the trauma hero's struggles and ultimate recovery are readily exploited as models of national triumph over adversity: war as the staging ground for representing American mettle. An adherence to generic expectations, what William Dean Howells described as the American taste for "a tragedy with a happy ending," fosters expectations beyond the story: predisposed to want uplifting tales of survival and recovery, civilians sanctify their soldiers or pathologize them as traumatized victims in need of "support." Such expectations fuel marketing campaigns: "self-help" and "survivor" memoirs flood America's literary marketplace with stories of recovery that follow tidy conventions—protagonists who take us on predictable journeys from psychic or physical wounding through struggle to ultimate triumph. These tropes and stereotypes are not merely "fictions" circulating through media and entertainment forms. They are discursive forms of power that fortify certain truth claims and invalidate others. Since controlling the meanings of the past involves ideological policing, soldiers' personal experiences can be recruited into broader efforts to control or interpret collective memory. This implicates soldier-memoirists, despite their intentions, in competing efforts to control, manage, and instrumentalize memory, as their narratives can be appropriated and exploited by "memory entrepreneurs" seeking legitimacy for a particular political agenda or rendering of the past (Jelin). The "I" that overcomes the horrors of war deflects attention away from a war's negative outcomes toward its heroic survivors. Veterans' shared memories, imperfect as memories are with gaps, inconsistencies, and embellishments, become part of a culture's discursive toolkit, the "scripts" that situate events within the national story and help positions for or against war "make sense."

THE PERSONAL IS POLITICAL

I do not mean to suggest that the memoirs discussed in this book all extoll overt political messages or act as forms of propaganda. My understanding of politics erodes crude distinctions between "public" and "private"—between affairs related to the state and those involving personal choices and experiences. As I noted earlier, politics is not just what happens in campaigns and elections, in government buildings or backroom dealmaking among elites. It mediates our daily encounters, making its presence felt in boardrooms and bedrooms, in schoolyard and prison yard. Feminists have long asserted the inextricable links between these domains, pointing to the many ways that politics is at work in routine social activities, interactions, and relationships. Some critics argue that the distinction between the personal and the political or between private and public is itself a fiction that supports an oppressive status quo. Here again veterans' memoirs offer important insights. Soldiers' memoirs suggest diverse ways that politics is performed, experienced, and transacted through the bodies of soldiers. In this sense, the conception and reception of the soldier's embodied experiences are one source of national identity formation, one means of giving emotional weight to notions about the American body politic.[12] Government policies help construct and police racialized and gendered bodies, which in turn frame public perceptions of bodies: whose bodies pose a threat, whose are unruly and in need of restriction and control, and whose can be admitted into the fold. This dynamic is reflected in veterans' memoirs, as policies come to be inscribed and enacted on the bodies of soldiers.

The body is a politically charged template for imparting meanings and ascribing cultural values. US military culture draws from certain preexisting assumptions about gendered bodies, informing institutional policies and practices with patriarchal norms that can be toxic to female service members.[13] As more female combat vets tell their own stories, these gender norms assume new meanings. The title of Mary Jennings Hegar's memoir *Shoot Like a Girl: One Woman's Dramatic Fight in Afghanistan and on the Homefront* intentionally disrupts gendered associations, while her story also exposes their enduring influence. Hegar, a decorated Air National Guard pilot who served three tours in Afghanistan, recounts the sexual assault she endured under the guise of an annual flight physical. The general doctor refuses to accept her ob-gyn's exam results from the previous week and threatens to fail her for "psychological reasons" (75). Terrified of losing her pilot's certification, Hegar is subjected to an aggressive, painful, humiliating gynecological "exam." He "had complete control over my future," she writes, and she felt powerless to stop him (76). Even after the doctor admits what he did, his chain of command protects him; a few months later he is even selected as the medical group's "Company Grade Officer of the Year" (80). The doctor was able to use a common weapon in the patriarchal arsenal: the pathologizing of female resistance or physical complaint as "hysteria."[14]

Such gendered articulations of weakness and pathology help sustain a military culture that impedes female service members' rise in the ranks. They articulate the gendered nature of militarized power and of the nation-state itself, "Reinforcing the imagery of masculinity—power, strength, blood, death and war embedded in the heroic soldier and breeding masculine cultural themes like honor, adventure, patriotism, cowardice and bravery" (Toktas 30). These attributions rely on gendered understandings of strength or ability that delimit female service members' contributions. Hegar counters that if the military is going to make decisions about who can do a job based on biology, then research suggests they should "make all their snipers and fighter pilots women" (54). While acknowledging the absurdity of such blanket ascriptions, she highlights how "equally absurd it is to bar women from certain jobs without even assessing them individually" (54). Hegar's experience with the doctor teaches her that "mental constraints can be as tight as physical ones" (76). She refuses to ever again conform to paradigms that constrain and devalue women: "I was proud of myself for shooting like a girl, damnit, and I planned to fly like a girl one day soon" (54).[15] Hegar would go on to earn a Distinguished Flying Cross with valor and a Purple Heart, but as her experiences suggest, gendered conceptual and discursive frameworks have coercive effects in both personal and professional contexts. Like many other veterans, Hegar continued her service through political activism. In 2017 she ran as the Democratic nominee against Republican John Carter for the US House of Representatives in the Thirty-First Congressional District in Texas and then again against Republican John Cornyn in 2020 for the US Senate. Although she did not win, she gave both men a run for their money, garnering more votes than any other Democrat ever had in Texas (Gilman). Hegar would also challenge the constitutionality of the Combat Exclusion Policy, which prevented her from ground combat training despite her combat experience and expertise as a pilot. The policy was finally repealed in 2013.

In addition to facile distinctions between the personal and the political, my approach in this book rejects a top-down understanding of political power. Such an approach creates a false binary privileging the state, its agents, and military brass; it ignores how power circulates through social relationships and how it is used, displayed, and exerted by individual actors at all levels of society rather than "contained" in any one social class or group. James Gibson recognizes that the knowledge produced by combat soldiers from lower ranks is multifaceted; their memoirs produce a form of knowledge often subjugated or displaced by official accounts (466). While readers may be skeptical of the personal interests, career incentives, and political agendas motivating leaders' accounts of war, they expect foot soldiers to "tell it like it is." We may admire the medals or the status of the top brass, but we do not see ourselves mirrored in their ranks; generals' accounts of war are studied by officers in war colleges and cited by military historians, but the infantryman's "worm's-eye view" appeals to a wide readership and makes an individual perspective plausible and compelling. Alex Vernon posits that we prefer to valorize common soldiers because they have "borne the lion's share of war's tragedies" at a time when so few Americans carry the burdens of war; sympathizing with their suffering can be "politically safer, analogous to 'supporting the troops' without supporting or even having a solid opinion (or understanding) of the operation" (*Arms*, 14). They also offer "reflections on the legitimation of and acquiescence (or otherwise) to the politics of militarism and the wider geopolitical ambitions of the state, from a position of relative subordination" (Woodward and Jenkins 495). War may be the "continuation of politics by other means" in Carl von Clausewitz's famous aphorism, but as Kevin McSorely reminds us, the reality of war is "politics incarnate, politics written on and experienced through the thinking, feeling bodies of men and women" (*War and the Body*, 3). Even when not overtly political, military memoirs invite political critique and analysis, as their claims to truth implicitly assert the authority of the speaker, situate the speaker in relation to others, and discursively mediate an event of national significance.

MEMOIR AND THE POLITICS OF EMOTION

Memoir has a rocky history, as critics have alternately hailed or lamented its popularity. The genre is celebrated for its "wisdom and self-knowledge" (Couser), debunked as a fleeting "literary craze" or denigrated as self-indulgent, whiney, or narcissistic. Scholars long ignored it as a form not worthy of serious attention, treating it as a minor form of autobiography, much like diaries, letters, or journals. Autobiography presumably belonged to the public sphere—memoir to the domestic, private sphere, with all that implies. Lee Quinby, for example, identifies autobiography as "a privileged aesthetic and ethical discourse of the modern era," while memoir is "a kind of poor relative" (299). In his study of memoir writing, Thomas Larson also characterizes the relationship between autobiography and memoir in familial terms: autobiography is the "patriarch, steadfast in its tenets and traditions," who does not want anything to do with its fledgling wild child, memoir (12). My favorite of these kinship metaphors is Daniel Mendelsohn's colorful description of the memoir's tawdry reputation: "Like a drunken guest at a wedding, it is constantly mortifying its soberer relatives (philosophy, history, literary fiction)—spilling family secrets, embarrassing old friends—motivated, it would seem, by an overpowering need to be the center of attention." Presumably worldly-wise, dispassionate men wrote autobiographies, while self-indulgent, sentimental women wrote memoirs.[16]

This notion that the memoir is implicitly a "feminine" (i.e., "sentimental") form is of course difficult to defend today—particularly in the context of military memoirs, a traditionally male-centered genre that relies on the exploits of battle-hardened no-nonsense warriors for its appeal. But it does help to explain why the war memoir experienced a sharp rise in popularity during the romantic period, suited as it was to an ethos that valued subjectivity and emotional expression. Neil Ramsey's seminal work on the rise of the military memoir during this period in England is particularly instructive. Ramsey sees the broader sentimental culture of the late eighteenth century as the "origin of a recognizable war literature that continues to shape our response to war today" (200). This affective sensibility informed Britain's cultural response to war—arousing sympathy for soldiers and fueling concern over the moral legitimacy of their suffering. It also accounted for the "emergence of the military memoir as a distinct and prominent literary genre," shifting its status as a marginal form to "a surprisingly dominant position in British literary culture" (193). While antiwar liberal opinion existed loosely before the military memoir's rise, the first peace movement emerged in the early 1800s, pressuring the government through tracts, articles, meetings, and petitions (5). Accounts of soldiers' suffering represented war's miseries and exposed its realities, giving rise to the popularity of antiwar memoirs. This commercially successful genre, with its soldier-narrator as "naïve witness," would profoundly shape nineteenth-century British culture's understanding of war. Ramsey argues that in these memoirs the soldier is constructed as "a man of feeling who represents war principally as an affective experience and who recoils in horror from its suffering" (25). These representations could be "politically problematic," Ramsey notes, "operating as a disturbing counter-narrative to a hegemonic national history" (26). As a result, the British state did not use or endorse these memoirs in its national narratives, instead relying on pageantry and military spectacle in their self-representations.

The tendency to relegate memoir to the "domestic" or "private" domain endures, however, its confessional tone underwriting its lesser status among many critics.[17] Memoir's emotional investments continue to cast doubt on the genre's critical validity, its reliance on memory and subjectivity the mark of its unreliability and irrationality. Laura Marcus contends that the dismissal of the memoir "is bound up with a typological distinction between those human beings who are capable of self-reflection and those who are not" (21). It is also bound up with power and powerlessness, which, as Vernon asserts, implicates not only women but also soldiers, who "have always found themselves subordinated, acted upon, subjected to the results of others' imposed wills—dependent, passive, even domesticated" (*Arms*, 20). Such gender-informed preconceptions ignore the political power memoirs can wield precisely because of their emotional pull—their ability to enthrall, motivate, and forge personal connections. Emotions always involve a kind of judgment, a personal evaluation of the significance of an incident or event (Solomon, *Passions*, xvii). This is particularly relevant in war memoirs, where responses such as empathy or outrage render a kind of judgment that has political resonance. Emotions fuel beliefs and can "stimulate people to action or allow them to approve of the actions of others in political contexts" (Frijda et al. 1). The persuasive power of veterans' memoirs resides not in their factual accuracy, as we tend to ignore empirical evidence that challenges what *feels true.*[18] As veteran-author Tim O'Brien puts it, reading the war story is a visceral experience.[19] The ability to elicit identificatory bonds through storytelling is the root of political power.[20] A war story's "emotional capital" can pay political dividends: reading one soldier's sensory account of a friend's death in battle can do more to influence our response to warmongers than any policy document on the pros and cons of nation-building.[21] This was driven home for me when I read Marcus Luttrell's *Lone Survivor*: while I was put off by Luttrell's rants against "liberals," I could not shed the emotional weight I carried for days after finishing his memoir. Luttrell's intrusive politics annoyed and alienated me, but the empathy stirred by his grief at the loss of close friends connected me to his humanity. This empathetic bond affected how I came to judge the man and far outweighed the off-putting effects of his politics.[22]

Research shows not only that emotion affects a variety of political behaviors but also that it can be a desirable force for civic competence. George Marcus's *The Sentimental Citizen: Emotion in Democratic Politics* rightly challenges the assumption that emotion is detrimental to good citizenship and deliberative democracy—merely a "trouble-maker intruding where it does not belong" (37). He rejects a binary that situates emotion as reason's antagonist, emphasizing instead the explicit and vital role it plays "in bonding citizen, party, party platform, and elected officials" (37). The claim that individuals adopt their political views through reasoned analysis ignores a wealth of research in the neurosciences that demonstrates the role of emotions in decision making and judgment. What sometimes passes as reasoning is more often rationalization, an attempt to reconcile preconceived notions with newly introduced evidence. As Drew Westen puts it, "*The political brain is an emotional brain*" (xv). While the "marketplace of ideas" may be a great place to shop for policies, Westen quips, it is the "marketplace of emotions" that matters most in American politics (36). For example, philosopher Richard Rorty posits empathy as the root of human rights politics, suggesting that the "emergence of human rights culture seems to owe nothing to increased moral knowledge and everything to hearing sad and sentimental stories" (118). Corey Robin explores fear as "a political idea" that serves as a "source of political vitality" and a "meeting ground of the intellect and the passions, of our morals and our politics" (24). Robert F. Brissenden goes so far as to trace the roots of modern secular humanism and liberal democracy to eighteenth-century sentimentalism, which produced emotionally riveting and inspiring essays, novels, and speeches that instigated political change. Emotions are the engine that fuels our concerns and launches social movements, the basis of the connections we forge as social and political subjects.

Since our emotional engagement is intensified when stories are based on "real life" people and events, the memoir is an ideal form for "converting" readers or promoting a cause.[23] Recounting their personal experiences of war in sensory, evocative prose, soldiers' memoirs wield persuasive power, their rhetorical force intensified by what David Shields calls "the lure and blur of the real" (4). Studies indicate that the perceived "reality" of media content, for example (i.e., documentaries, news programs, "reality" crime shows) has a stronger impact on viewers' attitudes, beliefs, and behaviors than fictional content (Potter 24). This effect occurs even when content is not factually accurate or is clearly fictionalized: creative writers understand that using first-person narrative, with events recounted through the main character's point of view, invites the closest relationship between reader and narrative voice. Their choice of first-person narrative voice seeks to elicit the reader's identification with the story's protagonist. Literary theorist and novelist David Lodge argues that readers' preference for the first-person narrative voice responds to contemporary philosophical and historical conditions: "In a world where nothing is certain, in which transcendental belief has been undermined by scientific materialism, and even the objectivity of science is qualified by relativity and uncertainty, the single human voice, telling its own story, can seem the only authentic way of rendering consciousness" (87). Of course, all prose narratives court their readers' sympathies and identifications, and as Lodge himself concedes, the first-person voice can be "just as artful, or artificial" as fiction's third-person point of view. But Lodge defends first-person narrative as the most effective literary technique for evoking empathy, and he does so by noting its affinity with memoir and testimonial. In his view, first-person narration "creates an illusion of reality, it commands the willing suspension of the reader's disbelief, by modeling itself on the discourses of personal witness: the confession, the diary, autobiography, the memoir, the deposition" (87–88). This literary technique, inherent in the memoir as a genre, promises readers privileged access to the inner life of the protagonists. The interiority and intimacy of the genre enhances its rhetorical force, inviting us to see and judge experiences through the witness's eyes, to align ourselves with his or her worldview.

I have argued that soldiers' memoirs contribute to public memory and public discourses—to a realm that is always already implicated in politics broadly defined. While looking to the past, memoir is in this sense always forward-looking, as implicit in the desire to bear witness is the conviction that we can make a difference, that our shared memories can offer something of use to those who follow in our wake. In her book *Welcome to the Suck: Narrating the American Soldier's Experience in Iraq*, Stacey Peebles contends that soldier-memoirists express a political disillusionment sparked by the Vietnam War but not exclusive to its veterans. In her view, Iraq War memoirs suggest that today's soldiers are "politically cynical, but personally idealistic," a claim that presumably does not refute her conviction that their "stories have the power to change our national narrative" (4). I would counter that given the miscalculations, fabrications, and failures that characterize much of America's postmodern war making, political cynicism could well be a national malady. But I would also challenge Peebles's interpretation of soldiers' memoirs as "politically cynical" and "personally idealistic," a view rooted in that diehard dichotomy between the personal and political, as if a soldier's actions on the battlefield or in domestic life were fully autonomous from the contingencies of place, culture, and power relations that structure our values, motivations, and behaviors. Even if the dividing line between the political and the personal were so clearly demarcated or stable—can political cynicism coexist with personal idealism? Can I distrust the motives and efficacy of all political actions or actors yet still aspire toward some transcendent set of values?

Perhaps, but this position demands a more complex understanding of cynicism. Reexamining its political valence in a postmodern world, Sharon Stanley reminds us not to skirt "over certain instabilities and tensions built into the very structure of cynical consciousness," tensions that suggest the possibility of "a more productive and dialogical cynicism, one that need not stand in absolute antithesis to any and all political action" (384). In their memoirs, veterans will often call out incompetence, hypocrisy, or failures of leadership, qualities that in a war zone can cost lives. The experience of war may strip away myths of glory and invulnerability, but the soldier's cynicism can nevertheless "retain a paradoxical investment in the very values he dismisses as naïve pieties." After all, Stanley argues, "corruption only gains substance if it can be read against some realizable standard of purity or integrity" (391). As a response to loss (of illusion, of trust in others' motives, of the potential for a just world), cynicism can mask a nostalgia for what was lost. The foundation of our political identity lies in the belief that individual choices and actions matter, that a better world is possible—regardless of how corrupt the present state of our politics or the failures of our leaders. Instead of a retreat from politics, cynicism might entail a certain kind of orientation toward political action, or as Stanley puts it, "a realistic capitulation to the corruption of the world." Veterans' cynicism is often strategic: mocking or discrediting their government's "noble goals," they do not necessarily relinquish the political space for mobilizing these values. Soldiers who have fought in war, Paul Fussell reminds us, possess "a mysterious shared ironic awareness manifesting itself in an instinctive skepticism about pretension, publicly enunciated truths, the vanities of learning, and the pomp of authority" (48). It is important, Stanley argues, to "distinguish between cynicism as a rhetorical performance and cynicism as a deeply rooted aspect of an individual's subjectivity. The individual who has perfected the jeering, mocking one-liner has not necessarily given up on politics—and the jeering, mocking one-liner might even be put to solid rabble-rousing use" (406). The gallows humor deployed by soldiers both in the barracks and in their writings is often a shield against vulnerability—a defense mechanism for coping with disillusionment, fear, or grief. But the villains and follies they expose, mock, and decry provide a clear-eyed picture of what needs fixing and may provoke a response from an otherwise apathetic or politically complacent American public. Army major Richard A. Lacquement Jr. suggests that American soldiers' cynicism and skepticism "might even be considered character strengths as they mark the independent spirit that makes U.S. troops flexible and innovative in battle" (7). In this sense, cynicism is a needed counterbalance to the dangers posed by Hollywood-style heroics, delusions of glory, or a blind faith in the nobility or competence of leaders. But most importantly, cynicism as an end (rather than a means) would spell the death of storytelling, for why bother sowing seeds in the desert? Why exercise a power that Peebles acknowledges can "change our national narrative"? In a world deemed irredeemably corrupt and hopeless, wherefore storytellers?

MAPPING THE TERRAIN: CHAPTER BREAKDOWN

The book's organizational framework arises from its thematic concerns, all centering on politics, broadly conceived. I begin by setting a historical context for my interest in veterans' diverse political subjectivities. In chapter 1, "Protestors, Patriots, and Culture Warriors: American Politics and the Citizen-Soldier," I show that American soldiers and veterans have consistently organized and participated in political activism. In a brief overview of this history, I trace some of the economic and social conditions that shaped veterans' civic identities and fueled their collective responses as citizens, focusing attention on the intersections of race, military service, and national politics. I include discussion of African American and Latino veteran activism, for despite a long history of military service, war commemorations and histories rarely include their perspectives. Yet their political activism reveals a more complex version of the American war story, with its democratizing themes and cast of steely-eyed White heroes. As I argue, this more complex history of political mobilizations and strategic alliances challenges the image of

American service members as detached, apolitical subjects uncompromised by or disconnected from their civic or racialized identities. It is further complicated by current events, as American soldiers are increasingly making their voices heard in a variety of settings: as proxies for political candidates or parties, organizers of grassroots movements, bloggers, and as candidates in both local and national campaigns.

I then turn to the politics of emotion, particularly shame and humiliation. In chapter 2, "The Fate Worse Than Death: Saving Face and the Affective Economy of War," I call attention to the dominant structure of feeling in post–World War II America that served as a backdrop to the Vietnam War: what I call its "pride economy." Evoked through political discourses commemorating the American warrior as savior and protector of the "free world," the pride economy engendered a reciprocal—even reactionary—anxiety of influence: the fear of not living up to this masculine ideal. As a result, face-saving maneuvers served as the thread binding a series of responses before, during, and after the Vietnam War, from securing popular support to foreign-policy decision making to the recruitment, training, and behavior of soldiers in the field. Reading three critically acclaimed war memoirs as case studies, Philip Caputo's *Rumor of War*, Tim O'Brien's *If I Die in a Combat Zone*, and Tobias Wolff's *In Pharaoh's Army*, I show how face-saving motivated personal choices and behaviors. Using declassified documents and historical accounts, I situate these literary works in conversation with political speeches, interviews, and memos showing how face-maintenance shaped leadership decisions, prioritized the preservation of national pride, and cost American soldiers' lives. Ironically, after the war, it was shame, not pride, that would dominate collective and personal memories of Vietnam.

Americans trust their military more than their government, news organizations, or even religious institutions, endowing it with a kind of soft power generally unacknowledged by political scientists, foreign policy experts, and military historians. Concurrently, a "support the troops" mantra makes criticism of the military or our nation's wars difficult, even unpatriotic, a predicament that political leaders are quick to exploit. These factors are further complicated by our current, "post-truth" political culture, where, as Lee McIntyre argues, "largely left-wing relativist and postmodernist attacks on the idea of truth . . . have now been co-opted by right-wing political operatives" (McIntyre 6).[24] In chapter 3, "Trusting the Messenger: Veterans' Memoirs and the Politics of Credibility," I call attention to these intersecting concerns. My reading of Marcus Luttrell's *Lone Survivor*, John Crawford's *The*

Last True Story I'll Ever Tell, and Michael Anthony's *Mass Casualties: A Young Medic's True Story of Death, Deception, and Dishonor in Iraq* contrasts the extent to which these writers assert, exploit, or subvert their own veracity. I first situate these works against the "credibility gap" initiated by the Vietnam War, arguing for Tim O'Brien's memoir *If I Die in a Combat Zone* as a critique against political certainty and absolutism. I then show how assumptions about truth as relativistic, contingent, or immutable—that is, skepticism or faith in context-transcendent notions of truth—frame post-9/11 military memoirs and model competing ways of responding to the state's authority.

Immigrants have served in the US military in every major conflict since the Revolutionary War, their service often seen as a test of loyalty to the nation and the very crucible of citizenship. Yet their stories are mostly absent from our national narratives. In chapter 4, "'Soldiers of Conviction': Duty, Dissent, and the Immigrant Soldier," I take up one of the most controversial issues affecting military personnel and polarizing Americans today, immigration, to explore questions about citizenship, cultural belonging, and duty through the rare perspective offered by foreign-born American soldiers' memoirs: Camilo Mejía's *Road from ar Ramadi: The Private Rebellion of Staff Sergeant Mejía: An Iraq War Memoir* and Robert Mencia's *From Here to Insanity: An Immigrant Boy Becomes a Citizen by Way of the Vietnam Draft.* I situate their stories in a broader political and social history, tracing some of the incentives that have driven noncitizens to enlist in the military, showing how political attitudes toward immigrants affect policymaking, and raising questions about the role of national and ethnic affinities in shaping concepts such as honor, heroism, and patriotism.

Chapter 5, "Silence amid the Din of War," focuses on Brian Turner's memoir *My Life as a Foreign Country* to explore the politics informing his poetics. Rather than theorizing the political and the aesthetic as separate realms (functioning in opposition, as if art's aesthetic aims necessarily conflict with or deny its politics or as if one must invariably subordinate the other), Turner places these two modes in dialogical relation, recognizing that politics has an inherently aesthetic dimension and aesthetics an inherently political one, and that both modes reflect "ways of doing things with words." Adopting literary devices (irony, symbolism, foreshadowing, flashback, etc.) as vehicles for oblique political commentary, I argue, Turner contributes to the diverse forms through which wars are represented and imagined. I conclude in chapter 6, "Beginnings: Stories That Need Telling," by pointing to recent changes in the military that promise new stories by female and LGBTQ combat veterans.

In the low-intensity conflicts that have become America's new normal, boundaries between combatants and noncombatants are blurred or shattered, alliances shift or dissolve within twenty-four-hour news cycles, and information is deployed as a weapon, a myth, an edge, a trope, and an asset (Gray 22). Treading this minefield of competing discourses, voices, and interests is complicated enough, but today's professional American soldier is also asked to play contradictory roles: to serve as nation builder and destroyer, savior and killer, sacrificial lamb and lion of war—to fit the image of the benevolent GI who hands out candy to kids in Baghdad, and of the stoic warrior of *Generation Kill*.[25] Civilians thank them, call them heroes, offer them free coffee, discounts, handshakes. Of course, Americans also tend to be fickle in our loyalties—ready to turn on our soldiers when they fail to live up to our myths or when wars turn too ugly or our side loses. But long after the small-town parades, the homecomings, the yellow ribbon campaigns, and regardless of what new burdens the vicissitudes of public opinion and political spin will place on them, soldiers will be telling war stories. Their voices will often be difficult to hear above the rousing calls to arms, the shock and awe of talking heads, and the shrill and bluster of warmongers. But if we listen, we will hear them.

Chapter 1

PROTESTORS, PATRIOTS, AND CULTURE WARRIORS
American Politics and the Citizen-Soldier

Maybe you didn't understand American foreign policy
or why we were at war. Maybe you never will. But it
doesn't matter. You held up your hand and said, "I'm
willing to die for these worthless civilians."

—Phil Klay, "Psychological Operations"

In recent years there has been a growing interest in the political attitudes, behaviors, and activism of military veterans. Some of this research seeks to understand the mechanisms that shape how veterans negotiate their identities as soldiers and the effects of military service on their civic participation or partisanship. My aim in this chapter is to explore the volatile mix of agendas and historical precedents motivating veterans' political activism on the home front. I focus on the ways that identity politics—especially challenges to and disruptions of traditional racial hierarchies—find expression in veterans' grassroots movements and organizations. These interplays between personal experience, group identification, and social power relations shape veterans' political subjectivities and postwar judgments. Political subjectivity denotes "how a single person or a group of actors is brought into a position to stake claims, to have a voice, and to be recognizable by authorities" (Krause and Schramm 115). It is shaped, in part, by historical, juridical, and social practices of inclusion or exclusion (often articulated through debates about citizenship or race) and by the emotions these evoke. Veterans' war stories tap into prevailing social anxieties and intraethnic politics, informing the meanings they attribute to military service. Their political agency is often spurred less by their experiences of war abroad than by how these experiences resonate with culture wars at home. Highlighting the experiences of Latinos and African

Americans, two racialized groups with a strong tradition of military service, my historical overview traces racial subtexts rendered invisible in collective memories of American wars. I then address the politicization of service members post-9/11, calling attention to aspirations and intersectional alliances galvanizing political mobilizations and activating dissident, reactionary, or even militant ethnonationalist movements.

Contrary to popular perception, veterans' and soldiers' large-scale political mobilizations precede the Vietnam War. Most relevant here is the extent to which the racial and ethnic makeup of earlier veterans' movements have been ignored, downplayed, or forgotten. While military service often united veterans seeking redress for shared grievances, racial and ethnic tensions sometimes hindered collective efforts. The first organized veterans' movement, the Grand Army of the Republic (GAR), was created by Civil War veterans to increase their political influence. Their activities focused on supporting candidates and working to secure pensions for former service members. It was the Union Army's first and largest veteran's organization, and despite resistance in former slave states, the first to include Black veterans as both members and elected spokesmen. This early coalition of veterans was an impressive accomplishment in its day, not only because of their organizational effectiveness but also because at a time when "race trumped virtually all other social identities, Black and White veterans created an interracial organization at both the national and local levels" (Gannon 6). However, despite GAR's achievements, race eventually splintered solidarity and eroded support from within their ranks. As GAR expanded into the southern states, maintaining an integrated organization became increasingly difficult, and internal debates divided members along deep-rooted racial fault lines. The national organization tried to uphold its position on full integration, but many White members dropped out in protest and officials feared that enforcing integrated posts came at the expense of the organization's broader aims. As Wallace E. Davies observed in a 1947 study, "When matters came to such a showdown, the debates in meetings showed that many preferred to retain and expand the White membership rather than to insist upon an equality of status for the colored recruits" (371). Some recent scholars, however, refute the more negative assessments of this racial experiment, focusing less on the prejudices, hostilities, and setbacks reflected in the Grand Army's history and highlighting the ways that many White veterans resisted or condemned the organization's attempt to segregate Black veterans, "citing both their shared comradeship and the shared cause they believed worthy of their sacrifice" (Gannon 32). GAR serves as a reminder that military service can engender new social relationships and strategic alliances.

After World War I, veterans again mobilized in efforts to secure discharge bonuses, pensions, and other compensation for service members. In 1930, journalist Oliver McGee Jr. noted veterans' status as emergent political actors, announcing in a *Commonweal* article, "The American veteran of the World War has arrived on the political scene and . . . brought a new force into political life" (40). The rise of large veterans' organizations such as the American Legion and Veterans of Foreign Wars (VFW) helped mediate veterans' relationship with the state and provide the "machinery" that helped them become a political force (Ortiz 4). By 1932, at the height of the Depression, the VFW lobbied the federal government to demand full payment of the deferred bonus veterans were promised in 1924. As tensions mounted in the face of massive unemployment and the government's piecemeal responses to their urgent needs, over twenty thousand World War I veterans descended on Washington, DC. They were met with violent suppression (two veterans were killed by police). General Douglas MacArthur was sent to restore order, which his cavalry did with machine guns, bayonets, and tear gas (Kindell 85). Although the protestors did not achieve their aims, their "Bonus movement" contributed to the creation of the GI Bill (Servicemen's Readjustment Act of 1944).[1] Further, veterans would gain visibility as a force to be reckoned with: Harry Truman, a VFW member and vice-presidential candidate in 1944, predicted that veterans would become "the most potent political factor in the country" (Ortiz 201–2). But the Bonus March itself faded from public memory despite its vast size and impact. One important reason for this relative obscurity is race: Bonus Expeditionary Force troops were integrated, alarming high-ranking political and military officials who saw this integrated political movement as a sign that "Negro and Jewish" communists were conspiring to spark a revolution (Dickson and Allen 7). This affected how the march would be interpreted and remembered.

THE FORCE AWAKENS: VIETNAM VETERANS AND THE STATE

Using tactics and tools not available to earlier generations, Vietnam War veterans and soldiers significantly altered the strategies and aims of their predecessors and engaged in a different kind of mobilization: active-duty soldiers would be dragged into the political fray at home, breaking a code of silent obedience through public displays of defiance. Soldiers and veterans participated in highly visible forms of organized dissent, including appearances in televised debates, testimony before Congress, op-eds in newspapers, public hearings, and "guerrilla theater" performances that dramatized their experiences in public locations. The GI antiwar movement published nearly three hundred underground newspapers, and active-duty troops participated in dozens of protests at military bases around the world. Antidraft organizations, such as the Boston Draft Resistance (the largest of its kind), as well as the sanctuary movement supported by churches, would help thousands of service members resist or protest the war.[2]

Although the Vietnam War marks a shift in veterans' political tactics, the culture wars at home frame how their efforts were perceived and later remembered. Now, over half a century later, public memories of Vietnam veterans' protests have comfortably settled around a familiar set of iconic images, most re-created in Hollywood films: veterans tossing their medals over the White House fence; thousands marching through the streets, some in wheelchairs or on crutches, demanding an end to the war; scores bearing witness before Congress, describing abuses and atrocities seen or committed. Like many aspects of these tumultuous years, these iconic images efface as well as reveal. They are useful in tidying up a messy, complicated history, offering shorthand knowledge about the past and a handy index of clichés. The story of Vietnam-era soldiers' and veterans' politicization is stripped of troublesome ambiguities, its diverse players divvied up into tidy pro- and antiwar factions. This binary fails to acknowledge the ambivalence, range, and fluidity of positions on the war. It also decontextualizes—for instance, obscuring the fact that in the early years, most draftees were willing to serve, and many young men even enlisted, enculturated as they were into a Cold War mindset that saw communism in stark terms.[3] Going to war was also the age-old path to manhood: for many young White men, it was a rite of passage modeled by their fathers and grandfathers, the very foundation of the lives they led as middle-class boys in a post–GI Bill America. For young Black and Latino men, military service offered a path toward achieving an American dream long deferred, whether through the tangible rewards of job training, college money, and housing grants or the symbolic capital offered by the uniform: pride, honor, respect.

While the latter eluded many Vietnam-era veterans by war's end, at the outset of the conflict most Americans were still enamored of the myth of the "Good War" and its corresponding images of men in uniform, what veteran and author Steven Rosales calls the "hagiography of the Second World War" (5). Himself a World War II veteran, Paul Fussell acknowledged that the Allied war had been "sanitized and romanticized almost beyond recognition by the sentimental, the loony patriotic, the ignorant, and the bloodthirsty" (ix). Vietnam War memoirs support this view, with many veteran-authors noting the influence that John Wayne war movies or stories about America's World War II heroes had on their decision making.[4] In *Jumping from Helicopters: A Vietnam War Memoir*, veteran John Stillman tells us that his father and both grandfathers had served, so he would daydream "about being a war hero" and feel proud at the thought of joining their ranks. He enlisted and was deployed in 1967. Similarly, veteran memoirist Charles Peter Hensler describes a childhood and adolescence shaped by the Cold War, a conflict described simply in terms of "East versus West, the 'Free World' against the Communists, Good versus Evil" (5). As he explains, "The war was heroic in the grand scheme of things, and those who served could bask in that glow" (66). In *Rumor of War*, Philip Caputo admits that at the outset of his deployment to Vietnam he envisioned himself "charging up some distant beachhead, like John Wayne in *Sands of Iwo Jima*, and then coming home a suntanned warrior with medals on my chest" (6). *Born on the Fourth of July*'s Ron Kovic cites the effect that World War II movies had on his decision to serve in Vietnam: "I'll never forget Audie Murphy in *To Hell and Back*. . . . He was so brave I had chills . . . wishing it were me up there" (54). Such widely shared images, which showcased America's power for good, complicated how many young men reacted initially to the Vietnam conflict. For many men of this generation, these films endorsed the image of the "white savior" that had long justified colonial and imperial military interventions.[5]

Many did object to the war on political grounds, but most believed that once again, yanks were being called on to save the world. This is not hyperbole: given the pervasiveness of the "domino theory" metaphor that framed Cold War rhetoric, many Americans believed that the "fall" of South Vietnam to the communist boogeymen could ultimately mean we would be fighting them on American turf.[6] Conceptual metaphors such as these "infiltrate" our thinking and approaches, providing "an underlying intellectual construct for framing the situation, for viewing the world, an outlook which creates some degree of order and expectations" (Shimko 665).[7] The idea of stopping the domino chain reaction was a unifying force in American culture and also contributed to the ways that many young men who had come of age in the 1950s and early 1960s responded to the call to arms.

Opposition to the Vietnam War grew steadily during the conflict, however, resistance sometimes taking the form of conscientious objection. Historians attribute the rising tide of antiwar resistance to several key factors—including the growing awareness that the war was not going well and that casualties were reaching critical mass. The media's role in exposing the public to these conditions played a role, as did the coverage of the 1968 Tet Offensive, when Viet Cong and North Vietnamese regulars overran numerous cities and towns that officials had insisted were "pacified." Most historians agree that this event marks a turning point in Americans' support for the war. It also intensified protests and acts of resistance among both veterans and active-duty soldiers, as many came to regard their civilian and military leaders as inept, duplicitous, or indifferent. Thus, the Vietnam War marks a change in military-civilian relations and in the ways that soldiers defined their role in the public sphere. Soldiers who protested were taking great risks; the free speech rights of active-duty military personnel are limited by regulation and tradition; the punishment for breaching those limits ranges from ostracism to court martial. Articles 88, 89, 91, 133 and 134 of the Uniform Code of Military Justice specifically address soldiers' public behavior, which now includes their use of social media comments and posts (Rodewig). Yet despite these restrictions, the discontent that first expressed itself in barracks and coffee houses would eventually spill into America's streets.

Popular memories about the antiwar movement tend to downplay the role veterans themselves played as political actors. Time and circumstance elide nuance, and generalizations about antiwar protestors revolve around three stereotypes straight out of central casting: the "spoiled" university student, the "radical" hippie, and, in president Richard Nixon's description, the "thugs." Vietnam veterans, on the other hand, are often cast as passive victims, mere receptacles of the scorn, mistreatment, or harassment of these unruly countercultural ("antitroop") forces. Such images have been useful in demonizing dissenters and supporting a no-questions-asked form of patriotism post-Vietnam. They also have proven effective in undermining the legitimacy and breadth of soldiers' and veterans' antiwar protests and discounting their political agency.[8] As Jerry Lembke argues, "the real story of solidarity between the anti-war movement and Vietnam veterans has to be told" (26). My aim is not to dismiss the ill treatment or neglect that many Vietnam veterans experienced on their return home but to complicate a well-worn script in which returning combat soldiers serve as depoliticized objects of pity or fear, as victims or sociopaths.

The tendency to generalize about Vietnam veterans also shapes memories about civilians who fought against the war. Michael S. Foley argues that "American collective memory of both the war and opposition to it has long been too simplistic, and draft resistance may be one of the least understood phenomena of the period" (6). In his view, Americans have demonized or misunderstood men who refused to serve in the conflict by conflating "draft dodgers," men who claimed deferments or escaped abroad to avoid military service, with "draft resisters," men who refused to cooperate with the Selective Service System and accepted the legal consequences of their civil disobedience. This leads Americans to dismiss resisters as selfish cowards, especially as "draft resistance has been virtually forgotten or, at best, understated by historians of the antiwar movement" (6). Books and films about the 1960s, Foley notes, highlight spectacular displays—the burning of draft cards—while ignoring the motives behind such acts of political dissent. Draft resisters, Foley contends, upheld American traditions founded on the belief that citizens have a duty to oppose illegal or immoral acts by the government. Taking great risks, draft resisters were "the antiwar movement's equivalent to the civil rights movement's Freedom Riders and lunch-counter sit-in participants" (9). Discourses sustaining an "us" versus "them" antagonism between antiwar civilians and active-duty soldiers or veterans, however, are politically useful, as they promote self-censorship among civilians not wanting to be identified as "antitroop" because of their opposition to a war. Yet relations between Vietnam veterans and antiwar civilians were not always adversarial and could even be mutually supportive. Vietnam veteran David Cortright, for example, "always found that the civilian anti-war movement people were very welcoming" (qtd. in Ellis and Smith). Army veteran Bill Branson joined the antiwar movement in 1970 and went on to serve on the board of Vietnam Veterans Against the War. He insists that joining the movement saved his life, as it did for many other veterans. Poet and veteran Bill Ehrhart credits postwar activism with giving him something constructive to do with his rage (Ellis and Smith).[9] For these and many other returning soldiers, political activism aided their recovery and reintegration.

Various movements would converge around intersecting injustices, aspirations, and identities, sparking competing and sometimes controversial political alliances. External social pressures and internal racial dynamics combined to shape soldiers' and veterans' politicization, reintegration, and postwar politics. In the next section, I situate Vietnam-era pro- and antiwar political activism within a broader racialized military history, focusing attention on draft-age

African American and Latino males. The legacy of World War II also informed their attitudes and decision making, but the lessons it imparted differed, complicated by their status as marginalized citizens navigating competing ethnic and national identities, obligations, and aspirations.

BLACK GIS AND THE LONG WAR AT HOME

Shall we be citizens in war, and aliens in peace?

—Frederick Douglass, "What the Black Man Wants"

For US-born Black men, the privileges and protections of citizenship have not always been a birthright. Generations of African Americans fought—in courtrooms, barracks, and streets—for the right to fight for their country as equals. Their path to full military integration and recognition has been a long and winding one, as White leaders vacillated between their need for troops during wartime and their fear and distrust of Black men with guns. Throughout much of this history, Black men's struggle for the "right to bear arms" was not about citizenship: it was a struggle for recognition of their humanity. While a detailed accounting of this history is beyond the scope of this study, even a cursory glance can help us take a longer view of Black veterans' politicization and subsequent military status.

The history of African Americans' military contributions begins with the birth of the nation itself. Official history recounts the Revolutionary War as a struggle for freedom from colonial rule, omitting an obvious contradiction: the concomitant enslavement of Black peoples. Nonsegregated Black troops fought in the Revolutionary War at Lexington, Concord, and Bunker Hill. Crispus Attucks, a fugitive slave, was the first soldier to die for the new nation. Yet by 1775, Southern states had forced concessions designating Black men as unsuitable for military service. After the implementation of a draft system with state quotas, some states allowed Blacks to serve as substitutes for White conscripts. Despite their wartime sacrifices, however, only Massachusetts and Vermont emancipated enslaved Blacks during the Revolutionary War, while others simply reneged on their promises (Graham 2–3). Most African Americans remained in bondage a century later, the Supreme Court ruling in the 1857 Dred Scott case that the "Negro race" was a "slave race" and that even freed Blacks had "no rights which a white man was bound to respect." Hoping to further their own quest for freedom and equality, Black men agitated for enlistment during the Civil War, and the Union Army accepted them in 1863; however they were segregated, given menial tasks, and paid less than Whites. In protest, they threatened mutiny in 1864, so Congress passed legislation retroactively equalizing their pay.

By the outbreak of World War I, however, "any black political advances during Reconstruction had been decisively reversed and black economic progress across most of the South had stalled" (Ellis 10). The disproportionate percentage of Black inductees during the war was the outcome of systemic racism, local policies, and limits on Black volunteer regiments. Whites were granted deferments at a much higher rate than Blacks; thus while they made up 10 percent of the population, African Americans comprised 14 percent of draftees (C. Williams). Further, physical disabilities that excluded White conscripts from service were often ignored for Blacks, relieving some of the enlistment burden for Whites. For example, the draft exemption board of Fulton County, Georgia, exempted only 6 of 202 African American applicants, while exempting 526 of 815 Whites (C. Williams).

After the Great War, the army's War College prepared a mobilization plan aimed at training 140,000 Black men, mostly for noncombat duties (with 30,000 left for "the experiment of combat duty"). But preconceptions about Black men remained an obstacle to full integration. For example, a 1925 memo to the chief of staff titled "The Use of Negro Man Power in War" conveyed the entrenched social attitudes informing military politics at the time. On the one hand, the War College recommendations noted that "the negro should be measured by the same standards applied to the white man." On the other, it reinforced racist assumptions about the Black man as "by nature subservient," unable to "control himself in the fear of danger" and "mentally inferior to the white man."[10] Nevertheless, about one million African American soldiers were among the sixteen million US soldiers who served during World War II. Of these, the vast majority were in segregated labor and supply units led by White commanders. They were not allowed to attend the "white" theater set up on base; Black MPs could not arrest Whites, while White MPs frequently arrested Black troops; they could not frequent the PX; and officers could not go to the Officer's Club. But their military experiences—serving in combat zones, living abroad, expanding their educational and job prospects, and enhancing their sense of purpose and worth—made it more difficult for these veterans to conform to the old racial order back home. Military service bolstered their political agency and self-confidence, intensifying Black veterans' calls for equal treatment. As Christopher S. Parker argues, "Black veterans' willingness to challenge white supremacy and resist Jim Crow rested to a significant extent upon their military experience" (4). As a result, many Black veterans joined the fight for justice at home: one-third of the leaders of the civil rights movement were World War II veterans, and, as Parker demonstrates, they also made up "a significant segment of the struggle's rank and file" (17). Countering the belief that military training is anathema to protest, nonconformity, or challenges to authority, Parker contends that soldiers' civic education in the military shapes postservice attitudes, often producing "citizens willing to fight for their fair share of the democracy for which they had sacrificed so much" (90).[11]

This is evident in other stories omitted from the grand narratives of World War II. When Congress authorized the Women's Army Auxiliary Corps (later renamed Women's Army Corps) in 1942, hundreds of women joined the war effort. But African American women who served faced discrimination for both their gender and their race. Their unequal and denigrating treatment as service members highlighted the disconnect between the myth of American democracy and its realities. The uniform held the promise of inclusion in the nation's civic and political life, and while this promise often remained unfulfilled, many Black female service members, like their male counterparts, gained a sense of accomplishment and self-worth. In her memoir *One Woman's Army: A Black Officer Remembers the WAC*, Charity Adams Earley, the first Black woman commissioned as an officer, describes both the bigotry and the glimpses of welcome she received from White male officers. But on her return stateside after the war, Adams is reminded "that our prewar enemy in our own military was not dead; it had just been quietly sleeping while we shared another common enemy. Racial discrimination had never even rested, but now the male ego was awake and active, and discrimination based on gender again appeared" (186). Adams wrote her memoir to commemorate the "trailblazing" women who, despite having "ventured into a service area where they were not really wanted," valiantly performed jobs normally assigned to men, and "survived racial prejudice and discrimination with dignity," had been "virtually ignored and forgotten" (183, 214). Yet they had also "opened a few doors" and "broken a few barriers" for the next generation (214). Adams's military experiences and achievements fostered in her "a strong sense of responsibility and personal dignity" (211).[12]

This personal development also vitalized a sense of political agency, the confidence to organize and resist discrimination or denigration, even at great risk to themselves and their careers. For example, in 1945 four African American Women Army Corps (WAC) privates—Mary Green, Anna Morrison,

Johnnie Murphy, and Alice Young—organized a strike with fifty other Black female service members. They described the appalling treatment of Black WACs at Fort Devens in Massachusetts and demanded better job opportunities in the military. Despite having been recruited to train as medical technicians, they were assigned only cleaning duties. As one hospital commander told Private Young, "I do not have colored Wacs as medical technicians. They are here to scrub and wash floors, wash dishes and do all the dirty work" (Bolzenius 2). These women braved court-martial rather than return to menial duties, opting to air their grievances in a military court, and in so doing garner considerable attention in the court of public opinion (113). Although they were sentenced to a one-year prison term and dishonorable discharge for their actions, the servicewomen managed to elicit broad support among both Black and White citizens. The intensely negative reactions to their sentencing forced the War Department to backtrack and seek a compromise to "assuage the public outcry" (125). The military saved face by not admitting wrongdoing while reversing the conviction on a legal technicality. But the women had achieved an important aim: their high-profile actions demonstrated "that African American servicewomen had documented rights in the U.S. military, and that they would use them to assert their full entitlements as citizen-soldiers" (151). Indeed, Black service members' civic activism would play a crucial role in desegregating the armed forces.[13]

However, such self-affirmation also fueled backlashes following both world wars, as White vigilantes targeted Black men in uniform and used violence to ensure that returning soldiers "knew their place." For example, during the "Red Summer" of 1919, White sailors carried out violent racist attacks targeting returning World War I Black veterans, whom they regarded as a threat to White supremacy. The initial rampage spread, as White mobs burned Black homes and businesses, and beat and even lynched African Americans across US cities. In response, Black veterans took up arms again— this time to defend their neighborhoods.[14] After World War II, the NAACP again reported numerous incidents of Black servicemen beaten, murdered, and disappeared. Sometimes beatings were conducted by police called to enforce Jim Crow laws against such "crimes" as "loud talking" and "cursing" (Phillips 90).[15] During the Korean conflict, Black men would again be drafted disproportionately (by 1951 nearly one in four new recruits were African American), more likely to see combat and become casualties, and promoted at lower rate (Westheider 42). They also faced racial violence within the ranks. Colonel David J. Clark encapsulates the Korean War for its African

American soldiers as "both a tragedy and triumph": a tragedy because they fought for others' rights while lacking them at home, but also a triumph in that "the wheels of change in America" seemed to be turning (qtd. in Black). This enduring pattern of racial progress followed by reactionary pushback set the stage for the explosive racial dynamics that propelled African American political activism during the Vietnam War.

At the outset of the Vietnam conflict, elevated levels of unemployment and the need for greater educational and vocational opportunities led many young Black men to enlist, with over 300,000 serving before the end of US involvement in 1973 (Lucks 196). Cultural conflicts and conditions at home informed Black soldiers' initial willingness to serve, as well as their subsequent disillusion and activism. A 1966 poll suggested that most young Black men had a positive view of the military and also viewed the draft more favorably than Whites did.[16] Paul Matthews, a platoon surgeon in Vietnam who went on to found Houston's Buffalo Soldiers National Museum, agrees that the "military has always been popular in the black community.... It was Frederick Douglass who said that if you put a uniform on a black man and a musket on his shoulder then you could not stop him being a citizen and a man" (qtd. in Jeffrey). The limited prospects at home and the intangible rewards of service—self-respect, honor—led many young Black men to reenlist at twice the rate of White men (Graham 24). Many volunteered for elite forces, comprising 40–45 percent of some paratrooper units (Grove 5). For many African Americans, military experiences during the Vietnam War fostered more positive inter-racial relationships, improving their career and educational prospects and social integration. In 1967, journalist Frank McGee spent several weeks living with soldiers of the 101st Airborne Division in Vietnam, observing Black and White soldiers. He saw interactions rarely seen stateside at that time, men "sharing supplies, telling stories and jokes, and generally empathizing with one another, whatever their race" (qtd. in Goodwin). The platoon, led by an African American from Mississippi, seemed to have overcome racial barriers to such an extent that McGhee wrote, "Nowhere in America have I seen Negroes and Whites as free, open and uninhibited with their associations. I saw no eyes clouded with resentment" (Goodwin). McGhee concluded that the army had achieved what America had not: "the elimination of race as a factor in human existence."

But relations were not always so harmonious, and not all Black soldiers were accepted by their White colleagues. For many Black service members, military experiences "accelerated and fueled [their] critiques of the war into a powerful social and racial justice movement at home" (Phillips 227). What they witnessed—the indifference, ignorance, or outright hostility of some soldiers toward the Vietnamese people (often referred to as "gooks") mirrored racist attitudes they experienced stateside.[17] As the *New York Times* reported in 1970, "Confederate flags, a 'white power' symbol in the military, are banned at some bases," but they are "freely displayed at others" (T. Johnson, "G.I.s in Germany"). Black soldiers were often subjected to harsher penalties for even minor infractions. In December 1969, African American soldiers represented 58 percent of prisoners at the infamous Long Binh Jail near Saigon (Goodwin). A 1972 Defense Department study found that they received 25.5 percent of nonjudicial punishments and 34.3 percent of court-martials (Goodwin). These injustices fomented discontent and triggered a political awakening that sometimes found expression in the militancy of Black nationalist or Black Power groups. Thus while in 1966 few African American soldiers identified with extreme militarism, by 1969 many were greeting each other using Black Power salutes (Graham 75). This change in attitudes and affiliations correlates with reenlistment rates: at the start of the war about 66 percent of Black soldiers reenlisted, whereas by 1970 that number had declined to 13 percent (Graham 75). Many sought out groups that could represent their interests and concerns, such as Unsatisfied Black Soldiers, the Minority Servicemen's Association, the Concerned Veterans Association, Black Brothers United, and the Black Liberation Front of the armed forces.[18] Having served in the first fully integrated military, where some Blacks occupied command positions over Whites, many of these veterans were primed to refuse a quiet return to the racial status quo.[19]

While critics often assume a causal relationship between rapid modernization processes, certain types of social cleavages, and subsequent political mobilizations, others call attention to the importance of available organizations in inducting new members and producing new patterns of behaviors. Rather than theorizing political subjectivity as the response to or product of social forces and strains, they shift the focus toward the importance of mobilizing agents in engaging the political orientations of individuals at given moments (Cameron 145–46). Civil rights organizations served as agents of political mobilization for many African American soldiers and veterans, providing vehicles for their frustrations with a military establishment and government perceived as unresponsive to their needs. Daniel S. Lucks contends that scholars have generally neglected the interplay between the antiwar protest movement and the civil rights movement, resulting in "a paucity of work on the relationship between the two" (2). Yet this interplay reminds us that identity is a shifting, multilayered construct in which race and gender, class and nationality, and other aspects of social identity intersect and often compete. For African American soldiers and veterans, military service often dictated a Sophie's choice between their national and racial identities. The desire to earn the respect or status denied to them back home contributed to their overrepresentation in elite combat units, and as a result, in early casualty figures during the Vietnam War. From 1961 to 1967, African Americans made up 11 to 12 percent of the US population but peaked at about 25 percent of combat casualties (T. Johnson, "U.S. Negro in Vietnam" 16). The perception that Blacks were being disproportionately targeted for the most dangerous missions gained traction over time, despite the military's actions to curtail Black casualties. This incited rebellions even before the assassination of Martin Luther King Jr., but later, when some White soldiers burned crosses and waved confederate flags in response to the news of King's death, many Black soldiers began to compare their experiences of racism and oppression with those of the Vietnamese. The more militant leaders of the civil rights movement aroused responses that did not align with King's nonviolent vision, "changing the character of Black-White relations in the military after 1967" and further contributing to the deterioration of race relations within the ranks (Bates 59). Black active-duty soldiers engaged in both subtle and overt acts of resistance, for example, participating in antiwar protests at an army base in 1969 as part of the "Fort Jackson Eight" or refusing orders to serve as guards for the Democratic National Convention in 1968 to avoid participating in the suppression of Black protestors. Military bases in the United States and abroad became the sites of race riots (Mershon and Schlossman 322). While several of the Black veterans interviewed for Wallace Terry's book *Bloods* point to the murder of Martin Luther King Jr. as a turning point in their attitude toward the war, Milton Bates notes that in September 1968, months before King's death, "two hundred black prisoners rioted in the army stockade at Long Binh, killing one White inmate and injuring several others" (60). This disturbance was the most widely publicized, but journalist Zalin Grant reported in 1968 that racial incidents were occurring on an almost daily basis, concluding that the "biggest threat is race riots, not the Vietcong" (qtd. in Goodwin). By 1969, "many were now prepared to take part in a riot or revolt (45 percent of black enlisted men) and join a militant group like the Black Panthers (31 percent of enlisted) when they returned home" (Bates 60). While these uprisings are usually recalled in dire terms—as symptoms of cultural and social breakdown or emotional trauma—they should be linked to a longer history of resistance and activism, one that ultimately "prompted the reconstruction and transformation of American political beliefs and cultural traditions" (Morris 1). Just as many World War II veterans joined and led civil rights organizations, Vietnam veterans paved the way for a new generation of citizen-soldiers. Their acts of rebellion resonated within military institutions and beyond, sometimes feeding into emergent international antiracist, antiimperialist, and Third World solidarity movements.

DIVIDED LOYALTIES: LATINO POLITICS, CULTURAL CITIZENSHIP, AND THE VIETNAM WAR

The military is part—often the most crucial part—of a political order. The absence or over-representation of any ethnic group in the military . . . should tell us something about that political order and how groups with widely different political resources cope with that order.
—Cynthia Enloe, *Ethnic Soldiers*

Latinos have served in the US military since the war of 1812, earning numerous commendations and medals throughout history. Yet their numbers before the Vietnam War can only be estimated, as the military did not keep records on Latinos service members prior to this time (Dansby et al. xix).[20] But here again World War II's cultural influence is noteworthy. Using surnames to identify Latino service members, one study estimates that approximately half a million Latinos fought in World War II (Allsup). For many minorities, and in particular for Mexican Americans who had long faced disparagement, prejudice, and marginalization, their military service during World War II was a "tremendous source of ethnic pride" (Oropeza, *Raza*, 13).[21] This is exemplified by veteran-author George Mariscal in a 1997 interview in which he recalls the impact that his father's war stories had on him growing up: "The military was a presence, always in my family, because all of my uncles had served, and my father was a World War II vet, a Marine Corps vet, and that was very important to him" (Rosales 95). For many other veterans, military service triggered substantive changes, including sustained efforts to "militate within existing structures for economic and social mobility" (Roach 26). After World War II, this heightened civic engagement helped invigorate civil rights campaigns, increased veterans' political activism, and paved the way for such groups as the League of United Latin American Citizens and the American GI Forum, a Latino veterans and civil rights organization founded in 1948.[22] Many believed that military service had validated their claims to full cultural citizenship, and some were inspired to run for public office in their efforts to improve their lot from within the system (Oropeza, *Raza*). They saw civic participation as a clear path toward political change as well as cultural recognition and acceptance.

What these veterans sought extends beyond the kind of legitimacy provided by one's birth certificate, naturalization papers, or other legal documents. Cultural citizenship involves more than one's relationship to the state. It involves social relations—the extent to which individuals are recognized as full members of the wider community, whatever their heritage or skin color; an acknowledged right to participate in the public sphere, to be seen and heard; and membership in "imagined communities"—affiliations based on beliefs about what defines the collective "we" and who belongs within its ideational boundaries. These boundaries are often articulated through the stories we tell about ourselves and our others. As I argue throughout this book, war stories contribute to visions of "Americanism," wielding a meaning-making power that is always contingent on which version of the American story is believed, by whom, and toward what ends. Much of the internal divisions that would splinter loyalties within the Latino community stemmed from this struggle over meaning. On the one hand, the story of Latinos' World War II heroism and loyalty buttressed assimilationist claims—endorsing the belief that duty and honor would achieve desired goals. On the other, stories highlighting America's historical racism, its internal colonization of darker-skinned peoples, and the extension of this power via imperialist wars abroad—clashed with the former.

When president Lyndon Johnson signed the Voting Rights Act into law on August 6, 1965, he called it a "triumph for freedom as huge as any victory that's ever been won on any battlefield" (841). The act outlawed discriminatory practices that prevented African Americans from exercising their right to vote under the Fifteenth Amendment, abolishing literacy tests and poll taxes and giving the federal government the power to take over voter registration if necessary. Passage of the Voting Rights Act had a significant, widespread impact: in Mississippi alone, voter turnout among African Americans rose from 6 percent in 1964 to 59 percent in 1969. Later amended to include protection of voting rights for non-English-speaking American citizens, the Voting Rights Act represented an important breakthrough for Latinos, particularly Mexican Americans—many with roots in the United States dating back centuries.[23] Yet the exclusionary attitudes that had kept Blacks and

Latinos from achieving full cultural citizenship persisted even as thousands were dying in a war "to defend freedom" in a country thousands of miles away. This disconnect between their own status as second-class citizens and their value as cannon fodder in foreign wars was not lost on a new generation. It gave credence to stories that differed significantly from laudatory tales of American meritocracy and noble intentions.

This was apparent in the stories gaining currency during the 1960s, as many young Chicanos came to reject their predecessors' accommodationist politics and repudiate military service as a path toward cultural recognition or legal rights. As Lorena Oropeza illustrates, the war in Vietnam was a defining event in this turn away from the political tactics that World War II had made popular, as "opposition to the war accelerated the transition from the politics of supplication to the politics of confrontation" (*Raza*, 49). Activists challenged the notion that their "route to equality, liberty, and freedom in the United States should rest on military service, unquestioning patriotism, and devotion to the nation" (45–46). Inspired by the tactics of Black Power advocates, Chicano activists "engaged in mass demonstrations, uncompromising speech, and an open celebration of their cultural inheritance to denounce inferior schools, paltry political representation, job discrimination, and abusive treatment by law enforcement" (48–49). These different visions for Latino social inclusion and recognition created divisions within the Mexican American community between pro- and antiwar factions, as activists who supported the traditional basis for their political claims sought to differentiate themselves from groups that opposed the war. For example, World War II veteran Vicente T. Ximenes, whom President Johnson had appointed to the Equal Employment Opportunity Commission and later as chair of the Inter-Agency Committee on Mexican American Affairs, represented the latter view. Asked by a reporter in 1968 about antiwar protestors who were burning draft cards, Ximenes responded, "[Mexican Americans] don't burn draft cards because we have none to burn—we volunteer" (qtd. in Oropeza, *Raza,* 58). Similarly, the founder of the American GI Forum, Hector P. Garcia, wrote in a 1967 letter to President Johnson that "the majority if not the total Mexican-American people approve of your present course of action in Vietnam" (62). Oropeza notes that most Forum members saw antiwar demonstrators as "un-American and unmanly." She describes a confrontation between Mexican American marchers in support of the war and antiwar activists during which forum members called protestors "pinkies" and "cowards" (*Raza,* 62).[24] The stories shaping their beliefs aligned with foundational stories about American freedom and justice for all—and more specifically, with official Cold War narratives justifying the current conflict.

In contrast, those who favored a confrontational approach in their struggle for recognition found it difficult to ignore the implications of the war, particularly its costs in blood and treasure. To many, Vietnam was a distraction from a war at home—the war on poverty.[25] Opposition to the war in Vietnam became an integral part of the Chicano movement's political platform, as its most prominent leaders aligned themselves with antiwar activists and African American oppositional groups. Rarely acknowledged in accounts of antiwar protest movements is the fact that some of the largest antiwar rallies of the 1960s and 1970s were organized by Chicano organizations (Mariscal 2). Like African American civil rights leaders, Chicano activists appealed to Latino service members by highlighting a less altruistic or noble American story. Drawing connections between the domestic subordination and oppression of racialized groups and foreign wars of oppression against Third World peoples, their stories implied that US Latinos had more in common with the Vietnamese than with their leaders in Washington. This identification was not simply economic—it was embodied, inscribed in the color of their skin. To many soldiers of color, it seemed that skin color was the only marker that truly differentiated friend from foe.[26] Latino draftees struggled to reconcile their commitment to political and social change, their family's tradition of military service, and competing definitions of national and ethnic loyalty.

But neither antiwar protests nor patriotic statements tell the whole story. Latino service members who enlisted to gain citizenship may have privately opposed the war but were loath to participate in public displays. While White men had images of John Wayne heroics to inspire or coerce them into military service, Latino males often inherited *machismo* cultural expectations, vestiges of which shaped their intimate relationships. George Mariscal identifies "warrior patriotism" as one of the most pernicious legacies of Mexican nationalist ideology. The idea that men must be ready to die for "la patria" inheres in traditional Mexican American relations, making it difficult to refuse military service, regardless of personal views. Mariscal argues, "The chant 'You don't have to go!' offered to minority draftees by the relatively privileged student leaders of the campus anti-war movement wholly ignored the intense pressures and contradictions felt by members of working-class communities of color" (28). As US Navy veteran and author Steven Rosales explains, "More conservative interpretations of machismo have cast a large shadow over many Mexican American men. . . . promoting military service as a steppingstone into manhood" (4). Refusing to serve was a blot not only on the individual draftee but on his family and culture. In my next chapter I take up the coercive force of such inducements in more detail, but here I want to note the additional layer of conformity expected from members of a minority group, as a personal decision or action is often interpreted as "representative" of the entire group's moral character or inherent deficiencies. An older generation of Mexican Americans, many of them World War II veterans, expected their sons to follow a tradition of military service and thus affirm their right to the privileges of citizenship—to "represent" *la raza* as worthy national subjects. Rosales illustrates this familial and cultural pressure through firsthand accounts included in his book, but the poignancy of this predicament is exemplified in a letter written by a World War II Mexican American veteran to his son who is refusing deployment to Vietnam: "Dear Son: Your mom and I are shocked to read your letter . . . we have never had a Herrera yet who refused to serve his country. Your family will never live it down and your life will be ruined. . . . Your objections will be widely publicized here in Texas and your family will probably have to move . . . to get over the embarrassment and humiliation of what you are doing" (123). Despite such inducements, the perception that the system of drafts and deferments discriminated against working-class and minority males sparked the emergence of a "politically engaged ethnic identity" during the Vietnam War (7). This combustible blend of heightened racial group consciousness, military experience, and social grievance would lead to the politicization and even radicalization of many veterans during and after the Vietnam War years.

Through interviews with scores of Chicano and Latino veterans, Rosales documents diverse outcomes of military service, including the "anger and disillusionment, and other negative and tragic consequences in addition to positive gains experienced by individual servicemen" (6). Many of the veterans Rosales interviewed saw their political transformation as the most prominent outcome of their military service (200). One Chicano Vietnam War vet's account of his disillusionment expresses a common theme: "My coming back from Nam gave me a real clear picture as to where I stood in this society. . . . As soon as I got out of Nam, I was going to protests . . . as a veteran and as a Chicano" (199). Mariscal admits that the most enduring outcome of his own service was his politicization: "What really did change for me was my political awareness. And that's only grown since then" (200). Charley Trujillo's oral history *Soldados: Chicanos in Viet Nam* includes many personal accounts by soldiers whose war experiences cast new light on their perception of America. Vietnam War army veteran Frank Delgado sums up feelings of disillusionment and betrayal: "When I first started fighting the war, I really believed we had a just cause, fighting communism and all of this bullshit they tell you. But after being there for a while, everything changed for me" (qtd. in Trujillo 153). Delgado believed that he was being used by a government and a people who did not care about him, a conviction that sparked his antiwar stance postdeployment.

Recalling these intraethnic group tensions reminds us that even within "pro" and "anti" war factions there were other fissures created by race, citizenship status, personal experiences, and familial bonds. It should complicate our understanding of Latinos' political aspirations and activism. Many Chicanos who served with distinction, such as Mexican American Alfredo Gonzalez, a Congressional Medal of Honor recipient killed in action during his second tour of duty in Vietnam, are held up as models of Mexican American courage and patriotism (the navy even commissioned a guided-missile destroyer, the USS *Gonzalez*, in his honor). But as a working-class Chicano, Sergeant Gonzalez's private view of the war was complicated by race: he dreaded killing Vietnamese people because "they worked the field and lived simple lives, like most Hispanics from the [Rio Grande] valley" (qtd. in Mariscal 4). Recognizing these competing aims, motives, and incentives destabilizes boundaries between "pro" and "anti" war camps and denaturalizes White men as the standard bearers of the military's political culture.

A "POSTRACE" MILITARY?

Clearly, the military's history of racial inclusion and merit-based opportunities is a "tale of two cities": one notable for its diversity and efforts toward racial integration, another a "conservative, authoritarian institution that is slow to change and continues to disadvantage minority groups, including racial minorities" (Ender et al. 230). Defenders will hold up prominent figures such as Colin Powell as evidence that since the Vietnam War, the military has functioned as a meritocracy in which race is irrelevant. Others will insist, as the NAACP did at the start of the Vietnam War, that "the integrated military remained the most successful of its civil rights gains" (Phillips 230). This assessment endures, expressed recently by Iraq war veteran and poet/novelist Kevin Powers in an interview: "The military was, after all, one of the first public institutions to implement racial desegregation. Not to say that those issues have been erased, but it has been among the most diverse areas of American life ever since. I realize that hasn't necessarily come about as a result of any kind of institutional beneficence. A lot of it is a reflection of economic divisions that are becoming further entrenched, but I do think that it has a net positive effect on the people who get a chance to interact with others in a way many people don't" (qtd. in Slater). Indeed it has not been "institutional beneficence" that led to needed changes. Soldiers and veterans organized, lobbied, resisted, and mobilized—showing that, as Harry Truman predicted, they would become a potent political force.

Today's all-volunteer military creates new opportunities and dilemmas for African American men and women. At the start of the Iraq and Afghanistan wars, they comprised 22 percent of all armed forces enlisted members while representing only 13 percent of civilians in the same age range (Rohal et al.). This is surprising given the lower percentage of Black citizens who supported the war in 2003: while 78 percent of Whites supported the invasion of Iraq, only 29 percent of Blacks were in favor; this lower support for US wars has endured to the present (Denton-Borhaug, "Beyond Iraq and Afghanistan" 129). Yet in 2019, Black Americans accounted for 17 percent of all 1,340,533 active-duty personnel according to the Pew Research Center. These numbers reflect two intersecting factors: on the one hand, stagnant wages and an enduring lack of educational and career options, and on the other, the enduring perception among many African Americans that "the military does a far better job of embracing egalitarianism than the rest of US society" (Jeffrey). But Black service members may still face unequal treatment and even racism that can spur them into action as citizens. Marine veteran Kyle Bibby's experiences, for example, sparked a political awakening: "In the military I saw lots of confederate flag tattoos that made me very uncomfortable, and the sorts of personalities that you might expect with them" (qtd. in Jeffrey). Bibby would go on to cofound, along with infantry veteran Richard Brookshire, the Black Veterans Project, which works to preserve the historical legacy of America's Black veterans and "advocates against racial inequities in the military and post-service" (Jeffrey). Brookshire's experiences both during and after the war fueled his political activism, as he tried to come "to terms with the social and racial climate of the country I was coming back to." Brookshire admits that he was inspired to join under the first Black president, but within a month of his return from Afghanistan in 2012, Trayvon Martin, an unarmed Black teenager, was shot and killed by a White man in Brookshire's hometown of Sanford, Florida. Brookshire's personal experiences as a veteran, combined with the enduring racism he witnessed stateside, motivated him to become more politically active. Brookshire's response bears out research showing that serving in the military can spur political participation in the United States, including among African Americans and Latinos, by enhancing organizational skills and promoting patriotism and civic duty (Leal and Teigen).[27]

In 2017, the advocacy group Protect Our Defenders found that Black service members were treated more harshly by the military's judicial system than their White counterparts. Black soldiers were 61 percent more likely than White soldiers to face court martial; Black airmen were 71 percent more likely than Whites in the air force to face court martial or nonjudicial punishment. Further, the promise of career advancement has not materialized, as only about 8 percent of military officers are Black (Brook).[28] Coretta Gray, a former officer in the US Air Force Judge Advocate General's Corps, connects these trends to the current political climate in America: "People are feeling more emboldened to act out their bias" (Jeffrey). Like many Latinos, African American service members experienced renewed hostilities following president Donald Trump's election. For example, White nationalists marched through the streets of Charlottesville, Virginia, during the "Unite the Right" rally in August 2017 waving Confederate battle flags, swastikas, Ku Klux Klan paraphernalia, and White nationalist banners, and with militia carrying semiautomatic weapons in what scholar Sam Perry called "a stunning visual display suggestive of the normalization of white supremacy in contemporary American politics" (57). One of the organizers of the rally was Unity and Security for America, a group whose website bemoans the "erosion of white power" (Bertrand). Another was a White supremacist organization, Identity Evropa, founded by ex-marine Nathan Damigo. Damigo served two tours in Iraq, and was dishonorably discharged after drug and assault charges landed him a six-year prison term. Interviewed for the HBO documentary *Wartorn: 1861–2010* (2010), Damigo admitted that he "felt betrayed by the government."[29] Marine lance corporal Vasillios G. Pistolis was dishonorably discharged after his violent participation at the Charlottesville rally as a member of the Atomwaffen Division, a neo-Nazi group whose members have been linked to five murders in the United States in 2017 and 2018 (Boghani et al.). The organization, created by former Florida Army National Guard private Brandon Russell, espouses hatred of minorities, gays, and Jews (Thompson). Members train using paramilitary tactics in preparation for what they believe is an impending race war; their training often comes from former or active members of the armed forces, whom they actively recruit. As I discuss in the next section, these movements often target soldiers and veterans who have become disenchanted with the government after stints in combat zones. Historically, membership in White power movements has surged with the return of veterans from combat (Thompson). After Charlottesville, the corps reminded service members that participation in White supremacist groups is prohibited.

President Donald Trump's tepid response to the events in Charlottesville, as well as his remark that there were "very fine people on both sides," seemingly equating the neo-Nazi demonstrators with the activists protesting racism, drew strong criticism from many commentators but earned praise from White nationalist leaders (Perry 68–69).[30] This set the stage for a rare display of dissent from high-ranking military officers concerned about the president's politicization of the armed forces. When an unarmed Black man, George Floyd, was killed by police in late May 2020, President Trump referred to the protestors as "terrorists" and tweeted, "Just spoke to Governor Tim Walz and told him that the Military is with him all the way. . . . when the looting starts, the shooting starts" (Sullivan). Having already deployed active-duty troops to "protect our borders" from a ragtag caravan of asylum seekers, President Trump threatened to invoke the Insurrection Act, which would authorize him to send active-duty military personnel to thwart civil unrest and "dominate" those he called "lowlifes and losers." Within a week of Floyd's death at the hands of White police officers, there were as many guardsmen on protest duty on US streets as there are active-duty troops in Iraq, Syria, and Afghanistan combined (Browne et al.). Military leaders were quick to respond. In an op-ed titled "I Cannot Remain Silent," admiral Mike Mullen, former chair of the Joint Chiefs of Staff, cautioned that the president's actions "risked further politicizing the men and women of our armed forces." Marine general James Mattis, who resigned as secretary of defense in 2018 in opposition to President Trump's Syria policies, wrote a scathing rebuke of the president's threats to use the military against Americans: "I swore an oath to support and defend the Constitution. Never did I dream that troops taking that same oath would be ordered under any circumstance to violate the Constitutional rights of their fellow citizens" (Goldberg). He warned of the dangers of militarizing government responses and thus eroding "the moral ground that ensures a trusted bond" between civilians and their military. In an interview on CNN's "State of the Union," retired army general Colin L. Powell, the first African American national security adviser, Joint Chiefs chairman, and secretary of state, called Mr. Trump's actions "dangerous for our democracy" and "dangerous for our country."

Veterans' groups would also take note: About Face (formerly Iraq Veterans Against the War) issued a public statement calling for the withdrawal of the Minnesota National Guard and denouncing police violence against "Black bodies and people of color." Their open letter to active-duty national guardsmen, signed by almost nine hundred veterans, reminded them that guardsmen "took an oath to defend the country from enemies foreign and domestic," then asked, "Are Black protesters the enemy of this country?"[31] Their website posted images of soldiers supporting the organization Black Lives Matter (fig. 1).

Individual service members also chimed in: US Marine veteran and recipient of two purple hearts Todd Winn stood in uniform outside the state capitol in Utah for hours with Floyd's last words, "I can't breathe," taped over his mouth. Winn, who is White, told reporters that he was not trying to "espouse any political ideology" but to uphold "the inalienable rights and protections all Americans should expect to be provided" (Crump).

Over 40 percent of active-duty and reserve personnel are people of color, and just as some Black service members resisted confronting protesters demonstrating against the Vietnam War or for civil rights, some active-duty personnel denounced the show of military force against Americans protesting police brutality against Black men. Kaleth O. Wright, chief master sergeant of the air force, for example, openly expressed concerns about racial injustice, both in civil society and in the military, through a series of Tweets: "Just like most of the Black Airmen and so many others in our ranks . . . I am outraged at watching another Black man die on television before our very eyes." He acknowledged his responsibility as a Black officer to address "the Air Force's own demons that include the racial disparities in military justice and discipline among our youngest Black male Airmen and the clear lack of diversity in our senior officer ranks."[32] In a *Task & Purpose* opinion piece cowritten with Lindsey Church, cofounder of Minority Veterans of America, veteran-memoirist Kayla Williams criticized the lack of official support from

Figure 1. Image posted by About Face Veterans organization in support of Black Lives Matter. AboutFaceVeterans.org.

major veterans' groups such as Vietnam Veterans of America or the Veterans of Foreign Wars (Williams and Church).[33] The GI Rights Hotline, About Face: Veterans Against the War, and Veterans for Peace reported numerous calls from troops concerned that they might have to use force against protestors. Army veteran and executive director of Veterans for Peace Garett Reppenhagen confirmed receiving queries from service members exploring their options: "Some have already made a decision not to deploy and not to report for duty," he said (qtd. in Jones). The group Vets VS Hate organized to counter what they perceive as President Trump's inadequate response to the rhetoric and violence of White nationalist groups.[34]

These responses suggest that many active-duty military personnel and veterans are organizing to counter bigotry at a time when other segments of society seem stuck in a time warp. Beyond partisan differences, veterans turn to political activism today based on the same ideals about patriotism and moral duty that motivated them to become soldiers in the first place. As Flores argues, "For veterans, activism is more than an activity for political expression; activism reminds veterans of who they are, where they come from, and fuels their hope for a better future" ("Politicization beyond Politics" 13). Their military experiences entail a level of sustained contact with a government institution that communicates to citizens a sense of rights and obligations, as well as "whether government is legitimate, how well it functions, how people like them are regarded in the political community (Mettler 60). This combination of factors contributes to the formation of diverse new social movements and feeds into other identity-based forms of political organization in the present.[35]

In recent years, the revival of divisive anti-immigrant and anti-Latino rhetoric has again complicated Latinos' relationships with their government, even as the United States remains entangled in protracted military conflicts abroad. We should note that once eligible to vote, naturalized Latinos register and vote more frequently than native-born Americans.[36] This level of political engagement may inform enlistment decisions, Latinos' postservice activism, and their sense of civic inclusion. After 9/11, the US military redoubled its outreach efforts toward Latinos, once again positioning itself as a path to achieve citizenship or educational and professional goals. For example, the "Strategic Partnership Plan for 2002–2007" prepared by the US Army Recruiting Command targeted Los Angeles and San Antonio for intensified recruitment efforts, noting that "priority areas are designated primarily as the cross section of weak labor opportunities and college-age population as determined by both [the] general and Hispanic population."[37] Such efforts paid off, as Latino active-duty personnel increased rapidly between 1980 and 2015.[38] But this trend could be reversed by rekindled culture wars on the home front, particularly the rise of White-nationalist and anti-immigrant hostility. As community organizer Rosalind Guillén puts it, "We're fighting a two-front battle out here. On one side we have the Minutemen, and at the same time, we're trying to stop Army recruiters from taking our kids" (qtd. in Lovato 26–27). Roberto Lovato contends that "growing numbers of Latinos, especially young Latinos, [are] joining the ranks of the counter-recruitment movement" (29). In his view, an increasingly antimilitaristic strain among US-born Latinos (especially Chicanos and Puerto Ricans), combined with anti-imperialist attitudes among recent "Latin American immigrants from El Salvador, the Dominican Republic and other sites of Cold War devastation," suggest that a "new politico-cultural sensibility is taking hold among Latinos throughout the country" (29). While that remains to be seen, an increase in hate crimes targeting Latinos, draconian immigration policies that kept thousands of children in detention centers separated from their parents and relatives, efforts to deport undocumented young Latinos brought to the United States as children ("Dreamers"), and President Trump's repeated threats to send troops to "secure" the border and even shoot illegal crossers—may dampen Latinos' enthusiasm for the military, undermine recruitment efforts, and kindle a political awakening among young Latino service members.[39]

ENEMIES FOREIGN AND DOMESTIC: WHITE NATIONALISM REDUX

In *For Liberty and the Republic: The American Citizen as Soldier, 1775–1861*, Ricardo Herrera traces a warrior ethos that reflects broader patterns in America's political culture. He argues, "This military ethos of republicanism, an ideology that was both derivative and representative of the larger body of American political beliefs and culture, illustrates American soldiers' faith in an insep-arable connection between bearing arms on behalf of the United States and holding citizenship in it" (x). This ethos affirms the warrior as one who belongs in and to the nation, legitimizing both the discourse of sacrifice and the state as an entity that must be defended. It sustains the conviction that soldiers' highest duty is to their country, and that defending the nation's borders and values is an expression of patriotism. This founding assumption has shaped veterans' postwar activism and extended their service to the nation beyond the limits and terms of enlistment. I contend that a citizen-soldier tradition is still deeply woven into the fabric of American culture. The post–World War II mythos of the US military as guardian of liberty promotes an idealistic vision that aligns bearing arms with the survival of democratic institutions, the rule of law, and the protection of "American values." A warrior ethos can endure long after military service or deployment, expressing itself in diverse ways. On the home front, it may translate into personal and public actions aimed at preserving the ideals of a participatory democracy. But this ethos can take a darker turn when the ideals soldiers fought and died for are compromised or betrayed, when the nation or citizenry has failed to measure up to their sacrifices, and when these grievances are fueled by economic hardship and eroded status or privilege. In its need to defend against an enemy, a warrior ethos can then bolster the impulse to scapegoat—to blame certain groups for the perceived decline of America's "greatness."

America's political culture harbors a warrior ethos that fuels a reactionary strain that, rather than defending the state, works toward its dismantling. Targeting the state—particularly the federal government—as the enemy of the people, these movements are born at the intersection where personal anguish and disappointment and a perception of threatened cultural identity converge. How "the people" is defined by these various movements varies, but my concern here is with the ways that racial, gendered discourses can trigger veterans' political mobilization. While many Vietnam War veterans defended their involvement in political demonstrations as a continuation of their service to the nation and a patriotic duty, a few took a different tack, registering their discontent by joining fringe "patriot" or antigovernment movements. Seeking ways to channel their anger, alienation, or shame, some enlisted in another kind of war—a culture war that pitted veterans against each other, their own government, and the nation itself. In her landmark study *Bring the War Home: The White Power Movement and Paramilitary America*, Kathleen Belew shows how the emergence of post–Vietnam War narratives centered on feelings of betrayal and crisis gave rise to alliances among antigovernment and raced-based nationalisms. Apocalyptic "race war" stories fueled alliances between KKK groups claiming to support a nation under White rule, and antistatists for whom White racial identity transcended national borders. Unlike the KKK, many of these movements did not profess loyalty to the state or patriotism to justify their actions; in fact, by 1983 some had openly declared war on the federal government. These narratives of betrayal and cultural decline found a voice during the Reagan administration among discontented conservatives organized as the "New Right." They also found voice among evangelicals, whose opposition to abortion, welfare, feminism, LGBTQ rights, and immigration aligned them with both the New Right and far-right extremists. Reagan's attempts to rehabilitate the memory of Vietnam by repackaging it as a "noble cause" fanned the flames of resentment, as many vets saw themselves as victims of government malfeasance and civilian contempt.

By the early 1990s, the far-right framing of the Vietnam War as a story of betrayal and crisis upended notions of the "triumphant American warrior" (Belew 22). It mobilized some veterans to form White power movements and militias that would reclaim lost honor and rehabilitate "White masculinity." In chapter 3, I show how framing the war as a story of humiliation and shame lay the groundwork both for acts of retribution among soldiers and leadership decision making. Belew focuses on how framing the war as a story of government treachery fueled the rise of paramilitary groups. Declaring war on the government itself, these groups actively enlisted "active duty troops as members and trainers" (24). They used the artifacts, materiel, and camouflage fatigues of the war, and applied combat methods modeled on the US Army training manuals. Some veterans "referred to their own experiences in the Vietnam War as justification for perpetrating racist violence at home" (24). Belew writes, "For white power activists, a shared story about Vietnam outweighed the historical reality of the war itself" (25). Veterans' grievances would coalesce around stories of dishonor and emasculation, "their" jobs going to immigrants, "their" women threatened by Black men. They would find voice in stories about spat-on warriors, with White GI's coming home to social and economic upheavals that would leave many of them unemployed or homeless. Having fought in a terrible war, these men returned to a home front intent on forgetting the war and moving on. Many needed someone to blame—women, Blacks, government bureaucrats, corrupt leaders, or the nation itself.

In recent years, White supremacist groups have become more extremist and more likely to advocate violent insurrection to achieve their goals. Cassie Miller, a research and investigations specialist for the Southern Poverty Law Center, explains that these groups actively recruit military members because "they need people with a knowledge of firearms, explosives and other military skills" (qtd. in Shane). A 2019 *Military Times* poll found that 36 percent of troops surveyed have personally seen evidence of White supremacist and racist ideologies in the military, a significant rise from the year before (22 percent in 2018).[40] Incidents included "specific examples like swastikas being drawn on service members' cars, tattoos affiliated with white supremacist groups, stickers supporting the Ku Klux Klan and Nazi-style salutes between individuals." Forty-six percent of the troops polled cited White nationalists as a greater national security threat than domestic "Islamic terrorism" (45 percent) or immigration (28 percent). The recruitment of military personnel to White-nationalist and "patriot" movements has attracted the attention of law enforcement officials, who recognize the threat such alignments represent. Daryl Johnson, a senior intelligence analyst with the Department of Homeland Security's Office of Intelligence and Analysis, reports that the financial crisis, along with the election of Barack Obama in 2008, fueled antigovernment and White-supremacist recruitment.[41] Johnson warned that veterans returning from multiple tours in Iraq and Afghanistan War might be particularly susceptible. He based this prediction on an FBI report showing that between Sept. 11, 2001 and 2008, 203 individuals with military experience had joined White-supremacist groups (Reitman). Dillon Ulysses Hopper, a marine corps veteran who served in Iraq and Afghanistan, founded Vanguard America, which the Anti-Defamation League describes as a White-supremacist neo-Nazi group. *Task & Purpose,* a military and veteran-focused digital news source, reported that Hopper first identified as a White supremacist in 2012, the year he started a three-and-a-half-year stint as a marine recruiter. Dillon claimed in a 2018 *Marine Corps Times* interview that his organization includes "many" veterans and some marines. In January 2020, army veteran Brian Lemley was arrested for conspiring, along with a Canadian soldier, to transport weapons and ammunition with intent to commit a crime. Both are members of a neo-Nazi organization, The Base, a militant group founded in mid-2018 that espouses Hitler's ideals and prepares members for a future race war in the United States.

Although this is a small fraction of the almost twenty-four million veteran population, the FBI acknowledges that "the 'prestige' that those with military or tactical skills held within White-supremacist groups made their influence much greater" (Reitman). They warn of extremist groups infiltrating the US military to exploit training that could help sympathizers carry out attacks. Johnson traced numerous incidents of violent extremism by veterans with White nationalist views, many using their knowledge of weapons and explosives in attacks targeting Muslims, immigrants, or people of color. But he also highlights another, opposite strain: right-wing extremists targeting military units, army personnel, national guard armories, and military recruiting stations in the United States. In these cases, extremists are acting on the belief that the military is collaborating with the federal government to strip citizens of their liberties, take away their guns, or train Blacks and other minorities for a future race war (Daryl Johnson 87). The significant gains that the military has made in its treatment and integration of minorities bolster these fears.

Most recently, the threat that such alignments pose was on full display during the violent January 6, 2021, attack on the US Capitol. Some of the rioters waved Confederate flags; among those attacking police and rampaging through the halls of Congress were members of the Proud Boys (an ultra-nationalist group founded by Stewart Rhodes, a former soldier), the Oath Keepers (a militia group that has pledged to ignite a civil war on behalf of Trump), as well as White nationalists who participated in the 2017 White power rally in Charlottesville, Virginia. According to an NPR investigation, of the 140 charged as of this writing, at least 27 (nearly 20 percent) served or are currently serving in the US military (Dreisbach and Anderson). To many of these veterans, their actions were in defense of their "commander and chief."

Yet veterans would also put their lives on the line in defense of the Capitol that day. Brian Sicknick, the police officer who died trying to prevent the mob from storming into the Capitol, was an Air National Guard veteran. Police officers Samuel Hahn and Tyrone Gross, both veterans, desperately tried to prevent rioters from entering the chamber as a group of veterans among the protesters yelled at them, "Remember your oath! You're breaking your oath!" Officer Hahn, a former marine, later remarked, "There was this cognitive dissonance between what I was doing and what the people screaming at me were doing, which is the very thing that is antithetical to that oath" (qtd. in Steinhauer). Eugene Goodman, the Black officer who strategically led the rioters away from the Senate floor and was praised for saving lives that day, served with the 101st Airborne in the Sunni triangle during one of the most dangerous periods of the Iraq War.

A MORE UNIFIED FRONT: POLITICAL COALITIONS AND CIVIC ENGAGEMENT

These opposing views among veterans about what constitutes "honoring the oath" reflect the broader fault lines polarizing both military and civilian segments of the population in America today. Fortunately, most political activism among active-duty soldiers and veterans aims to preserve the state as a functioning, legitimate entity. These organized movements reflect broader coalitions and operate more openly. In recent conflicts, active-duty soldiers and veterans have taken a visible role in shaping civil society, voicing their support or opposition to America's wars and challenging a traditional separation between civilian and military sectors. This vocal and politicized climate for soldiers coincides with Americans' more favorable view of the military. Whereas Vietnam veterans often faced a hostile reception at home, today's soldiers are generally hailed as heroes—even in the absence of any clear victory or "mission accomplished."

Veterans of the Iraq and Afghanistan wars have organized resistance groups not against the state or any particular social identity but against their wars, most notably, Iraq Veterans Against the War (IVAW).[42] IVAW was founded on July 30, 2004, at the annual Veterans for Peace convention in St. Louis, Missouri, by seven Iraq War veterans. IVAW's stated goals extend beyond better benefits and healthcare for veterans, relatively "safe" territory, moving instead into overtly political terrain: demanding the "immediate withdrawal of all occupying forces in Iraq," "reparations for the human and structural damages Iraq has suffered, and stopping the corporate pillaging of Iraq so that their people can control their own lives and future." IVAW has also passed resolutions opposing the war in Afghanistan and calling for the prosecution of the Bush administration for war crimes. Another vet-founded organization, Vets for Freedom, which aligns itself with the Republican Party, works in support of the military missions in Iraq and Afghanistan.[43] Founded as a political advocacy group, they were most active between 2006 and 2010, less so after the "official" withdrawal of American troops from Iraq in December 2011. Their website, no longer active, was hosted by a firm that previously worked for the 2004 Bush-Cheney reelection campaign and the Republican National Committee. It described the group as "a nonprofit organization whose mission is to promote the unbiased, nonpartisan truth of military operations in Iraq and Afghanistan" and "to educate the public and mobilize public support for the Global War on Terror" (D. Johnson).

Because the United States now wages wars with an all-volunteer force, many Americans assume that troops are generally "pro-mission." Thus, today's professional soldier is often contrasted with Vietnam's unruly draftees, with the Vietnam vet's patriotism, loyalty, and discipline seen as sadly wanting. Many Americans would be surprised to learn that disagreement with government war policies remains widespread among its troops. For example, a 2006 Zogby International poll among troops in Iraq found only 23 percent supported White House policy, while 72 percent said that all US troops should be pulled out within one year (Suellentrop). Volunteer soldiers do face greater constraints than Vietnam-era conscripts and draft-induced volunteers, especially as many who volunteer for the military are married or have children (Cortright, "Conscience and War" 506). Nevertheless, the digital age magnifies their ability to reach hearts and minds, extending soldiers' access in ways that Vietnam War veterans could not have imagined. Social media, blogs, and other digital platforms help active-duty soldiers and veterans express their views and inform political discourse, complicating their relationship with military and government leaders. For example, Garett Reppenhagen started his "Fight to Survive" blog in 2004 while he was serving as a sniper in Iraq. The site's mission statement read, "This site is the mouthpiece for a group of soldiers who are fighting in a war they oppose for a President they didn't elect while the petrochemical complex turns the blood of their fallen comrades into oil" (Cortright, "Conscience and War" 507). Such acts defy restrictions on soldiers participating in public dissent while in uniform. They can implicate military personnel in partisan politics and confound their relationship to the state, the military, and the civilian population.

There have also been various efforts to increase the number of veterans elected to state and national office. While in the 1970s about 70 percent of congressional members were veterans, this percentage dwindled to historic lows as veterans of World War II and Korea retired.[44] According to the Military Officers Association of America, the presence of veterans in Congress peaked in 1977, when 412 veterans were members of the 95th Congress (Southall). In a recent article, CNN's senior political analyst David Gergen notes, "In today's House of Representatives, only 19 percent have worn a uniform." Gergen argues that since "voters lean heavily in favor of men and women who have worn a military uniform," electing more veterans can help restore Americans' trust in public officials, changing for the better "what may be the most dysfunctional and least trusted US institution: our Congress." Two organizations devoted to electing more veterans include New Politics, which focuses on recruiting and training candidates to run for office, and With Honor, which describes itself as a cross-partisan organization that aims to provide critical financial support to help vets win their campaigns. According to With Honor's website, there are "close to 200 next-generation veterans answering the call to serve again and running for Congress in 2018."[45] Another veteran-founded organization, VoteVets.org, recognizes that "veterans have a stake in the top issues of the day" and works to ensure their voices are heard, not only through partnerships with progressive groups but also through political advocacy on behalf of veterans running for public office.[46] These efforts are compounded by the fact that the nation's military veterans vote at higher rates and comprise more than 10 percent of the voting electorate (Krueger and Pedraza; Teigen). Many veterans see their political activism not as a departure from their role as soldiers but as an extension of it. They often frame their involvement in terms of service to the nation or to their fellow soldiers, rather than to a political party or ideology.[47] In the 2018 elections, at least 170 veterans received major-party nominations for national office, and at least 75 won. Representative Seth Moulton, a Democrat and marine corps veteran, created the Serve America PAC to recruit veterans to run for office. Moulton became a marine corps officer after graduating from Harvard in 2001, and although he opposed the Iraq War, he served four tours out of a sense of duty and because he wanted to set an example of public service. He explains the moment he decided to run for political office this way: "It was after a difficult day in Najaf in 2004. A young marine in my platoon said, 'Sir, you should run for Congress someday. So this shit doesn't happen again'" (qtd in Dovere). This postservice commitment is also evident in Iraq War veteran Tammy Duckworth, an Illinois senator who was on the short list as a potential running mate for Joe Biden. Duckworth flew combat missions as a helicopter pilot in Iraq, losing both her legs when her Blackhawk was hit by a rocket-propelled grenade. In addition to serving as an elected official, she volunteers at local food pantries and community service projects. Clearly, Americans are turning to their veterans at a time when the nation is deeply polarized and suspicious of government leaders—and many are again answering the call.

Chapter 2

THE FATE WORSE THAN DEATH
Saving Face and the Affective Economy of War

I'm talking about having looked over the brink and
seen the bottom of the pit and realized the truth of that
linchpin of Stoic thought: that the thing that brings
down a man is not *pain* but *shame!*

—James B. Stockdale, *Courage under Fire*

In the opening scene of the 1970 film *Patton*, the World War II general
(played by George C. Scott) stands before a huge American flag and tells his
men, "Americans love a winner and will not tolerate a loser. . . . That's why
Americans have never lost and will never lose a war: because the very thought
of losing is hateful to Americans." It is ironic that this film was playing in
theaters as Americans were indeed losing a war, a time when thousands of
soldiers were dying in a conflict that would never earn them the love reserved
for winners. They were a generation raised on the promise of victory, in what
Tom Engelhardt has described as any American boy's inheritance in post–
World War II America: a "victory culture" repeatedly celebrated onscreen,
recounted in war stories, and taught in schools. Hadn't they learned that
president Franklin D. Roosevelt promised, even after the attack on Pearl
Harbor, that our nation's "righteous might" would achieve "inevitable" and
"absolute victory"? (qtd. in Hofstadter 401–3). And when Allied troops landed
on Normandy's beaches on June 6, 1944, on their way to liberating Europe,
general Dwight D. Eisenhower made it clear that Americans would "accept
nothing less than full victory" ("Transcript"). Decades later, president Lyndon
Johnson would deploy the marines in 1965 with the assurance that "America
wins the wars she undertakes. Make no mistake about that" (Greene 122).
Richard Nixon echoed this refrain in 1970 when he assured Republican
congressional leaders that he would "not be the first President of the United
States to lose a war" (qtd. in Heale 183).

But subsequent generations of American warriors have not experienced an all-out victory since that "good war." America's postmodern wars have ended in stalemates, compromises, and negotiated settlements, in messy and anticlimactic "agreements" without clear winners or spectacular victory parades. World War II casts a long shadow over those who have waged wars of attrition, counterinsurgency, and "low-intensity conflict," wars with undeclared beginnings and uncertain ends. It looms large as an impossible standard: legendary battles, illustrious leaders, yanks defeating evil incarnate. The nation's victory in World War II steeped the citizenry in an ethos of pride that profoundly shaped our collective self-image. But while political leaders still pepper their speeches with the language of salvation bequeathed, in part, by World War II, American Wars from Korea and Vietnam to Iraq and Afghanistan have been sustained by a far less altruistic vernacular of salvation: the need to "save face." It is with this need—with what it produces, suppresses, or exploits—that this chapter is concerned.

"Saving face" involves the need to avoid the negative judgments and subsequent shame we experience when a weakness, flaw, or failure is publicly exposed. The face in this sense is a metonym for the self, both as presented *to* others and as perceived *by* others. The concept of face captures the embodied nature of shame, the ways that it turns a body into a "body-for-others" (*corps pour autrui*, Sartre). It also reflects its interrelational nature: the face is not simply a personal attribute nor a public display—it is always constituted by the interplay of inner and outer, subject and object, by how the self measures up in relation to another and to culturally inscribed standards, norms, and values.[1] Shame "is not a discrete intrapsychic structure," notes Eve Sedgwick, "but a kind of free radical that . . . attaches to and permanently intensifies or alters the meaning of—of almost anything" (59). Relevant here is how shame "attaches" itself to acts of retaliatory and redemptive violence and to gendered conceptions of honor, power, duty, and courage. An obligation to avoid or compensate for the loss of face—for being exposed as weak, cowardly, or deficient in the eyes of others, is the thread that binds citizens and states in an affective economy of war. Despite the political and rhetorical capital that America's leaders invest in fostering national pride, I contend that it is the flip side of this coin—shame—that pays real dividends. While the dread of losing face is rarely acknowledged by political leaders, soldiers themselves often admit to its sway. Their subjective accounts can disclose valuable insights into the underside of pride and patriotism—into the strategic emotional cues that mobilize certain behaviors and perpetuate war making.

Focusing on the Vietnam War as a case study, I begin by commenting on the role of self-assessment emotions, particularly shame and pride, in eliciting social and political compliance. I suggest some of the ways that American foreign policy before and after the war consistently involved shame-avoidance strategies, maneuvers, and gestures aimed at recovering, redeeming, or deflecting the loss of face and projecting an image of American power on the world stage. I suggest that the need to save face served as catalyst for US involvement, then structured the terms of engagement and prolonged the conflict even when doing so did not serve national interests. My reading of three award-winning veterans' memoirs, Philip Caputo's *Rumor of War*, Tim O'Brien's *If I Die in a Combat Zone*, and Tobias Wolff's *In Pharaoh's Army*, showcases how the need to save face also activates a range of individual responses and incentives, compelling acts of compliance, complicity, and even violence. I examine the mutually sustaining and coproductive role of a pride/shame currency in constituting subjectivity, drawing from theories that understand emotions as evaluations or judgments central to our ethical reasoning and decision-making processes. While political scientists, foreign policy experts, and military leaders tend to neglect subjective accounts such as these in their analyses, I believe that soldiers' memoirs help us better understand the emotional incentives that inform judgments and decision making. Their memoirs reveal how a coercive system of debits and credits, subsidized by the currency of shame and pride, sustains the emotional economy of war, shaping the recruitment and training of soldiers, their actions in the field, and underlying acts of both heroism and atrocity.

Veering from the study of emotions as psychobiological processes, I build on Sara Ahmed's concept of emotions as cultural practices, that is, as part of the complex body of forces that produce and express shared meanings. Ahmed's influential works theorize the ways that emotions produce "affective economies" through which we negotiate our relationships with others. The concept of affective economies suggests that emotions function as a form of capital that circulates to "align individuals with communities." Ahmed contends that emotions "mediate the relationships between the psychic and the social, and between the individual and the collective" ("Affective Economies" 119). Her claim extends beyond noting that emotions are psychological *and* social, individual *and* collective. Instead, Ahmed posits them as "crucial to the very constitution of the psychic and the social" (*Cultural Politics* 10). That is, emotions are not "in" the individual or the social, they are an *effect* that allows us to distinguish an "inside" and an "outside" in the first place. These transactions of displacement and difference mediate the boundaries between bodily and social space; they form the basis of our social identity and of the debts and obligations it imposes.

Raymond Williams's concept of a "structure of feeling" is also useful in linking Vietnam War narratives to a broader politics of affect. Williams uses the word "feeling" to distinguish "meanings and values as they are actively lived and felt" (35) from concepts such as "world-view" or "ideology." A structure of feeling can become part of the "bedrock of reality" for viewers as it represents "a social experience which is still in process, often indeed not yet recognized as social but taken to be private, idiosyncratic, and even isolating" (36). By "experience" Williams does not mean an unmediated sensation; instead, he suggests that our identification with others is a mediated, second-order response linked to social structures and social formations. Williams's concept shifts the analysis of social and cultural forms toward the affective processes that make up lived experience, emphasizing how these are mediated and structured. "As a matter of cultural theory," he argues, "this is a way of defining forms and conventions in art and literature as inalienable elements of a social material process: not by derivation from other social forms and pre-forms, but a social formation of a specific kind which may in turn be seen as the articulation (often the only fully available articulation) of structures of feeling which as living processes are much more widely experienced" (37).

Veterans' memoirs chronicle the ways that America's narratives of national pride and honor, its "structure of feeling," becomes intertwined with individual motives and expectations. Their personal stories bear witness to the dishonor that haunted the sons of the "Greatest Generation" who fought in America's first "lost war." Cultural narratives within a society coproduce and speak through personal narratives, which in turn reflect a complex chorus of stories and predispositions appropriated from broader national themes. In the currency of American war, pride is the payment we earn for transacting certain versions of masculinity, courage, or heroism; shame is the price we pay for not paying the debt we presumably owe our nation, right or wrong. Failure to meet these terms ruptures the social bond, estranging individuals from their community.

Studies of war traditionally rely on rationalistic, structural, and organizational models for their analyses. For example, a "realist" international-relations approach tends to attribute conflict to some actual shift in power (military, economic, or political); game theory strategizes war in quantitative terms, assuming actors make rational choices to achieve sum gains. But the "reasons" given to justify war and the tactics used to wage it are often secondary, cognitive responses to emotional cues. As Rose McDermott explains, "While its importance in political science has frequently been either dismissed or ignored in favor of theories that privilege rational reasoning, emotion can provide an alternate basis for explaining and predicting political choice and action" (691). If we ignore the impact of emotion, she warns, "it will continue to exert a systematic, unspoken, and pervasive impact on decision making" (702). Subjective accounts of war can complement and enrich historical, political, and military analyses, which alone cannot decipher the often-irrational human actions and choices made in the process of waging wars, particularly as violent acts are so often contrary to self-interest. In fact, a wealth of research affirms the pragmatic futility of most violence, as it rarely achieves desired outcomes.[2] Rational choice theories focus almost exclusively on structures and their effects on relationships between states, paying little heed to the roles played by decision makers themselves, and then only as "rational" agents acting in pursuit of national interests. Alex Hybel reminds us, however, that foreign policy is not about acts "initiated by unreal, abstract individuals, but by men and women with strong interests and beliefs, different attitudes about how problems should be adduced, and diverse decision-making capabilities" (19). Rationalist accounts cannot explain why political leaders make decisions that go against stated goals or national interests; in attributing a causal logic to war, they neglect the emotional roots of human actions.[3] The Vietnam War, for example, was a "perfect" war in terms of its application of technology and rationality, argues James Gibson: "Machine-system meets machine-system and the largest, fastest, most technologically advanced system will win. Any other outcome becomes unthinkable" (23, 27). According to this logic, only one outcome was possible—the pacification and ultimate defeat of North Vietnam. Gibson analyzes the "point system" soldiers used in the field, the mathematical "body count," as well reports and documents generated during the conflict. His analysis of general William Westmoreland's 1967 report to President Johnson, for example, concludes that it "presents Technowar as a production system that can be rationally managed and warfare as a kind of activity that can be scientifically determined by constructing computer models. . . . What constitutes their knowledge is an array of numbers—numbers of US and allied forces, numbers of VC and NVA forces, body counts, kill ratios—numbers that appear scientific" (155–56). Yet despite this well-crafted logical system, the war failed to produce favorable outcomes for the United States. In fact, it left in its wake conflicting narratives of shame and pride that leaders deployed to sponsor a series of redemptive acts of violence.

The emphasis on a rationalist framework in political analysis also tends to exclude the role of gender from serious consideration. In doing so, it legitimates a discourse framed by male political actors and symbolic or passive roles for women. In response, feminist theorists brought the question of gender to the forefront of political analyses, challenging the state-centered focus that has dominated international relations scholarship and charging that IR remains "one of the most gender-blind, indeed crudely patriarchal of all the institutionalized forms of contemporary social and political analysis" (Walker 179). Their analyses reveal a variety of ways that gender discourses are deployed in theorizing "the international" as well as the integral connections between gender and nationalism.[4] Susan Jeffords asserts that "there has been no period, especially in the determination of U.S. foreign policy, when gender has not been a factor" (91). It is a primary factor in the construction of a "national history where enemies have often been demonized as 'feminine' or domestic heroes celebrated as 'manly,' where presidential characters have been evaluated in terms of . . . their 'macho' style" (92). As my reading of veterans' memoirs suggests, gendered binaries (strength/weakness, action/passivity, power/vulnerability) structure the meanings we attribute to the concept of "saving face." Social roles are central in the dynamics of shaming, as preserving "face" in international and interpersonal relations means that players must "do their gender right" (Butler 178). The "face" to be preserved in these narratives is itself gendered to project strength, power, agency. This is what the performance of "manhood" entails, a heightened awareness of and adherence to cultural scripts. Manhood is culturally inscribed as a precarious social status role that requires continuous validation; it is tenuous and easily lost via certain transgressions or shortcomings (Vandello et al.). Soldiers' accounts suggest that "losing face" is experienced as a figurative unmasking that exposes flaws in their successful performance of manhood.[5]

DE/FACING HISTORY, RE-FACING AMERICA: VIETNAM AND THE LEGACY OF SHAME

My conscience told me to run, but some irrational and powerful force was resisting, like a weight pushing me toward the war. What it came down to, stupidly, was a sense of shame. Hot, stupid shame.

—Tim O'Brien, "On the Rainy River"

In his victory speech following the 1991 Persian Gulf War, president George H. W. Bush proclaimed it a proud day to be an American. The president's speech officially heralded a new structure of feeling in America, one more suited to an imperial power's spectacular reemergence on the world stage. It pronounced an official end to the "Vietnam syndrome," a malaise that had presumably stricken the American psyche for a generation. Here was the antidote for what ailed us, Bush's speech assured us, the means to restore the nation's rightful status. Americans could finally trade in the sackcloth of shame for the mantle of pride: our victory had buried the specter of Vietnam forever "in the desert sands of the Arabian Peninsula" (Bush 197). There are several problems, of course, with President Bush's optimistic rendering of this event and its outcomes, but of interest here is the extent to which it relies on public memory of the Vietnam War as a psychodrama of shame. The "we" that Bush hails into being is meant to recall the sting of shame associated with this past—not because of what "we" did (carpet bombings, napalm, the massacre of civilians) but because of what we failed to do: win the war. His speech invokes a strategic movement away from the memory of past indignity and toward a mutual recovery of pride. This way of remembering Vietnam participates in the system of debits and credits I alluded to earlier. America's loss of face imposed a debt that demanded payback: a victory, a successful enactment of "hard" power on the world stage. President Bush's victory speech aimed to redeem—or more precisely "reface"—America's tarnished national image.

The Vietnam War is still one of the most debated events in American culture. As Walter Capps puts it, the war is like "a bone stuck in the throat of Americans. We can neither swallow and digest it, nor spit out the experience and be done with it" ("Postscript" 318). The fractious and contentious nature of the war has produced little or no consensus about its meanings or legacy. Historians, military analysts, and political scientists still dispute the ideological roots of the conflict (communism, nationalism), assess various logistical and military tactics (Nixon's "Vietnamization," Westmoreland's strategy of attrition, Kissinger's peace accords), and debate why the war was lost (media coverage, war protestors, civilian policymakers). Perhaps the only conclusion that goes unchallenged is that Americans suffered a "humiliating" defeat. Thus, the editors of the *Weekly Standard* could blithely assert that "virtually all Americans agree" the Vietnam War was "a national humiliation."[6]

This assumption forms a kind of conventional wisdom about the war's emotional legacy. Iconic images of horror and defeat—body bags and Zippo raids and massacred civilians—frame collective memories. The nation's loss of face is reified in the Hollywood film stereotype of the Vietnam veteran, whose wounded body and psyche sign for the nation's shame. Spat on by ungrateful antiwar protestors, shackled by the policies of civilian whiz kids in Washington, America's protagonists in these tales form a sad cast of dishonored warriors. In this iconography of defeat, the soldier's body bears the burden of a shame disavowed by their leaders. As the affect of indignity, shame turns the self against the self (Kaufman vii). That is, we believe we deserve our shame because of some moral failing, inadequacy, or lapse in judgment. Referring to America's lingering memory of Vietnam as an "illness" whose "fevers" are felt in veterans' war stories, Samuel Hynes distinguishes Vietnam from other modern wars—not just because the United States lost, "but because in the loss there was humiliation" and the "burden of complicity in a nation's moral failure" (177). Humiliation and shame are the twin pillars that sustain and reinforce collective memories of the 'Nam, the emotional fodder that allows leaders to deflect accountability for poor outcomes. Although the Vietnam War cost over fifty-eight thousand American and two to three million Vietnamese lives, restoring national pride takes center stage in the politics of face, deflecting the shame that may otherwise take root. The denial of shame in a community leads to its coded expression, in which shame conceptions emerge as narratives of honor, humiliation, and revenge (Scheff). The story of America's loss of face in Vietnam reemerges in political rhetoric whenever leaders seek to rally militaristic strains in the American character or to justify prolonging military ventures abroad. Repeatedly, US presidents have invoked America's alleged deficit after Vietnam to exact more blood and treasure. As Ben Mor points out, "Discredited performances (such as military failures) call for facework, and the subsequent use of force then becomes, at least partly, a means of impression management to reclaim an identity, legitimate a role, and regain self-esteem" (95). Exploiting the myth of war as curative, leaders use the recovery or maintenance of face as justification for initiating or prolonging wars, and thus "cure" the Vietnam syndrome. For example, in a memorandum to president Gerald Ford titled "Lessons of Vietnam," Henry Kissinger argued that because of the loss in Vietnam, the United States "may be compelled to support other situations much more strongly in order to repair the damage and to take tougher stands in order to make others believe in us again" (qtd. in Berman 282). In 1975, as a bloody battle raged and Saigon was overrun, President Ford delivered a speech aimed at restoring "the sense of pride that existed before Vietnam" (Ford 568). Harking back to the War of 1812, Ford reminded us that "we had suffered humiliation" but "the illustrious victory in the battle of New Orleans" was "a powerful restorative to national pride." Thus, by implication the next war could help pay down the "debt" imposed by our defeat in Vietnam. President Ronald Reagan collected interest on this debt, drawing on the memory of America's humiliation in Vietnam to justify military interventions. "America is back, standing tall," he declared after America's invasion of the tiny island of Grenada ("Address"). This theme also played out in Richard Nixon's *No More Vietnams*, in which he praises Reagan for exorcizing the "ghost of Vietnam" by halting "America's first international losing streak" (212). Several wars later the Gulf War seemed likely to pay off the debt—as it showcased American firepower and produced sensational images of retreating (emasculated) Iraqi soldiers. But alas, in 2007, when pressured about a timeline for withdrawing troops from Iraq, president George W. Bush resurrected that old IOU: we needed to "stay the course" to avoid repeating the upheaval of our retreat from Vietnam.[7]

It is important to acknowledge the power differentials that underscore the need to save face in any international conflict. The more that a nation values military dominance as a sign of worthiness, the sharper the sting of losing face in the theater of war. Further, the more that a people regard their "superior" national status as normative and justified, the more likely we are to endorse violent retaliation as a means to restore our "rightful" place in the world. America's economic status, its founding myths of exceptionalism, its relatively unchallenged technological supremacy, and the confidence with which its citizens rank theirs the "best" economic and political system on earth—all situate the nation within global geographies of power. This correlates with the high degree of patriotic pride that Americans express as a people.[8] We take pride in the supremacy of our democratic system of government, conceive of ourselves as a fair-minded, egalitarian people, and assume that the "American way of life" has almost universal appeal. Our enabling fictions preserve and warrant this collective self-image, extolling the virtues of our uniqueness, superiority, and moral authority. The myth of American exceptionalism is called on to rouse the national will, provoke a sense of shared purpose, or justify interventions. Just as it founded the first settlers' claims to the land and granted them moral authority over native peoples, it founds an enduring set of moral and political assumptions. Thus, Woodrow Wilson could claim with conviction that the United States had been "chosen, and prominently chosen, to show the way to the nations of the world how they shall walk in the paths of liberty."[9] Similarly, secretary of state Madeleine Albright, describing America's role in the world almost a century later, could declare with equal measure, "If we have to use force, it is because we are America. We are the indispensable nation. We stand tall. We see further into the future."[10] This asymmetrical power relationship framed foreign policy before and during the Vietnam War, informing attitudes and predispositions in the military and civilian leadership.

Historian David Kaiser contends that in the early 1960s "the United States probably enjoyed more prestige than at any time during the twentieth century" (1). This high degree of status not only informed popular attitudes toward the enemy but also shaped decision making at the highest levels of our government. As Kaiser explains, "American soldiers went to action in Vietnam with the gigantic weight of American industry behind them. Never before in history was so much strength amassed in such a small corner of the globe against an opponent apparently so inconsequential. If Ho Chi Minh described this war with the French as a struggle between 'grasshoppers and elephants,' he was now a microbe facing a leviathan" (435). This imbalance was not lost on US leaders. As a result, the need to save face forced the hands of Kennedy, Johnson, and Nixon, as each grappled with the options available to a great nation at war with an adversary deemed technologically and economically "inferior"—a conflict fought by "little men in black pajamas."[11] America's prestige, which then secretary of state Dean Acheson called "the shadow cast by power," had substantive effects (Sheehan 443). For example, in March 1965, John McNaughton, secretary of defense Robert McNamara's top aide during the Vietnam War, summarized the administration's view in a memo quantifying the reasons why the United States should go to war in Vietnam. The reasons for escalating the war were weighted as follows: 10 percent to bring the people of South Vietnam a better, freer way of life; 20 percent to keep the area from China; and 70 percent to avoid a humiliating blow to our reputation (Schelling 535). After Johnson's massive bombing campaign, Operation Rolling Thunder, failed to subdue North Vietnam, McNaughton made the administration's primary objective clear: "The important aim now," he wrote, "is to avoid a humiliating U.S. defeat" (qtd. in Sheehan 535). Years later, in a 1970 speech justifying the escalation of the war into Cambodia, Nixon implied that by failing to act aggressively, America would be seen as "a second-rate power" and "all other nations will be on notice that despite its overwhelming power the United States, when a real crisis comes, will be found wanting." Thus, he assured us, "We will not be humiliated. We will not be defeated" ("Speech on Cambodia"). The emotional incentive driving such remarks was not lost on senator J. William Fulbright: "When President Johnson used to declare that he would not be the first American President to lose a war, and when President Nixon warns, as he did on November 3, against 'this first defeat in American history,' they are not talking about the national interest but about the national ego and their own standings in history."[12]

The Vietnam syndrome, which diagnosed Americans' unwillingness to become entangled in new conflicts as a debilitating affliction, implied that only forceful action could bring about the nation's "recovery" from its humiliated state. Self-destructive or inappropriate actions can be justified by a fear of passivity, which, as Sara Ahmed argues, "is tied to the fear of emotionality, in which weakness is defined in terms of a tendency to be shaped by others" (*Cultural Politics* 2). Gender is the matrix through which passivity is aligned with loss of face: the syndrome's dispirited, defeated subjects evoke images of the nation as passive, emotionally vulnerable, and therefore "feminized." Gender helps to sketch a "face" worthy of salvation and calibrate affective responses. We should note the emotional minefield that this rhetorical strategy treads, however, as our responses to a feminized object must be adequately managed for "appropriate" effect. The Vietnam syndrome elicits identification with and sympathy for a feminized national self that must be redeemed from its fallen state. As a feminized *victim* of humiliation, America merits salvation, whereas feminized *enemy nations* merit only disdain. Leaders invoke fervent militarism or mobilize compassionate actions through a skillful maneuvering of gendered codes; since these often produce contradictory discourses, they must be carefully managed. Violence against a "feminized" enemy can be legitimized by deploying a "wimps and pussies" rhetoric that casts opponents as unworthy of mercy, respect, or dignity. The "face" of such an enemy is not worth saving or redeeming, as in this case, feminization implies inferiority— not vulnerability or victimization. But leaders must also be careful not to undermine their justifications for using force, to come across as bullies, or to make a victory against the effeminate enemy appear too easy. Thus the enemy is also bestowed sufficient power and prowess (i.e., "masculinity") to pose a threat and thus warrant preemptive violence, while not endowing him with a kind of "manhood" that elicits admiration. The "Oriental" was often depicted as a cunning, ruthless killer who, as General Westmoreland put it, "doesn't put the same high price on life as does a Westerner" (qtd. in D. Jackson). This made them unworthy of sympathy (feminine) or honor (masculine). However, the discourse of "feminized" victims in need of our paternal salvation is useful in amassing support for US military interventions, eliciting the citizenry's sympathy for oppressed "women and children" long enough to justify invading their country. Early versions of this narrative cited the threat posed by Indian "savages" and "heathens" to Christian virtue (usually embodied as White women). During the Vietnam War, the mass destruction of homes, crops, and collateral damage against "women and children" were presented as the only means to "save them" from the Communists. "Saving" Afghan women from the Taliban or from Saddam Hussein's "rape camps" was a dominant theme in garnering support for US invasions of both countries. Clearly, the "face" that merits saving must be carefully delineated.

Although Thomas Schelling describes "face" as a "country's reputation for action," he also refers to it as a kind of false pride that "often tempts a government's officials to take irrational risks or to do undignified things—to bully some small country that insults them, for example" (124). This dynamic also influenced policy and attitudes before and during the war.

Lyndon Johnson referred to Vietnam as "a raggedy-ass fourth-rate country," while Nixon assured his Republican colleagues that "America will not tolerate being pushed around by anybody, anyplace" ("Republican Convention Speech"). Declarations of this sort only made the prospect of losing face more dreadful. Historian Fredrik Logevall contends that "what [Johnson] really feared was the personal humiliation that he believed would come with failure in Vietnam. He saw the war as a test of his own manliness" (393). Similarly, as late as 1972, President Nixon's decision to mine the harbors of North Vietnam and cut off the flow of supplies to Hanoi (which *Time* called the "most momentous military decision" of his presidency) was said to have grown "out of an almost obsessive fear of national and personal humiliation in Viet Nam."[13]

Blema Steinberg's *Shame and Humiliation: Presidential Decision Making on Vietnam* is the only extended study of Vietnam to date focused on the emotional dynamics involved in policymaking. Steinberg's analysis argues for the critical role that the dread of losing face played in motivating both Johnson and Nixon. In her view, both leaders exhibited narcissistic personalities that made them highly susceptible to shame and humiliation. Steinberg insists that while cognitive abilities are important, "if highly charged emotional states color leaders' perception of their environment, the outcome will be policies that reflect that bias to the detriment of more reasoned choices" (309). Describing the men's personal and professional backgrounds in some detail, Steinberg demonstrates how their conduct of the war reflected the need to restore self-worth, seek a "vindictive triumph," and avoid "losing face" at all costs. As Steinberg points out, "Narcissistic personalities may favor aggressive foreign policies to avoid shame and humiliation for failing to act (Johnson in 1965) or after they have been shamed and humiliated (Nixon 1969–70)" (308).

Steinberg's analysis of personal memoirs, letters, declassified documents, and memos offers compelling evidence of both men's extreme vulnerability the loss of face.

The Vietnam War was waged by "whiz kids" enamored of their own rationality and arithmetic calculations, men confident in their belief "that sheer intelligence and rationality could answer and solve anything" (Halberstam 57). But if the war would not be won by reason, it might certainly have been lost to the pull of emotion, especially to the double-edged sword of pride and shame. This dynamic was in full display on April 18, 1971, when thousands of Vietnam War veterans marched to the Capitol, "bedecked with their nation's highest honors" (Nicosia 106–7). What would normally serve as a display of military pride and honorable service to country, on this day conveyed veterans' rebuttal of such claims. They marched to the Capitol to reject the "payment" they had earned for their service—for their medals had become, in the words of Jack Smith, the first veteran to return his medals, "a symbol of dishonor, shame, and inhumanity" (qtd. in Nicosia 141). Publicly exposed and denounced for their ineptitude, negligence, hypocrisy, or misguided leadership, America's military and political institutions were shaken to their core, and along with them, Americans' own self-image. Perhaps this accounts for the ways that blame had to be deflected years later, turned away from those who gave orders to those who followed them. Images of Vietnam veterans as "malcontents, liars, wackos, [and] losers" (Swiers 198) placed the burden of shame on soldiers, effectively letting leaders and civilians off the hook.

The loss of face on the world stage—prestige, status, or sovereignty—influences subsequent moral appraisals and judgments, eliciting certain emotional responses and precluding others. Not surprisingly, leadership decisions made in retaliation for real or imagined humiliations produce disastrous results, sometimes prompting government actions that do not serve national interests. Further, the effects of a damaged national identity can persist for generations, as leaders seek to impose their will, justify foreign interventions, or quell dissent at home. This historical memory grounded in the loss of face entraps Americans in a cyclical tale of compensatory violence, fueling nationalistic enmity through time. As Walter Capps argues in *The Unfinished War: Vietnam and the American Conscience*, the Vietnam War experience would be the chief shaper of postwar politics, fueling the rise of the religious right in the 1970s and Reagan's policies and interventions in places such as El Salvador, Grenada, and Nicaragua. Political leaders still resurrect Vietnam as a cautionary tale of shameful defeat or a failure of will, often accompanied by the promise that *this* war is "not going to be another Vietnam."[14]

FACE AND THE CALL TO ARMS

They carried the soldier's greatest fear, which was the fear of blushing. Men killed, and died, because they were embarrassed not to. It was what had brought them to the war in the first place . . . no dreams of glory or honor, just to avoid the blush of dishonor.
—Tim O'Brien, *The Things They Carried*

Philip Caputo admits early in *A Rumor of War* that he enlisted in the marines with the same motive that had "pushed young men into armies ever since armies were invented: I needed to prove something—my courage, my toughness, my manhood" (6).[15] This desire to prove his worth in accordance with a set of gendered expectations was further fueled by watching John Wayne heroics on film. Commenting on some of the factors that drove young men to enlist, Caputo recognizes the need for a "guaranteed annual income, free medical care, free clothing" (28). But he also believes that "something else, less tangible but just as valuable" was at stake: "self-respect" (28). He describes his boyhood admiration for the rough fighting men of early America, dreaming "of that savage, heroic time" and wishing he "had lived then, before America became a land of salesmen and shopping centers." Caputo concludes that such hero worship stemmed from his bored, suburban life, for "having known nothing but security, comfort, and peace, I hungered for danger, challenges, and violence" (5). He reiterates this in interviews over the years. For example, in one interview he claims that the first war movie he saw, *Sands of Iwo Jima*, stands out as one of most vivid memories of his childhood and influenced his attitude toward war. Caputo admits that the film shaped his "conception . . . that the United States stood only for what was true, good, and right and that we were the great liberators of the world from totalitarian tyranny" (qtd. in Herzog, *Writing Vietnam* 4). He also remarks that he emulated the World War II veterans he knew growing up, for they "had done something that was extraordinary" (10).

The rhetoric of war draws on the language of honor, courage, duty, and sacrifice to evoke pride and extol the virtues of military service. Pride is, after all, the public face of the nation, the emotion most often elicited in attempts to justify, endorse, and wage war. It is the coveted prize, the reward promised by recruitment posters hailing young men like Caputo (and now women) into an exclusive fraternity (into the ranks of "the few, the proud").[16] In Caputo's words, he was "seduced into uniform" by the "age of Kennedy's Camelot" (xiv). He was also swayed by the myth of American righteousness, confident that this assured a just victory: "Asian guerillas did not stand a chance against U.S. Marines. . . . There was nothing we could not do because we were Americans, and for the same reason, whatever we did was right" (69–70). Soldiers pay an emotional price for admission to this exclusive club, as the pride associated with belonging to the world's most powerful military is always tinged with the potential shame of not living up to this standard. Military training capitalizes on this emotional economy through disciplinary processes involving pride and shame, reward and punishment, ascription and differentiation.

Erika Carlsen points out that military culture "reinforces, supports, and re-creates patriarchal gender relations" and "in its enforcement of state and non-state hierarchies, [it] legitimates violence as an accepted conflict-solving method" (474). Reflecting on his marine training, Caputo notes that the rigorous, often painful psychological and physical trials they endured were meant to separate the honorable (read: the "manly") from the shameful. The latter—"collectively known as 'unsats,' for unsatisfactory"—were shunned because they carried "the virus of weakness" (11). Shame in this sense is a kind of contagion, a disease that requires a tactic of isolation and dissociation. Caputo admits that what terrified him most was not the fear of dying but the possibility of being "found wanting": "We were shouted at, kicked, humiliated and harassed constantly," he writes. "I endured these torments because I was driven by an overwhelming desire to succeed, no matter what. That awful word–*unsa*—haunted me. I was more afraid of it than I was of Sergeant McClellan. Nothing . . . could be as bad as having to . . . admit to my family that I had failed" (10). In the series of rebukes and reprimands he receives throughout his training, Caputo recognizes an affective economy of debits and credits: "They instilled in me a lasting fear of criticism and, conversely, a hunger for praise" (35). By the end of his training Caputo realizes that while "Napoleon once said he could make men die for little pieces of ribbon," he was "ready to die for considerably less, for a few favorable remarks." But Caputo admits that what he most dreaded was the emasculating affection his mother would show him if he failed to measure up to the marines' standards. In forging a marine corps—a military body defined by strength and hardness, the soldier extirpates any trace of the feminine. Discipline in this sense begins with self-abnegation, with absolute surrender to the authority of the stern father figure who punishes and rewards.

Those who survive these trials—who meet the expectations demanded of them—emerge from training as a disciplined, coherent *corps* or body. While this serves to align and fortify them in combat, it also marks their investment in the ongoing system of deficits and credits that will shape their behavior on the field. Acts of compliance—following orders without question, even morally questionable ones—can score credits (commendations, favorable evaluations). Any hint of passivity, helplessness, or vulnerability can register as weakness and thus evoke shame, a deficit that prompts compensatory displays of power meant to restore agency and control. This view of passivity as a sign of weakness and inferiority comes to affect the way Caputo judges the Vietnamese. For example, as they ransack a villager's home, he at first performs his role as American "good guy," tidying up the wreckage they were leaving in their wake: "See, lady, we're not like the French. We're all-American good-guy GI Joes. You should learn to like us. We're Yanks, and Yanks like to be liked. We'll tear this place apart if we have to, but we'll put it back in its place" (89). When the people do not react as expected, appearing to the action-driven marines as indifferent, passive, even stoic in the face of devastation and abuse, the men are repulsed, reenacting their training by relegating the Vietnamese people to the same feminized, rejected status of the "unsats." Caputo begins to dissociate and differentiate himself emotionally, asking, "Why feel compassion for people who feel nothing for themselves?" (134).

Action, no matter how senseless, helps ward off feelings of helplessness. Shamed by their inability to either predict or prevent the deaths of their friends, for example, the marines sometimes compensate for their deficiency through violent retaliations, displacing and disavowing their anger and sorrow. Ben Kilborne explains this critical distinction between shame and guilt in terms of the threat these pose to internal orientation: "With guilt, there is a sense of who is doing what to whom; one feels guilty for having done something to someone. By contrast, shame draws more directly on the wellspring of human helplessness; consequently, shame is characterized by an inability to locate 'the enemy' except as a sense of defectiveness of the self or in the form of splitting" (179). Thus, when Caputo and his men are ambushed, they burn a nearby village to the ground—exacting a toll on the villagers and achieving no military gains. But Caputo realizes that the destruction was "more than an act of madness committed in the heat of battle. It was an act of retribution as well" (110). He acknowledges that these violent retaliations were simply "payback" for their own inability to control the Vietnamese: "You let the VC use your village for an ambush site, I think, and now you're paying the price. . . . These villagers aided the VC, and we taught them a lesson. We were learning to hate" (119). On another occasion, pushed to the brink of endurance, the platoon explodes in a "collective emotional detonation" that leaves behind "a long swath of smoldering ashes, charred tree trunks" (304). Caputo admits that he "burned with a hatred for the Viet Cong and with an emotion that dwells in most of us, one closer to the surface than we care to admit: a desire for retribution. I did not hate the enemy for their politics, but for murdering Simpson, for executing that boy whose body had been found in the river, for blasting the life out of Walt Levy. . . . I wanted a chance to kill somebody" (219). Caputo notes the "inner quietude" they felt after they had exacted their payback in a cathartic release of pentup rage. "We had relieved our pain by inflicting it on others. But that sense of relief was inextricably mingled with guilt and shame. Being men again, we again felt human emotions. We were ashamed of what we had done" (305). As debt collectors, the soldiers can score a few credits on the official balance sheet, particularly in an accounting system run on "body counts." But this system exacts a heavy toll on the soldiers, who pay for it in a deficit of emotion. As Caputo puts it, "a callus began to grow around our hearts, a kind of emotional flak jacket that blunted the blows and stings of pity" (96).

In his postscript, Caputo notes the "cartoonish" view that prevailed by "the time Saigon fell in 1975" of the Vietnam veteran "as a drug-addicted, undisciplined loser, the tattered standard-bearer of America's first defeat" (349). He concludes that America's loss of face had left Americans struggling to "integrate the war or its consequences into our collective and individual consciousness" (354). A soldier's preconceptions or expectations can "provide a yardstick of estimated costs" of battle (Kellett 22). Caputo concludes that "our self-image as progressive, virtuous, and triumphant people exempt from the burdens and tragedies of history came apart in Vietnam, and we had no way to integrate the war or its consequences into our collective and individual consciousness" (353–54). Having served in Vietnam in 1965–66 and then returned as a journalist at the war's conclusion a decade later, Caputo is struck by "the humiliation of our exit" compared to "the high confidence with which we had entered" (xiii). Yet in his preface, Caputo rejects the notion that his memoir has any political intent (xiii).[17] Later working as a war correspondent, Caputo would seek out dangerous situations, reporting on events in Afghanistan. Yet the fear of losing face eventually morphed into guilt—a kind of survivor's guilt that haunts him. In an interview, he admits, "I felt a lot of personal guilt about Vietnam. Even just by surviving it. By constantly risking myself, by escaping from these situations, I was redeeming myself" (Bajak). He admits, however, that veterans' war stories can help us reach across the ideological divisions and polarities generated by the Vietnam War, can "change the tone and direction of the Vietnam debate, from a stale exchange of ideological rhetoric to a more open and honest discussion of the war's meaning, its legacy, its effects on all of us" (Caputo, "Goodnight" 22). In his view, the writer's literary mission is to reveal "emotional truths," which "are as important as facts."

While Caputo enlisted in what he first envisioned as a war against tyranny, Tim O'Brien's vastly different attitude toward the Vietnam War is evident in the opening pages of *If I Die in a Combat Zone*. O'Brien believed the war was wrongly conceived and poorly justified (18). Unlike Caputo, O'Brien was drafted. But planning his escape to Canada, O'Brien comes to the realization that he cannot run away. O'Brien explains that he was born into a World War II culture of triumph: "I was bred with the haste and dispatch and careless muscle flexing of a nation giving bridle to its own good fortune and success. I was fed by the spoils of 1945 victory" (11). He could not face his parents, for one, both of whom had served in World War II. His concern for what his family, friends, and hometown neighbors would think of him trumps all other imperatives, including ideological. "More," he writes, "I owed the prairie something. For twenty-one years I'd lived under its laws, accepted its education, eaten its food" (18). O'Brien has repeated versions of this justification in lectures and interviews through the years, for example, in a speech he gave at Brown University, where he described "crying with the knowledge that I'd be going to Vietnam, that I was essentially a coward" because he could not escape the draft by going to Canada, in part because of "raw embarrassment, a fear of blushing, a fear of some old farmer in my town saying to another farmer, 'Did you hear what the O'Brien kid did? The sissy went to Canada.'" He adds, "Men died in Vietnam, by the way, out of the same fear—you know, not out of nobility or patriotism . . . they charged bunkers and machine gun nests, just because they would be embarrassed not to, later on, in front of their buddies" ("President's Lecture"). Like other soldiers before and after him, O'Brien's need to save face in the eyes of his family and hometown—to pay the debt that he feels he owes—is greater than his fear of dying in battle.

O'Brien arrives in Vietnam in 1969 and faces intense combat with Alpha Company. He struggles to make sense of what he sees as a senseless war. O'Brien asks to speak with the battalion commander to express his opposition to the war but is ordered to see the chaplain first because "the chaplain weeds out the pussies from men with real problems . . . seems this year. . . . it's all coming up pussies, and the poor chaplain . . . is busy as hell, trying to weed out the pussies. Good Lord ought to take pity on the chaplain, ought to stop manufacturing so damn many pussies up there" (55). When he finally meets with the chaplain to express his moral qualms, he is reminded of the debt he owes: "If you accept . . . that America is one hellava great country, well, then, you follow what she tells you" (58). O'Brien concludes that "we come to war afraid to admit we are not Achilles, that we are not brave, not heroes . . . fear of weakness, fear that to avoid war is to avoid manhood" (38).

James Gilligan explains that "violence 'speaks' of an intolerable condition of human shame and rage, blinding rage that speaks through the body" (55). Violent acts arise in this context as a means to "diminish the intensity of shame" (111). In the chapter "My Lai in May," O'Brien describes the moral and physical breakdown of Alpha Company; witnessing the death of fellow soldiers and weighed down by grief, loss, and rage, the men feel increasingly powerless. Diminished in their own eyes by their inability to protect or save their own, their unacknowledged shame triggers what Thomas Scheff identifies as a shame/rage cycle of humiliated fury. On a mission to "pay back" the debt imposed by their losses, O'Brien offers this sobering description: "In the next days it took little provocation for us to flick the flint of our Zippo lighters. . . . and on bad days the hamlets of Pinkville burned, taking our revenge in fire" (119). The soldiers' ability to feel compassion deteriorates with each act of violence, and many succumb to a bitter loathing of the Vietnamese. Research affirms that "in an effort to escape painful feeling of shame, shamed individuals are apt to defensively 'turn the tables,' externalizing blame and anger outward onto a convenient scapegoat" (Tangney et al. 27). Robert Solomon reminds us that revenge plays on metaphors of debt, balance, and pollution. The debt metaphor requires a "paying back" of like for like ("Justice" 141). Thus when two popular soldiers are blown up, the men exact payment from the nearest Vietnamese: "Men put their fists into the faces of the . . . two frightened women living in the guilty hamlet, and when the troops were through with them, they hacked off chunks of thick black hair. The men were crying, doing this" (119). Caught in the pull and tug of contrary impulses—hate and grief, self-preservation and compassion, honor and shame—the soldiers struggle to maintain the rigid dichotomies that killing demands. Following an assault, they approach a dying North Vietnamese Army soldier—a young woman. The man who shot her kneels at her side, swats flies away, shades her face, strokes her lustrous black hair, holds a canteen to her lips, and cools her forehead with a trickle of water from his canteen. Their mutual humanity is evident here, a moment that contrasts the demonizing rhetoric of war. As they load her dead body onto a helicopter, however, humor serves to compensate for their momentary display of grief or shame: "Damn she is pretty.... We could have shot an ugly old man instead" (114). Mark Heberle argues that O'Brien positions himself as both "bystander/observer and register of shame," assuming a dual role as writer and moral reflector that complicates and ultimately displaces his identity as soldier."[18] I would argue that O'Brien is implicated in these acts precisely because he is a soldier; in telling this story, however, he bears witness to his own shame and complicity.

William Ian Miller contends that "shame bears a close connection with courageous motivation" and may indeed "be its chief motivator" (*Courage*, 70). In an affective economy of war, shame and humiliation work to ensnare individuals and nations in a system of debt and obligation. Miller and others have noted that honor societies employ shaming penalties as part of a local system of order, using the process to distinguish the honorable from the dishonorable. Miller's analysis of the Icelandic sagas, for example, argues that in these social settings male honor had to be consistently won, reclaimed, and displayed; humiliation was strictly understood as a violation of masculine honor and figured "prominently in social and psychic mechanisms of control" (*Humiliation*, 148). Suggesting the reciprocity involved in such exchanges, Miller shows that frequently "the obligation to pay back what one owes" after a loss of face is "inextricably bound up with violence" (xi). In Miller's sense humiliation is a kind of "negative gift" that demands repayment; honor codes uphold rigid norms of reciprocity in which humiliation imposes a debt that must be paid in kind. He explains that "gifts are obligation creating, more viscerally so than contracts" and that "honor, humiliation, and the obligation to pay back what one owes" are "inextricably bound up with violence" (xi). Our refusal or inability to reciprocate the "negative gift" poses a threat to face; it signals a loss of sovereignty and agency, burdening us with shame. In terms of political capital, the real or perceived humiliation of one nation by another is indeed the gift that keeps on giving.

It seems logical to assume that more individualistic cultures would produce subjectivities less susceptible to the approval or opprobrium of others, less concerned with maintaining a prescribed "public face" at all costs. Underlying this assumption is the understanding that in "traditional" societies, where rigid hierarchies and honor codes are a central feature of social and political life, the dread of public exposure is more acute than in "modern" individualistic nations such as the United States. Traditional societies ("shame cultures") are presumably more likely to be governed by the dictates or judgments of others, and thus more concerned with "face maintenance." Most Americans would explicitly reject the notion that what others think or say about us is worth killing or dying for. An American husband who murders his unfaithful wife because her deceit shamed and thus dishonored him is unlikely to be exculpated in a court of law. And though our legal systems do employ humiliation as an aspect of punishment—posting the names and photos of sexual predators online, conducting cavity searches on unruly inmates, and so on—Americans long ago gave up town square hangings and public stoning. But even the most "modern" nations endorse or commit acts of violence to save face, attributing "irrational" behaviors to their enemies while judging their own actions as necessary and just. In these settings, Miller reminds us, honor has "hidden its face, moved to the back regions of consciousness," though it remains "available for use by nation-states to justify hostility" (*Humiliation*, x). The desire for reciprocity is tendered as means to replenish the nation or group's bankrupt ego. In this exchange, cultural citizenship means that we "are liable for the debits and credits of our national heritage" (Leicht 247). This debt is then imposed on soldiers—who become expendable currency in a bankrupt system.[19] While O'Brien disagreed with the war, he answered the call to arms because he could not bear the shame that his refusal would reap; he had to save face—his own, his family's, and his nation's; this debt was greater than his obligation to his moral conviction or even self-preservation. His memoir decries this decision to save face as an act of cowardice; "proper courage" O'Brien concludes, is "acting wisely when fear would have a man act otherwise" (136).

Tobias Wolff's *In Pharaoh's Army* offers a vastly different take on the need to save face as obligation and impetus. Unlike Caputo and O'Brien, Wolff maintains an ironic distance throughout his narrative, sprinkling his memoir with humorous accounts of his wartime antics (such as stealing a television set from an officers' lounge so he could watch the *Bonanza* Thanksgiving special) and consistently proclaiming his lack of military skills, bravery, and credibility. More concerned than Caputo or O'Brien with aspects of his personal life before and after the war, Wolff's narrative seems bent on undermining any illusion of honorable motives or heroic causes. Instead, we learn about his con-man father, his dysfunctional relationships with women, his "lousy grades and fatuous contempt" for rules as a teen, and his drunken exploits. Unlike Caputo or O'Brien, Wolff has no romantic illusions about the military or desire for glory on the battlefield. He even admits that despite serving as an officer with the Special Forces, he "was completely incompetent to lead a Special Forces team" (8). But while he maintains this self-deprecating, sardonic tone throughout much of the narrative, his impudence masks the same need for external validation that has compelled men to march into wars throughout history.

Wolff's enlistment is ostensibly prompted by what he calls the need for "legitimacy"—a need that he links to his desire to be a writer. Experience, Wolff contends, seemed the "radical source of authority in the writers whose company [he] wanted to join" (44). Aspiring to "the most bankable" experiences of all—those borne of war—he emulates writers such as Norman Mailer, Ernest Hemingway, Erich Maria Remarque, and others shaped by their wartime experiences. But perhaps most compelling is Wolff's need to make up for his father's deficiencies, to burnish a family name sullied by his father's disastrously poor choices. As Michael Carr explains, the "nearest English synonyms of the apt figurative *face* are *prestige, honor, respect, dignity, status, reputation, social acceptance,* or *good name*" (87–88). Wolff admits that his "father's unflinching devolution from ace airplane designer to welsher, grifter, convict—appalled me" (45). For all his admitted "bohemian posturing," he did not see his father as a "hero or saint of defiance against bourgeois proprieties. He had ruined his good name, which happened to be my name as well" (45). Through his petty crimes and peccadillos, Wolff's father had accrued a debt that Wolff needed to pay off. By enlisting in the military and, just as importantly, serving in combat, he could balance his accounts "among respectable men." Wolff confesses that he "wanted to be a man of honor," unlike his father, and that military service seemed "the indisputable certificate of citizenship and probity" (46).

Wolff undergoes the familiar hazing that characterizes military training: when a recruit in another company dies of heatstroke, the drill sergeant asks his men, "Shitbirds, why did that troop croak?" and the men duly answer, "Because he was a pussy, Sergeant" (47). He finds himself growing stronger, and he claims that part of his "strength came from contempt for weakness" (48). Like Caputo and O'Brien, Wolff learns quickly to dissociate himself from those who can't pull their own weight, to mark his progress by their humiliations. Upon his arrival in Vietnam, Wolff is assigned to a South Vietnamese artillery battalion as an adviser, though he speaks Vietnamese "like a seven-year-old child with a freakish military vocabulary" (8). Wolff admits that he does not even "know exactly what advice [he is] supposed to be giving, or to whom" (14). But he sees the assignment as "a reprieve" since he won't be sent into the heart of the action with the Special Forces and because his own incompetence makes him "scared stiff" to lead men into combat. Yet he admits, "I lacked the courage to confess my incompetence as the price of getting out. I was ready to be killed, even, perhaps, get others killed, to avoid that humiliation" (8). Though the transfer gives him a way out of this predicament, he asks to be sent back to the Special Forces, "to wherever the latest disaster had created an opening," because "it was honor itself that [he] wanted, true honor, not some passable counterfeit" (9).

Face maintenance demands keen attention to performance, as the point is not so much being honorable or brave or powerful but appearing to be so before others. On the one hand, Wolff takes an ironic tone when his performance draws on the historical power differentials that elevate his status among the Vietnamese. Strutting his tall, lanky body through the streets of My Tho, for instance, the twenty-year-old Wolff admits that he "took pleasure in being one of a very few White men among these dark folk, big among the small, rich among the poor. My special position did not make me feel arrogant, not at first. It made me feel benevolent, generous, protective as if I were surrounded by children, as I often was—crowds of them, shy but curious, taking turns stroking my hairy arms, and, as a special treat, my mustache. In My Tho I had a sense of myself as father, even as lord, the very sensation that, even more than all their holdings here, must have made the thought of losing this place unbearable to the French." On the other hand, Wolff understands that this racialized and gendered ("fatherly") supremacy is an illusion—a performance scripted by historical and cultural myths. While Wolff claims disdain for this "counterfeit" currency, he also admits that as part of the Special Forces team he could "do a fair impersonation of a man who knew his stuff" but that "the act wouldn't hold up forever" because he didn't believe it himself (53). No longer inhabiting his "pose" Wolff distances himself from the "outrageous fraud" the soldiers enact in their "performance" (49). When one of the instructors receives orders shipping him back for another combat tour in Vietnam, Wolff is struck by the extent to which the performance dissolves to expose the man's fear. More intriguing perhaps is that the instructor doesn't lose face because he admits his fear, as the men seem to share a knowledge that allows them to accept a truth masked by their performance. Wolff asks, "And if this sergeant, who was the real thing, had reason to be afraid, what about me? What would happen when my account came due and I had to be in truth the wily, nerveless killer I pretended to be?" (55). Later, when his best friend Hugh Pierce is killed in action, Wolff is again reminded of the price that men pay for honor, admitting that he was alive not because of skill or bravery but quite the opposite, "because [the Viet Cong] didn't consider me worth killing" (87). As the face of empire further dissolves in its confrontation with an encroaching defeat, Wolff describes men in the grips of despair: "A sourness had settled over the base, spoiling and coarsening the men. The resolute imperial will was all played out here at the empire's fringe, lost in rancor and mud. Here were pharaohs' chariots engulfed; his horsemen confused; and all his magnificence dismayed" (23).

Despite his attempts to play the part expected of him by his nation, Wolff's mask fails to fool the South Vietnamese. At a farewell dinner presumably meant to honor his service, his Vietnamese hosts instead parody Wolff's act, mocking him through exaggerated praise and toasting his "implacable enmity toward the communist insurgents, [his] skill as a leader of men, [his] reckless courage under fire" (186). In an ultimate loss of face, Wolff realizes that the tasty meat served to him during this "honorary dinner" is the dog he had befriended during his tour.

In an interview years later, Wolff would reflect on the moral quality of his literary work, noting that "it has to do with will and the exercise of choice within one's will. The choices we make tend to narrow down a myriad of opportunities to just a few, and those choices tend to reinforce themselves in whatever direction we've started to go, including the wrong direction" (Wolff, "Interview"). Certainly Wolff's initial choice to enlist, driven as it was by the desire to earn "true honor," would bind him to other choices along the way. During his tour of duty, he participates in and witnesses acts that challenge his conception of honor and the legitimacy of the war itself. This seems to make the search for some affirmation of their truth and value more compelling. But Wolff recognizes the futility and folly of such wrong-headed tenacity. Referring to president George W. Bush's choice to invade Iraq, Wolff remarks, "Our present government likes to lecture us on the virtue of *staying the course*. Well, maybe it's not such a good idea to stay the course if you're headed toward the rocks. There's something to be said for changing course if you're about to drive your ship onto the shoals."

Stories of American atrocities have made their way into film and memory over the years, each casting light not on who "we" are as a nation but, in Cynthia Weber's phrase, on who we "wish we had never been" (5). Many would impress on us the extremes to which we might go to secure our place within a cohesive group and avoid their condemnation, cautionary tales reminding us that intrinsic moral motivations (our sense of right and wrong) may not withstand the pressures exerted by extrinsic expectations—our need to "save face" in the eyes of our fellow group members. While shame is the price we pay for not living up to a standard—our own as well as our society's—it is also a necessary debt collector. Without shame's policing role a society cannot survive. We need shame to keep us in line, to establish the boundaries that individual members of a society dare not cross. But shame is also a weapon as deadly as any other, capable of reducing the individual to a state of self-loathing and paralysis, a bludgeon that can fracture an individual's sense of self. Face maintenance can compel us to act, even if wrongly, to avoid exposing our own flawed decisions or human folly. But shame, when acknowledged rather than disavowed, can also help to reorient and rehabilitate. By 1969, many active-duty soldiers were painfully aware that they were fighting and dying in Vietnam because their leaders needed to save face. Rather than admit their mistakes or "cut their losses" and bring them home, both US presidents had continued a war that they knew was likely unwinnable. They were not only willing to "destroy the village in order to save it," but to destroy American soldiers' lives to avoid exposing their failure. Thus on November 9, 1969, two days before Veterans Day, antiwar GI's posted a petition signed by 1,365 active-duty servicemen in *The New York Times* that read, in part, "We are opposed to American involvement in the war in Vietnam. We resent the needless wasting of lives to save face for the politicians in Washington" (Cortright, "I Never Expected"). Public admissions of shame—such as the "Winter Soldier" testimonies—would unmask the pretense of moral supremacy, registering a first step toward healing and reconciliation. Many veterans would channel their feelings of disillusionment and shame into political activism—for example, Jan Barry, a former West Point cadet, founded Vietnam Veterans Against the War; Ron Kovic organized provocative acts of public resistance to protest the war; and thousands of soldiers joined the GI movement, which formed antiwar groups such as GIs for Peace, the American Servicemen's Union, and Movement for a Democratic Military.[20]

But throughout the conflict, leaders' face-saving maneuvers made conciliation unlikely, since neither side would seek nonviolent solutions to their conflict for fear of appearing "weak." Thus, the dread of losing face curtailed the potential to negotiate a peace. For among the most troublesome obstacles confronted in negotiations are "the intangible issues related to loss of face. In some instances, protecting against loss of face becomes so central an issue that it swamps the importance of the tangible issues at stake and generates intense conflicts that can impede progress toward agreement and increase substantially the costs of conflict resolution" (B. Brown 275). This dynamic was in evidence in the early lead up to the Vietnam War, as President Kennedy's attempts to seek compromise in the "dangerous mess" he inherited were immediately decried as "appeasement" (Kaiser 101). Further, Michael Lind argues that "in the aftermath of the humiliations in Cuba and Germany, the Kennedy administration felt compelled to demonstrate U.S. resolve in the Indochina theater of the Cold War" (13). The fear of losing face would ultimately outweigh the fear of communism—the oft repeated justification for the war.

Not much has changed in this system of debits and credits, as saving face often still trumps saving lives. For example, in ongoing efforts to negotiate peace between Israel and the Palestinians, James Kirbow argues, "radicals are willing to remain engaged in a state of perpetual conflict and unending hardship, even if only to save face and avoid the appearance of 'weakness.'" Similarly, Neil Altman reminds us that people throughout history have been "willing and even eager to fight, kill, and die to protect their honor and sense of self-respect." Psychologically, people fight to avoid "the humiliation of being crushed, overwhelmed by force, and threatened with psychological annihilation." The affective economy I have outlined here also finances the broader dynamics of the "global war on terror" and undermines attempts at conciliation or negotiation. As one reporter points out, "The story of how a superpower looks for a dignified way out of a messy and often unpopular foreign conflict has become a historical genre of sorts" (Glantz). Politicians peddle the belief that ending combat dishonors the dead, that to honor their sacrifices we cannot "cut and run." During the 2008 presidential campaign, for example, John McCain and Sarah Palin often remarked that Americans don't surrender, and Palin maintained that talking of withdrawal was equivalent to waving "the white flag" or even treason. As the United States entered the eighteenth year of involvement in Iraq and Afghanistan, a bipartisan chorus of voices denounced President Trump's moves to pull all the troops out of the region. Such a "retreat" was criticized using rationale tied to strategic and moral claims, but in my view the underlying motives involve a deeply entrenched fear of losing face.

Though rarely acknowledged as a prime motivating factor in US foreign policy and war making, Americans' collective need to sustain our self-esteem or "righteous" status in the world remains compelling. Given the emotional and moral costs of such face-saving transactions, we would do well to consider how much more we are willing to pay. This begins by challenging the notion that war making is more honorable than peacemaking—and that America's power in the world resides in the former and not the latter.

Chapter 3

TRUSTING THE MESSENGER
Veterans' Memoirs and the Politics of Credibility

> At the most general level, power is the ability to
> influence the behavior of others to get the outcomes
> one wants.
>
> —Joseph Nye, *Soft Power: The Means to Success in World Politics*

Most analyses of American global power revolve around its tangible resources—
for example, its economic clout or military capabilities. But America's power
also depends on intangibles: on its symbolic capital, the influence it wields
globally through its diverse cultural forms, its values, and its credibility. In
international affairs, credibility is "among the most critical of all U.S. foreign
policy objectives" (McMahon 455). The belief that America can be trusted to
honor its commitments or follow through on its threats bolsters the nation's
persuasive power, improving its ability to build alliances, garner support,
and gain leverage in negotiations. Credibility is an aspect of what Joseph
Nye calls "soft power," a kind of power that "co-opts" rather than "coerces,"
an intangible asset in preserving US economic and security interests (*Soft
Power*, 5). American leaders explain and justify a wide range of "diplomatic
and military decisions by invoking the hallowed principle of credibility"
(McMahon 455). It has served as rationale for initiating and prolonging conflicts from the Vietnam War to Iraq and Afghanistan. While some scholars
underestimate or discount its prominence in foreign policy, others argue that
credibility is the main currency of US international power, "the geopolitical
coin of the realm for America" (Brands et al. 3).[1]

But credibility is more than a tool for foreign policymakers or a worthy
goal for nations. It is a form of power that can be wielded by individuals and
groups, a tool of persuasion that works not only on behalf of power—but also
as a check on the exercise of power. If "truth is the first casualty of war," then
credibility is a precious asset not only in waging war but also in resisting or

promoting its attendant deceptions and myths. This chapter proposes that veterans wield a kind of power mostly overlooked by political scientists, foreign policy experts, and military historians, a soft power that works "indirectly by shaping the environment for policy" (Nye, *Soft Power*, 99). While the military is the face of America's hard power abroad, I contend that its veterans can reflect what Nye calls "the second face of power" at home. As witnesses to and participants in the nation's wars, their credibility with Americans represents a soft power that extends beyond mere influence, for it arises from "shared values, and the justness and duty of contributing to the achievement of those values" (Nye, *Soft Power*, 64). This form of power is more susceptible to and reliant on prevailing dispositions and attitudes than hard power. But it is also most important in contemporary democratic settings, where power is "more dispersed" and "opinions matter," where the "ability to share information—and to be believed" shapes power politics. As Nye points out, in these contexts, politics is ultimately "about whose story wins" (*Soft Power*, 106).

Persuasion is a critical dimension of politics, and the memoir's ability to evoke empathy or outrage (pathos) serves as the kindling that can ignite political action. But it is another rhetorical element—ethos—that allows the fire to spread. Issues related to ethos, including authorial intent and credibility, are central to the memoir as both rhetorical and performative strategies. What readers accept as "true" and "authentic" is slippery, of course, subject to matters that are, broadly speaking, political. Such determinations involve relations of power and privilege—that is, whose stories or perspectives are deemed credible and what "we" (culturally-situated, contingent subjects) accept as plausible at any given time. We accept a witness's account not simply because of the credibility ascribed to the individual and the plausibility of what they recount. Less noted is the extent to which our own background beliefs shape these two components, both of which rely on cultural assumptions about the way the world works, about the extent to which a speaker's truth claims align or cohere with our own preconceptions and biases. That is, we tend to ascribe different levels of epistemic status to social groups. This shapes how we evaluate a speaker's credibility—whose accounts are deemed suspect or reliable, whose versions of "reality" claim legitimacy. In this sense, veteran-memoirists are well positioned as trusted sources.

In what follows, I consider ways that veteran-authors both exploit and subvert narrative and political credibility. My discussion of Tim O'Brien's *If I Die in a Combat Zone*, Marcus Luttrell's *Lone Survivor*, John Crawford's *The*

Last True Story I'll Ever Tell, and Michael Anthony's *Mass Casualties: A Young Medic's True Story of Death, Deception, and Dishonor in Iraq* explores the diverse ways that these writers deploy their "soft power" to counter or endorse official narratives and influence readers' judgments about the effectiveness and legitimacy of American military interventions abroad. Their memoirs model competing ways of responding to the state's authority, the myths of war, and the veracity readers seek in first person accounts. I begin by commenting on the erosion of credibility during the Vietnam War and then suggest how veterans' elevated credibility quotient in post-9/11 American society shapes their rhetorical and narrative strategies. I argue that political, cultural, as well as market forces and personal experience coalesce in our war stories, implicating them in a broader politics of persuasion. Veterans' soft power is subject to the moods of a fickle citizenry, but their stories endure as critical mechanisms of influence, articulating cultural and individual self-references and orientations for political action.

THE DISCREDITED WAR: VIETNAM AND THE WANING OF AMERICAN CREDIBILITY

Now we have a problem in trying to make our power credible, and Vietnam looks like the place.

—President John Kennedy, *New York Times* interview, June 1961

If, as Robert D. Kaplan proposes, in postmodern counterinsurgency wars "victory is awarded to those who weave the most compelling narrative," then the Vietnam War represents not only a military defeat, but also a failed story. The war never produced a tidy, credible story, mired as it was by its dubious legitimacy and undeclared status. The mythic tales that framed Americans' memories of World War II no longer held, called into question by our leaders' questionable motives, policies, and justifications. Such moments of crisis or "dislocations" destabilize a discourse by events it is unable to integrate, domesticate, or symbolize (Carpentier 6). Blurring the lines between reality and delusion, facts and deception, the military and the government engaged in a systematic campaign of disinformation, distortion, and dishonesty.[2] Officials continually heralded an impending victory, while privately cognizant of the contrary outcome. Months before the 1968 Tet Offensive, a coordinated and widespread offensive by People's Army of Vietnam and National Liberation Front forces, general William Westmoreland reassured the American public that the enemy stood at "the beginning of a great defeat." Cover-ups and lies were normalized to mask negative outcomes and save face. As the war's putative architect, defense secretary Robert McNamara, admitted privately, "The picture of the world's greatest superpower killing or seriously injuring a thousand non-combatants a week, while trying to pound a tiny backward nation into submission on an issue whose merits are hotly disputed, is not a pretty one" (qtd. in Arendt, "Lying" 2). Subsequent war makers would attempt to revise this history by winning "on the battlefield of memory what they lost on the battlefields of war" (Hayden 11). Thus as president Ronald Reagan ordered military interventions into Central America, he repackaged past lies as new truths: Vietnam had been a "noble cause" and the United States "didn't lose that war" ("Remarks"). These disjunctions between triumphal fictions and the reality of defeat, between words and deeds, contributed to the problem of credibility.[3]

The Vietnam War ushered the erosion of anchoring stories, a disruption of the triumphalist historical narrative that Tom Engelhardt identifies as "the American war story." Vietnam disrupted the structural integrity of America's dominant war story, with its linear plot (toward freedom and democracy), triumphal themes, and self-glorifications. The nation's "heroic war ethos" had shaped and sustained a "culture of victory" that would find its graveyard in Vietnam (4). With the collapse of America's victory culture, Engelhardt argues, the triumphal war story's "codes were jumbled, its roles redistributed, its certitudes dismantled, and new kinds of potential space opened up that proved, finally, less liberating than frightening" (15). This may explain why Vietnam War memoirs were often rejected by publishers who believed that no one wanted to read about—or remember—Vietnam. John Wood points out that even after the commercial and critical success of Caputo's *Rumor of War* in 1977, and despite their importance, Vietnam veteran memoirs initially "received inadequate treatment by scholars" (4).[4] The Vietnam War lacked the structuring elements of a good war story: grand battles, savior heroes, and decisive victories. Even decades later, it still culls ambivalent feelings and judgments. Opinions about those who served in the war have also fluctuated, as attitudes toward the war were mirrored in Americans' views of their soldiers (Shipler). Early in the conflict they were generally seen as "saviors" of the South Vietnamese people. As the war dragged on, attitudes changed to reflect disillusionment with the war, and many veterans were treated with cold indifference or outright hostility.

Leo Bersani argues that mimetic fiction constructs "a secret complicity between the novelist and his society's illusions about its own order . . .

providing [society] with strategies for containing (and repressing) its disorder within significantly structured stories about itself" (247). But the postmodern breakdown of narrative itself, which saw its apotheosis in the Vietnam War, complicates soldiers' attempts to give meaning and purpose to their experiences. As Vietnam War veteran-author Charles Peter Hensler points out, with his war "there was no Pearl Harbor to avenge. We had no symbol of evil incarnate, aka Adolf Hitler, for moral justification" (88). The story of America's "first terrible postmodern war" could not be told using traditional paradigms, did not lend itself to coherent narratives or clear moral epiphanies (Jameson 38). Dualisms of good and evil, civilian and combatant, victor and vanquished that had structured traditional war stories were radically destabilized; expanded media coverage, rather than fostering more clarity and understanding, often increased confusion and cognitive dissonance, as no source of information could be taken as stable, absolute, or innocent. Laurence Kowalewski explains, "When the authorities start to collapse the boundaries between history and invention, the very ideas of fact and truth become tarnished with an officially endorsed relativism" (1). Postmodern war is itself characterized by such relativism and uncertainty: the lack of stable markers (uniforms or other identifying information, clearly demarcated war zones), murky legal distinctions (POWs versus "enemy combatants," torture versus "enhanced interrogation"), and equivocal justifications (9/11, WMDs, Saddam Hussein, oil). As former Special Forces officer and military historian Keith Dickson points out, "None of the certainties of modernist war exist now. The enemy is unknown and invisible. . . . The battlespace is undefined and resists any attempts to bring it into a rational structure." Dickson explains that technological and social transformations drastically changed the context of warfare, as "power is defined by how much information is controlled to define and shape what is known" and "truth is irrelevant at worst and contingent or situational at best." Postmodern war, critics argue, dismisses the possibility of objective knowledge and truth as goals of inquiry; beyond its technological distinctions, it plays out against a broader crisis of authority.

Tim O'Brien's memoir *If I Die in a Combat Zone*, published in 1973, epitomizes a sensibility born of the moral and epistemological ambiguities of the Vietnam War. In a nod to the dictates of realism, O'Brien courts our credibility by sprinkling details about equipment and weaponry strategically throughout his text: descriptions of "the M-14 antipersonnel mine, nicknamed the 'toe popper,'" or the "Bouncing Betty," for example, all pay tribute to conventions of the military memoir. He includes descriptions of the landscape, such as when he explains that Pinkville was "named for its flat acreage of grass and rice paddy" (126). But O'Brien also destabilizes his narrative, discrediting the reliability and validity of his account, admitting that he cannot conjure exact memories. While veteran-memoirists typically build credibility through the authenticity and realism of their accounts, truth claims increasing the likelihood that their stories will be published, O'Brien casts doubt on his ability to impart enduring truths about war.[5] "Can a foot soldier teach anything important about war," he asks, "merely for having been there? I think not" (23). He concedes that all a soldier can do is tell war stories, and in the telling offer "unprofound scraps of truth." Continually undercutting his authority as someone "who was there," O'Brien foregrounds the contingencies, gaps, and embellishments that shape not only memory but all representation. In answer to an interviewer's question of what is "true" or "real" in his stories, O'Brien responds simply, "If you believe it, it's real; if you don't, it isn't" (qtd. in Young, "Textual Truth").

Scholars have focused attention on how indeterminacy shapes O'Brien's fiction, yet most have ignored the extent to which it functions to deauthorize his autobiographical voice as well. This is surprising given that, in my view, O'Brien's *If I Die in a Combat Zone* marks the emergence of the postmodern military memoir as a literary form. His aesthetic ethos highlights the contradictory role of the postmodern war memoir as both a "remembering" (with claims of authenticity and truth) and a "representation" (a selective, unreliable, performative act). He derides an overreliance on verisimilitude, opting to capture what he calls elsewhere "story truths," which invoke emotional connection, rather than "happening truths," which claim accuracy and adherence to facts ("Good Form" 172). In O'Brien's ironic postmodern vision, "realistic" accounts may be false, fiction's "lies" or memory's gaps may contain "scraps of truth," and such judgments are ultimately tenuous. As he writes in "How to Tell a True War Story," "A thing may happen and be a total lie; another thing may not happen and be truer than the truth" (80).

At the same time, O'Brien understands the power he wields as storyteller, admitting, "I'm a believer in the power of stories, whether they're true, or embellished, and exaggerated, or utterly made up. A good story has a power . . . that transcends the question of factuality or actuality" (Lomperis 53). Through "the magic of a story" he argues, we cross the affective boundaries of self, feeling *with* and even *as* other: "It is one thing to understand that the American war in Vietnam was morally ambiguous and morally complicated," he says. "It is another thing to feel personally ensnared in those ambiguities and

complication" ("Conversation").[6] This tension between asserting his authority and subverting it poses an ethical challenge: O'Brien posits the need to
question truth claims without abandoning his search for meaning and moral
choice making, processes integral to political agency. As he remarks in "The
Vietnam in Me," "The world must be written about as it is or not written
about at all" (2). But his narrative ethics also serves as a reminder that to
read a story is to bear "some responsibility for believing oneself addressed
and thus answerable—to the text itself, or to one's reading of it" (Newton 45).
O'Brien's struggle to wrest moments of clarity (to salvage "scraps of truth"
from fragments of sensory, embodied memories: "Men die. Fear hurts and
humiliates. It is hard to be brave. It is hard to know what bravery *is*" [*If I Die*
23]) stems from his conviction that stories matter, that they wield a form
of power. But he cannot—will not—attempt to impart absolutizing truth
claims about his war.[7]

Although O'Brien disavows totalizing truths, his memoir is nonetheless
anchored by the moral dilemma he poses in the opening pages: whether to
desert or fight in a war he believed was wrong. Despite his political objections,
O'Brien would serve with the Third Platoon, Company A, Fifth Battalion,
Infantry Regiment—the Charlie Company Battalion that had committed the
My Lai Massacre a year earlier (August 16, 1968). During his fourteen-month
deployment (1969–70), he was wounded twice and earned a Purple Heart. Yet
O'Brien never validates his choice with moral platitudes about patriotism,
self-sacrifice, or wisdom gained. Instead, throughout his memoir, he grapples
with the meaning of courage, short-circuiting readers' desire to interpret his
choice as courageous: "I had reasons to oppose the war in Vietnam. . . . the
conviction seemed right. And, if right, was my apparent courage in enduring merely a well-disguised cowardice?" (139). While readers may attempt to
"make meaning" out of O'Brien's choice—attributing some higher purpose to
his service, justifying or decrying his decision—the narrative never rewards
such expectations, never offers the closure readers seek.

Marilyn Wesley rightfully notes that O'Brien's fiction resists "the cultural
closure imposed by the traditional war narrative" and "identifies Vietnam as
a continuing struggle over representation" (1). But unlike his fiction, Wesley
adds, O'Brien's memoir fails in its criticism of war because of its adherence to
verisimilitude. She argues that O'Brien's efforts to "transfer" and "translate"
the experience of war to the reader reinforces the "sense of an apprehensible
truth" through its "reliance on representational codes which annul subversive analysis" (3). Wesley identifies O'Brien's characterization of the noble

officer, Captain Johansen, and preoccupation with the theme of courage as "traditional devices which repress the disturbing impact of violence in Vietnam." Although Wesley concedes that O'Brien depicts various officers whom the military would want to disown ("the insensitive Colonel Daud; the dangerous, bumbling ROTC-trained Captain Smith; a racist first sergeant fragged by black infantrymen; the maniacal Major Callicles; and the war-loving lieutenant, 'Mad Mark'" (4), she insists that O'Brien's admiration for Captain Johansen imposes order on the chaos and violence of the war. In her view, O'Brien's memoir adheres to the tropes of American military power as represented by Captain Johansen: "Johansen's example extends from personal achievement to public principle. As the generic 'officer' of traditional war narrative, he embodies the US military project as a form of fairminded paternal intervention" (4). Wesley concludes that O'Brien's "thematic investment repeats the traditional trope of war as the uniquely desirable setting for the ultimate determination of a young man's mettle" (5). Thus while O'Brien attempts an ethical critique of the Vietnam war, "his challenge is discredited by the effect of the formal realism and the traditional narrative tropes of *If I Die in a Combat Zone*, which transform his memoir into the conventional account of a young soldier within the military tradition" (5).

Wesley's critique overlooks several literary devices O'Brien uses throughout his narrative to disrupt such tidy conclusions, often the same devices Wesley praises in her discussion of O'Brien's fiction. For example, O'Brien's memoir repeatedly "deflects the ascription of moral purpose to the violent events of war" (6). First, reading Captain Johansen as the reification of American military honor and thus as evidence of O'Brien's conformance to the tropes and myths of war ignores the extent to which Johansen is characterized not in terms of his functional identity but as an individual who exists quite apart from his role as a military officer. Unlike others included in O'Brien's recollections, Johansen is not depersonalized or abstracted. In fact, O'Brien uses the pronoun "I" only in his prewar chapter, then switches to "we" throughout most of the wartime narrative, only to return to "I" after he has completed his tour. As a soldier, he is stripped of personal identity, subordinated to his function: "We followed the man in front like a blind man after his dog. . . . The man to the front is civilization. He is the United States of America and every friend you have ever known." (*If I Die* 87–88). The soldiers—and the narrator himself—have lost their autonomy and sovereignty; they are pawns in a game without clear rules or winners. O'Brien makes a point of explaining that the soldiers refer to each other by their nicknames: Kid, Water Buffalo,

Buddy Wolf, and Buddy Barney. Only Captain Johansen and O'Brien's close friend during training, Erik, are singled out as individuals. Other officers are identified in mock reference to their roles: "NCOs who go through a crash two-month program to earn their stripes are called 'Instant Ncos'; hence the platoon's squad leaders were named Ready Whip, Nestle's Quick, and Shake and Bake" (80–81). Yet O'Brien tells us that Johansen is separated from others "by a deadfall canyon of character and temperament." Rather than embodying a model of the national Self, shared purpose, or a paternal connection to the men, he is "quite alone" and without "companions" (133). His presence is a stark reminder of the absence O'Brien perceives—the lack of any redeeming moral authority or purpose in his war. While Wesley notes that the conventional war story evades moral accountability "through the narrative attribution of cause and effect," Johansen's valor and decency change nothing, have no relation whatever to the execution or outcomes of the war (8). In fact, it is an anomaly, the distinguishing feature that separates Johansen from others and from O'Brien himself, who seems confounded by the presence of authenticity and courage in a world so devoid of both.

From the outset, O'Brien unmasks deceptive myths and tropes. For example, the chapter "Pro Patria" makes ironic reference to the "obligations" imposed on individuals by home and nation. O'Brien's distrust of any romanticized image of America is evident: while he describes his hometown with references to Fourth of July celebrations and Thanksgiving parades, this idyllic image of small-town life reeks of conformity and alienation—of a stifling routine that, as Alex Vernon points out, is conveyed through O'Brien's diction: words such as "desolate, flat, tepid, small, strangled, shut in, lassoed, with lights off and curtains drawn" register O'Brien's rejection and distaste for "Norman Rockwell–like" depictions of America and suggest "O'Brien's ambiguous relationship to his homeland" ("Submission" 167–68). Rather than abiding by the conventions of war stories he heard growing up, O'Brien distances himself from these traditions. Thus, during his training, O'Brien "vigorously defined himself against the army, both the sergeants and officers above him and his fellow trainees" (163). Rather than reinscribing the tropes of solidarity and shared purpose that frame traditional war stories, O'Brien subverts these. Describing the aftermath of an ambush that resulted only in two soldiers being "blown to pieces as they swept the village," O'Brien writes simply, "That was Alpha Company's most successful ambush" (98). This deadpan delivery mocks official statements repeated by political and military leaders proclaiming successes—despite mounting casualties suggesting the opposite.

Disrupting the traditional binary oppositions that structure conventional war narratives (us versus them, good versus evil), O'Brien signals the changeability and permeability of these boundaries, showing how "good guys" are also capable of committing atrocities. The notion of American power as a force for good or the claims about "winning hearts and minds" unravel in the face of war's realities. After two popular soldiers are blown up, the men exact payment from the nearest Vietnamese: "Men put their fists into the faces of the . . . two frightened women living in the guilty hamlet, and when the troops were through with them, they hacked off chunks of thick black hair. The men were crying, doing this" (*If I Die* 119). This scene captures the men's potential for both violence and grief, destabilizing the polarities used to justify "our" violence against a "savage" other. Such paradigms endow our side with noble intentions and moral causality, while stripping "the enemy" of reason, justification, or complexity. O'Brien refuses to abide by such conventions, leaving us disoriented and confused, unable to anchor our judgments to familiar bearings. After O'Brien and his men channel their pent-up rage and grief by burning down a hamlet, he does not explain or rationalize the act, but simply writes, "It was good to walk from Pinkville and to see fire behind Alpha Company. It was good, just as pure hate is good" (119). In the morally ambiguous landscape of O'Brien's memoir, language itself is suspect, as familiar words assume new, ambivalent, even opposite meanings. Who is "good"? What is "courage"? Who can know?

Summing up the war upon his departure, O'Brien offers only "scraps" of knowledge gained: "Dead bodies are heavy, and it is better not to touch them; fear is paralysis, but it is better to be afraid than to move out to die, all limbs functioning and heart thumping and charging and having your chest torn open for all the work" (207–8). There is no glory here, no flag waving or parading in this return to the world: "It's the same, precisely the same, as the arrival," he notes (206). He is haunted by his own complicity in a lie—asking, "Was my apparent courage . . . merely a well-disguised cowardice" for failing to "utter a dramatic and certain and courageous no to the war?" (139). O'Brien never mentions the Bronze Star or Purple Heart he was awarded: like veterans who tossed their medals over the White House fence in protest, perhaps O'Brien believes these badges of honor lend an air of legitimacy to "bright and shining lies."[8]

Years later, in distinguishing fiction from postmodern memoir, writer Hugh Ryan would ask how, in a world perceived "as a collection of competing truths," does a writer "honestly write a work of nonfiction?" Ryan responds that postmodern memoirists must be willing to accept the inexplicable, the incoherent—to admit *they do not know*: "In fiction, the author has a monopoly on truth. Great nonfiction, on the other hand, can never be truth in the literal sense of the word. It can only be a truth, a story in an arena of a thousand stories battling to document the same moments." Memoir has always eluded fixed boundaries—between artifice and art, between the intentional "lie" and the embellished "truth"—but also between the public and the private, personal history and history writ large. The genre defies these categories for assorted reasons, not the least of which is our understanding that memories are not simple reenactments mirroring actual events; they are stories we tell about our past, attempts to construct coherent narratives out of fragments excerpted from life experiences. Postmodern memoirists "are consciously creating books in which the unreliable narrator is themselves. . . . exploring those areas where the metanarrative of truth is at best useless, and at worst, stands in the way of actual comprehension" (Ryan). O'Brien has admitted that he finds the "distinction between fiction and nonfiction" problematic, especially as "truth itself—whatever that might be—is elusive and mutable" ("Conversation" 221). I would argue that O'Brien's epistemic uncertainty— his willingness to cede his authorial power and credibility—extends beyond generic contingencies or epistemological shifts. O'Brien's mode of telling has a political edge: it is an implicit recognition that other sensibilities and sources of knowledge are not only possible but necessary, and that misplaced credulity can have devastating outcomes. Indeed, when deception is normalized, incredulity may be the safer choice and uncertainty the more ethical stance.

In an interview, O'Brien rages against the forces of deception that fuel unjust wars. "That little tirade I gave earlier about government lying," he says, "was a kind of post-traumatic stress syndrome resulting from witnessing the consequences of deceit, incompetence, and blundering. The consequences are your friends dying, and you're watching Vietnamese die" (qtd. in Herzog, *Writing Vietnam*, 112). Bluster and "belligerent rhetoric" serve only those whose "handsome young son or lovely young daughter will never end up in a plastic body bag" ("Conversation"). Undermining his own credibility, O'Brien rejects the righteous certitudes that justify oppressive regimes of power; subverting readers' acquiescence to the author as authority, he challenges those who disavow moral responsibility through willful ignorance, passive resignation, or comforting illusions. If our understanding of war is to extend beyond the metanarratives that have always accompanied it, O'Brien suggests, readers—and by extension civilians—need to confront their own complicity in the collective fiction making that keeps us beholden to war. Having heard its pitchmen selling their singular versions of truth, and seen firsthand the effects of blind faith in its wares, O'Brien urges us to reject their siren's call.

Ironically, O'Brien's admission that he cannot impart any universal or transcendent truths makes his narrative more credible. In the absence of any stable anchor on which to secure claims of "objectivity" or universality or permanence, and in the wake of a disastrous war in Vietnam waged on the credibility of "whiz kids," O'Brien's admissions of doubt and fallibility endow his narrative with an aura of authenticity that makes readers more receptive, a kind of soft power that *attracts*. His uncertainty mirrors our own, fostering identification and trust. This strategy produces what Megan Brown calls the "ethos paradox." In *American Autobiography after 9/11*, Brown contends that "narrative strategies showing that an autobiographical text is itself constituted and contingent can strengthen that text's credibility/air of authenticity" (21). She concedes that in disrupting readers' expectations memoirists risk undermining their own authority, but I would argue that in O'Brien's memoir, that is the point. Speaking through his stories, O'Brien acknowledges, "It's a question of credibility. Often the crazy stuff is true and the normal stuff isn't, because the normal stuff is necessary to make you believe the truly incredible craziness" ("How to Tell a True War Story" 68). O'Brien's memoir incites readers to take an active role in piecing together fragments of history and memory, to locate their own "scraps of truth." It reminds us that "bright shining lies" got us into the Vietnam War, kept us there long after leaders knew the war was lost, and cost over fifty-eight thousand American soldiers their lives. O'Brien's memoir, like his fiction, is a resounding "rebel call against absolutism" (Franklin).

IN SOLDIERS WE TRUST: POST-TRUTH IN/CREDULITY

We like non-fiction because we live in fictitious times.

—David Shields, *Reality Hunger*

The "credibility gap" that became apparent during the Vietnam War has grown into a chasm in the wake of another war justified with manipulated intelligence, doctored photos, and downright lies. The weapons of mass destruction and mushroom clouds conjured up as pretext for invading Iraq echoed LBJ's Gulf of Tonkin and Cold War rhetoric, but this time America's eroded credibility hindered efforts to persuade crucial allies to join president George W.

Bush's "coalition of the willing."[9] More recently, Joseph Nye argues that Donald Trump's lack of credibility further compromises America's status abroad and weakens its soft power, as "the president's looseness with the truth has debased the currency of trust that is needed in a crisis, and his continual disdain for our allies means we have fewer friends" ("No, President Trump").[10] But other authorities and information sources fare no better. Confidence in traditional institutions is at an all-time low, as Americans distrust not just their own government but also media, corporations, and even religious institutions.[11] As a result, we regard our leaders and fellow citizens with outright cynicism: we "know" politicians lie, the rich cheat on their taxes, and the poor defraud the government. Since no one trusts anyone from the other side of the political aisle, gridlock is the new normal in Congress.

Paradoxically, distrust makes us more gullible, as Americans increasingly turn to alternative and partisan media outlets.[12] Nostalgic for the solace of certitude, we encase ourselves in political echo chambers where like-minded talking heads and pseudoexperts are granted license with the facts. The more partisan we are, the more trapped we become in a polarizing feedback loop, believing absurd claims about political opponents while rejecting whole-sale any counter evidence.[13] Here the measure of credibility is simple: does the information comply with the receiver's worldview or party line? One is reminded of Joseph Addison's words in 1716: describing the partisan divide in his day, the English essayist bemoaned the "political faith" of those who are blindly "nourished . . . by fiction and delusion" if it pleases their political sensibilities. Addison's remark that the citizenry is primed to "hate one half of the Nation" rings eerily true in America three hundred years later.

This volatile combination of forces—a deeply polarized citizenry, a mood of distrust, the prevalence of "fiction and delusion"—is most troublesome when a nation is at war. While fake news and doctored photos are not unique to postmodern wars (the printing press and the camera introduced staged battle scenes, yellow journalism, and government propaganda presented as "newsreels"), new media technologies democratize the business of producing and circulating sensational falsehoods.[14] The Trump administration provided ample kindling to the fires of distrust—denigrating journalists as "enemies of the people" and waging a war of words on major news outlets such as CNN ("Clinton News Network"), MSNBC ("Commiecast"), and the *New York Times* ("Failing New York Times") among others.[15] Jonathan Ladd points out that "those practicing conventional, objective journalism are . . . dramatically less trusted by the public, face harsh and persistent political criticism, and must compete with less conventional news sources as well as many other entertainment options" (2). Ladd demonstrates the partisan nature of this declining trust in media: in the 1950s both Republicans and Democrats expressed the belief that the media were generally fair in their accounts of events, but by the later decades of the twentieth century the polarization of the party system increased attacks on media fairness by politicians and political activists.[16] Since persuasion depends on the extent to which the source of information is deemed credible, distrust leads the citizenry to resist new messages about national conditions in major policy areas. Beliefs about what policies are needed or what outcomes these achieve may be less accurate, shaped by partisanship rather than facts or verifiable evidence (190). I would add that the government's use of "embedded journalists" also controls the media's access while allowing some televised operations to be staged for public entertainment.[17] These combined factors splinter communities into dueling camps mired in suspicion and paranoia.

Yet in this highly polarized "post-truth" environment, Americans of all political stripes are in the mood to trust their military. In particular, civilians now grant soldiers and veterans a level of credibility unmatched by any other group.[18] This high credibility quotient translates into a kind of soft power as veterans, even those never deployed to a combat zone, are asked to opine on everything war-related, from strategy to weaponry to policy. They can deploy their identity as veterans to help their political views resonate with the American public and provide "boots on the ground" credibility (D. Flores 13). Their moral authority can "legitimize their articulation of 'facts,'" lend credence to select political figures, and "legitimize broader social movements" (13). This positions veterans' memoirs in a category once reserved for the news media. Philip Melling contends that in the aftermath of the Vietnam War, Americans' intense distrust of government and media sources elevated the veteran memoirist to the status of "investigative writer," a figure best qualified to document "his knowledge of events and perceptions of the truth" (53–54). Thomas Larson is similarly optimistic about the memoir's standing in such a context, noting that it "is taking the lead, among other dissenting voices, against any form of media misrepresentation" (*Boom!* 188). Veterans are a trusted brand in America: they are asked to serve as impromptu news pundits, give speeches at political rallies, and even run for office themselves.

For their part, civilians are expected to extend uncritical, even jingoistic support to the military. Without a draft, only about one half of 1 percent of the US population has been on active military duty at any time during almost two decades of sustained conflict. "At the dawn of the twenty-first century," writes retired army major Adrian R. Lewis, "America's wars resembled the wars of the seventeenth-century monarchs, where kings elected to go to war, a small professional army fought them, and the people were uninvolved."[19] Despite this disconnect, or because of it, American militarism has morphed into a kind of secular religion that elevates the soldier "to the status of national icon, the apotheosis of all that is great and good about contemporary America" (Bacevitch 23). Pleas to "Support the Troops" interpellate us as American consumers, hailing us into the ranks of citizenship with what Michael Schwalbe calls "micro militarism." Citing examples of America's ubiquitous proliferation of its war culture, Schwalbe cites trivial, day-to-day appeals that add up to "normalize militarism on a large scale": ATM receipts with "Support the Troops" posted under our checking account balance, and requests for donations at the grocery checkout counter. Despite even the best intentions (to recognize the service of military men and women), the consequences of such practices are far from trivial, Schwalbe insists, as the pervasiveness of these exhortations teaches Americans "that war and violence and soldiering are not political matters subject to contention or debate." Instead, they are "normal parts of who we are and what we do as a people, and anyone who questions this is . . . unpatriotic, a traitor." Interestingly, America's revitalized militarism also shapes how soldiers respond to visual representations of war. Veteran author Anthony Swofford contends that to soldiers, all war movies "are pro-war, no matter what the supposed message" because "the magic brutality of the films" is "pornography for the military man" (6–7). These combined cultural trends make criticism of the military or attempts to "demythify" wars difficult, even blasphemous—a predicament that political leaders are quick to exploit.

Since 2001 over two million men and women have served in Iraq and Afghanistan, but for most Americans, these wars are just background noise. Our negligence prompts ritual acts of contrition—usually in hollow expressions of gratitude. Carrying the burdens of war, soldiers and veterans comprise an exclusive group of one-percenters. Against a precarious backdrop of perpetual war, the soldier's singular voice invites us back into a world where political choices have personal consequences, where personal actions reverberate nationally and can have repercussions on the world stage. Iraq veteran-author Roy Scranton understands why readers seek out veteran-writers for their special knowledge of war. But he bristles at the idea that soldiers should serve as moral authorities for a civilian population in search of some idealized portrait of America. He disputes the notion that their versions of truth are sacrosanct: "We cannot just keep worshipping veterans. They're just people who did a dirty, nasty, demanding job" (qtd. in Lawrence). Scranton, whose perspective on the Iraq War is unabashedly political, rejects "thank a soldier" clichés and the broader myths or omissions that this can perpetuate. He insists, "Anyone . . . talking about morality and the Iraq War needs to account for the gross irresponsibility, outright lies, and pointless waste of human life that characterized that conflict" ("Choosing War"). But challenging deeply held beliefs or criticizing the war effort in this way poses risks—as memoirists who do so may forfeit their credibility.[20]

In the process, these veteran-writers may also compromise their market value, especially as a glut of war memoirs written in the style of spectacular action films sensationalize killing and glorify recklessness as heroism. This subgenre, which Iraq war veteran and author Brian Van Reet refers to as the "kill memoir," often features a Navy SEAL protagonist-hero and focuses on graphic and often exaggerated accounts of military exploits. Popular entertainment for noncombatants, these "shock and awe" narratives reflect the sensationalistic, media-savvy hyperreality associated with postmodern war making. Van Reet argues that these memoirs, which have flooded the market, do nothing to reveal truths about the effects of war or its toll on soldiers. Instead, playing into civilians' morbid curiosity about killing in combat, "these books simply answer in the most spectacularly affirmative way possible: 'Did I kill anybody? Hell, yeah. His name was Osama bin Laden. Maybe you heard of him.'"[21] Van Reet notes that this genre relies on a two-part formula: the claim to authenticity (autobiography, memoir, firsthand) and "the assurance that the reader will learn the intimate details of taking human life." In his review of Dillard Johnson's *Carnivore: A Memoir by One of the Deadliest American Soldiers of All Time*, Van Reet comments on the promotional campaign for the book: the publisher, William Morrow, hyped up Sergeant Johnson's experiences as commander of a Bradley fighting vehicle during the 2003 invasion of Iraq, claiming in their marketing materials that Johnson killed 2,746 enemy combatants in Iraq, a figure widely disputed. The "kill memoir," Van Reet remarks, "offers the spectacle of high body counts and terrorists twitching on the floor as proof that we are winning" and "reinforces the military-civilian divide." Here killing is both just and entertaining, a myth that is useful in marketing wars as thrilling spectacles for civilian consumption. This also fosters what Ken Plummer calls the "dark side" of the autobiographical form, as war experiences become "commodities—literally stories that may be exchanged or sold" (100). As a result, writers may resort to a series of clichés that meet readers' expectations, producing formulaic war stories that are "endlessly recycled, repeated, replayed." Thus contemporary soldier-writers are incentivized to produce fast-paced, action-movie-style war stories on the one hand, and authentic, "true" accounts of their experiences on the other.

Veteran memoirs that portray "our side" as weak or ineffective are also less likely to be turned into profitable Hollywood war movies.[22] Rather than judged as authentic, these memoirs are less credible among Americans who believe that the US military is "the world's greatest force for good."[23] For example, Iraq and Afghanistan war films such as Kimberly Peirce's *Stop-Loss*, Paul Haggis's *In the Valley of Elah*, and Paul Greengrass's *Green Zone*, which are critical of the wars, did not fare well at the box office. Clint Eastwood's *American Sniper* (2014), based on the best-selling memoir by Iraq War veteran Chris Kyle (2012), by contrast, earned $105.3 million its opening weekend, more than every R-rated movie in history except *The Matrix Reloaded* (Lang). Kyle, a SEAL sharpshooter who served four tours in Iraq, is credited with the most confirmed "kills" of any sniper in American military history.[24] His memoir was the subject of much controversy, not only because of Kyle's unapologetic stance regarding his 160 "kills" ("I couldn't give a flying fuck about the Iraqis") but also because several claims he made are disputed—including one widely circulated by his publisher, journalists, and Kyle himself that all profits from the memoir were donated to the families of fallen soldiers.[25]

Of interest here are the political implications of sanctifying soldiers and veterans, especially the extent to which it promotes the kind of credulity that O'Brien warns against: a civilian population primed for new myths and deceptions. As O'Brien puts it, "Evil has no place, it seems, in our national mythology. We erase it. We use ellipses. We salute ourselves and take pride in America the White Knight, America the Lone Ranger, America's sleek laser-guided weaponry beating up on Saddam and his legion of devils" ("Vietnam in Me"). In today's "kill memoirs," the "white knight" may also be a Black army ranger, as in *The Reaper: Autobiography of One of the Deadliest Special Ops Snipers*, by "legendary sniper" Nicholas Irving, the first African American to serve as a special ops in the Third Ranger Battalion. Just eighteen years old when deployed, Irving killed a record thirty-three Taliban in a single Afghanistan deployment, making him one of the deadliest snipers in American history. His memoir is coauthored by Gary Brozek, who also cowrote Irving's second book, *Way of the Reaper: My Greatest Untold Missions and the Art of Being a Sniper*, and who, coincidentally, is included on the Conservative Book Club's directory of recommended authors.[26] Irving would go on to play a cadre leader on Fox's reality television series *American Grit* and was featured in various TV, newspaper, and magazine interviews. Rapper Jay-Z planned to produce a six-hour miniseries based on Irving's first book. But the Weinstein Company had acquired the rights to Irving's memoir less than a week after it was published, and Harvey Weinstein's conviction on sexual assault charges led Irving to back out of the project. NBC bought the rights, but in late 2017 Irving reported on his podcast that the miniseries had been scrapped and a movie based on the book was in preproduction. Irving also worked with director Doug Liman as consultant on the movie *The Wall,* a military thriller about two snipers. In *The Reaper,* Irving admits there is a tendency to exaggerate and create military "myths and legends," noting that someone had misattributed "more than seven hundred kills" to him (4). While he admits he would have wanted to make that contribution to keeping his comrades safe, he asserts that his memoir will "keep things real" (5).[27] But what most of these memoirs downplay—and what readers rarely glimpse—is the aftermath of "legendary kill numbers" for the men achieving them. Irving would struggle with alcohol dependency and attempt suicide after his discharge. Unlike most "kill memoir" authors, he admits feeling remorse, and notes, "I had one question that I pushed out of my mind until after I'd decided to leave the Army and begun finding comfort and courage in the bottom of too many bottles of booze: Was I a good man or a bad man?" (*Way of the Reaper* 166).

But in most depictions of US military snipers as "legendary killers," the iconic White Knight figure is indeed "White" (Black or Latino male "killers" are likely to inspire dread, not patriotism). Kyle fit the "all American hero" physical type, and his marketing as a "white Knight" is evident in Michael J. Mooney's 2015 biography of Kyle.[28] Mooney refers to Kyle as "a living, breathing mythological figure—a legend" (*Life and Legend of Chris Kyle* 8). Any questions about the legitimacy of the war, the morality of celebrating "kill ratios," or the credibility of Kyle himself seem sacrilegious after reading Mooney's panegyric, as Kyle the man is lost to the mythic warrior who "performed near miracles on the battlefield" on behalf of an American military "fighting for good, fighting against evil, fighting for freedom and for something bigger" (7). While critics debate Kyle's credibility, most readers (and viewers of the film) are enamored of his stoic heroism, "legendary" status, and absolute conviction (e.g., "SAVAGE, DESPICABLE EVIL. THAT'S WHAT WE WERE FIGHTING in Iraq" (*American Sniper* 8; caps in original).[29] Mooney's biography was a *New York Times* bestseller and has been called "an honest portrayal" (The Blaze).

Regardless of how we judge Kyle's credibility or views, however, Afghanistan War veteran and writer Brock McIntosh argues that what should concern us is not the lies Kyle told but the lies he *believed*: lies about WMDs in Iraq, lies about Iraq as culpable for 9/11, and the "lie that people do evil things because they are evil." He goes on to write that the controversy over Kyle's memoir deflects attention from those who crafted lies that "created a trail of blowback leading from dumb war to dumb war, and that have sent 2.5 million veterans to fight a 'war on terror' that persists in Iraq, Afghanistan, Yemen, Syria and Pakistan." He also directs his anger at the film, which "recycles propagandistic fiction under the guise of a 'true story.'" In McIntosh's view, the film's screenwriter, Jason Hall, tailored Kyle's story "to promote his moral fantasy world and deny legitimacy to veterans critical of the war."[30] Resorting to the same old absolutes, "every Iraqi in the movie—including the women and children—are either evil, butchering insurgents or collaborators. . . . They're all 'savages.'" McIntosh notes that Eastwood's film punishes anyone who is skeptical of the war (the only soldier who expresses skepticism is shot in the head) and rewards moral absolutism and righteousness ("Either [Kyle] kills a child or the child kills Marines").

While Eastwood's film aims to bring Kyle's Iraq War memoir to the screen, its moral universe is moored to World War II, a good-versus-evil moral framework that disallows nonbelievers. Its political effects are disguised by the claim that its only intent is to tell a soldier's "real story." The movie's creative team contends that the film does not contain a political message, and Eastwood himself claims that he made an antiwar film. But audience reception of both the film and the memoir suggest otherwise: Kyle was invited to "hang out" with George W. Bush, Republican Party officials promoted the film at political events, and conservative viewers treated it with "unconsidered, rah-rah reverence" (West).[31]

THE RETURN OF THE GREAT AMERICAN WAR STORY: MARCUS LUTTRELL'S *LONE SURVIVOR*

I'm telling you stories. Trust me.

—Jeanette Winterson, *Oranges Aren't the Only Fruit*

Many memoirs written by Iraq and Afghanistan war veterans retain the ambivalence, frustration, and anguish of previous generations of soldiers, but they are less likely to question the cause itself. This may reflect the broader mood, for despite opposition to the Iraq War, Americans are circumspect about antiwar displays for fear that these can be construed as antitroop. The hero worship that passes for patriotism in post-9/11 America has also displaced the Vietnam War from popular consciousness, as World War II resumes its role as the preeminent war (Bleakney 26–29). O'Brien suggests that today's veteran-memoirists often "look at war as an aspect of glory, of finding honor." In his view, "It's almost an old-fashioned, Victorian way of looking at war" (qtd. in Bumiller, "Well-Written War"). This return to a pre–World War II mindset is evident in Marcus Luttrell's bestselling Afghanistan war memoir *Lone Survivor*. Like Kyle, Luttrell is a self-described "American patriot" who is absolutely convinced that our cause is just and our leaders speak truth.[32] While on a mission in the Afghan mountains to capture or kill an al Qaeda leader, Luttrell and three Navy SEAL teammates are ambushed by Taliban fighters. He witnesses the deaths of his friends, an experience, he tells us, that leaves "a gaping hollow . . . in my life for the rest of my days" (402). Staunch in his conviction that they were fighting "on the front line of the battle against world terror," Luttrell is proud "to defend his country and carry out the wishes of his commander-in-chief" (44). There is no place for moral or political ambiguity in Luttrell's world. "I'm an American," he writes, "and when the bell sounds, I will come out fighting for my country and for my teammates. If necessary, to the death" (7). His credibility is founded on a warrior code of honor, and more specifically, a "SEAL ethos" (92) rooted in loyalty, duty, courage, and an "unspoken invincibility, the silent code of the elite warriors of the U.S. Armed Forces" (9–10). Membership in this warrior elite establishes Luttrell's personal character and moral authority. While O'Brien grapples with the meaning of courage, reflecting on its motives and outcomes, or blurs the lines between us and them—Luttrell has no doubt about who the good guys are and what they are fighting for. He asserts that Navy SEALS "can be trusted" to "know about bad guys . . . who they are" and "do what's necessary" (42). In Luttrell's world, the stakes are clear: SEALS are bound to a warrior code of honor, while the enemy "would sell their own mothers for fifty bucks" (28).

But the dichotomies that structure Luttrell's rhetoric extend beyond the nature of the enemy or the justness of the war. Sprinkled throughout his text are angry denunciations of antiwar protestors, "liberals," and the "rules of engagement" created by "liberal politicians" who worry "about the human rights of some cold-hearted terrorist fanatic" (41). When Luttrell and his men come upon three Afghan goat herders during their mission, they debate whether to turn them loose or kill them so they won't betray the SEAL team's location to the Taliban. "The military decision was clear," Luttrell avers; "these guys could not leave there alive" (231). While Luttrell acknowledges that his "Christian soul" is in conflict with his "warrior's soul" (234, 232), the quandary he describes is not strictly moral (whether killing them is wrong). Their decision to release the men, which proves fatal, stems from their fear that "the liberal media back in the U.S.A." will get hold of the story and they will be charged with murder, despite the potential threat the Afghans posed to the SEALS and their mission (232). Luttrell rhetorically positions "us," that is, "good" Americans who trust and support the troops, in contradistinction to an internal enemy—those who question or besmirch the warrior's ethos. The politics of such a framework is clear: "liberals" are aligned with the enemy who threaten our soldiers and, by extension, America's survival. Having voted to let the men go, Luttrell opines, "was the stupidest, most southern-fried, lame-brained decision" he ever made. "I'd turned into a fucking liberal, a half-assed, no-logic nitwit" (236).

Scholars have explored the ways that foreign wars unify a nation's people against a common enemy, fueling nationalistic or even xenophobic strains. However, the reverse is also true: wars ignite *internal* divisions and value conflicts, deepening preexisting religious, social, or ideological rifts. They strike "a blow to the basic tissues of social life that damages the bonds attaching people together and impairs the prevailing sense of communality" (Erikson 153). Hostility and blame for negative outcomes are then projected onto members of one's own community or nation. At worst, these socioemotional ruptures spiral into bloody civil disputes or internecine conflicts. But they also affect individual memories, shaping how subjects interpret events and assign culpability for negative outcomes or lingering emotional pain. Trauma can shatter trust and social ties, generating "social polarization between individuals, communities and groups as those belonging to out-groups become the negative 'other'" (Parent 33). This breakdown informs Luttrell's polarizing frames: he assigns blame not only to external groups—terrorists and insurgents—but also to internal "outgroups" that do not share his "faith": liberals, media, and government bureaucrats who impose rules of engagement that he deems "a clear and present danger" to American troops (39). In international relations, such polarized forms of remembrance fuel conflicts and hinder peace negotiations. In personal relations, they construct intranational boundaries, impeding reintegration and healing. The psychological consequences of this polarization are cognitive (stereotypes, perceived homogeneity, disavowal of internal differences or complexity) and emotional (anger, resentment).

Failure to acknowledge contingency and ambiguity hinders postconflict rehabilitation and intergroup reconciliation.

Luttrell witnesses his teammates' valiant efforts to survive against overwhelming odds. His way of remembering imposes order and purpose on the tragedy he witnessed, a strategy that gives Luttrell's narrative ideological cohesion and certainty. While O'Brien rejects what he calls the "politics of certainty" that led us into the Vietnam War, Luttrell's certainty is his anchor—a means to stabilize his narrative and impose meaning on traumatic events. But it is also his albatross, an impediment that impedes healing. Luttrell's polarizing rhetoric is typical in nationalist appeals, working to partition the world into irreconcilable binaries ("You are either with us or you are with the terrorists").[33] Stripped of causal logic, motives, or context that can help explain why they fight, a dehumanized enemy makes it "possible for normal, morally upright and even usually idealistic people to perform acts of destructive cruelty" (Zimbardo 3). Luttrell himself shrugs off the abuse and torture exposed at Abu Ghraib prison: "Was there ever a greater uproar than the one that broke out over Abu Ghraib? In the bigger scheme of things, in the context of all the death and destruction that Muslim extremists have visited upon this world, a bunch of Iraqi prisoners being humiliated does not ring my personal alarm bell" (313).

Ironically, a competing memory disrupts Luttrell's polarized worldview: he owes his life to Pashtuns, the ethnic group from which most Taliban soldiers are drawn. In this sense, Luttrell's memoir inadvertently performs an act of cultural translation, as readers glimpse the face of an enemy that does not conform to the strict dichotomies that structure his narrative. The Afghans who shelter and protect the seriously wounded Luttrell, at great risk to themselves and their families, destabilize his "savage other" rhetoric and potentially undermine his credibility. Luttrell rightfully acknowledges his debt to the brave Pashtun elders who accept responsibility for his care and protection, explaining that Pashtun villagers are bound to their own centuries-old code of honor known as *lokhay*, a system that aligns with Luttrell's warrior ethos. He identifies with the tribe's uncompromised adherence to a shared honor code that includes loyalty to family and tribe, a tradition of fierce independence, and respect for tribal authority. Luttrell never reflects on how these traits, when rooted in a fundamentalist worldview, can fuel both sides of the conflict. He and these men who protect him mirror each other's uncompromising faith in their god, their righteousness, and their cause. They share deference to an authority founded on a coherent, transcendent set of ideals and expectations.

Such experiences of connection with the "enemy" have the potential to aid soldiers' postwar recovery by fostering a "rehumanization" (of both self and other) that can "heal the burdens of psychic injury" (Lyons 195). In their analysis of the Iraq and Afghanistan "Winter Soldier" 2008 event (modeled after the Vietnam War era investigations by that name), for example, Stephanie Decker and John Paul point to the veterans' use of these tactics. Members of Iraq Veterans Against the War gave testimonies about the effects of war on Iraqi and Afghanistan civilians and detailed war crimes or abuse that they personally participated in or witnessed. Decker and Paul conclude that the testimonies helped to "rehumanize Iraqis by asking their audience to take the perspective of Iraqis" (328). These rehumanization tactics emphasize "shared commonalties," "engaging others' perspectives," "promoting empathy," and "combating stereotypes" (323–24). Through these acts of recognition, the face of the other is no longer an indistinct amalgam of negative preconceptions. As Kevin McSorley puts it, it is "when corporeal co-presence occurs that the boundaries of enmity and friendship may blur, and an alternative empathetic recognition of humanity . . . may emerge. . . . that may undermine the binary oppositions that war sets up" (7). McSorley's description echoes Emmanuel Levinas's "ethics of encounter": the face of the other demands recognition. But as Levinas reminds us, the ethics of encounter "hardens its skin as soon as we move to the political world" (Levinas and Kearney 29–30). This is the realm where borders are drawn and made impermeable, where a certain kind of political subject is hailed into being.

Luttrell's status as a hero, a warrior, and a "patriot" gives him moral authority and credibility; his devotion to "America" as sacred ideal elicits an attitude of sanctity and models unquestioning loyalty and obedience to the nation/state. It reflects the kind of nationalism that Jacques Ellul characterized as "political religion," whereby the nation or state represents the "supreme power which pronounces truth and justice and has the power of life and death over its members" (80). In Luttrell's worldview, "the enemy" poses an existential threat that makes the sacrifice of "our" soldiers inevitable. Moral certainty stands as his bulwark against despair in an epic battle against evil that gives meaning to their sacrifice. Words such as "sacrifice," "hallowed ground," and "sacred honor" reflect an attempt to bridge the metaphysical gap separating the physical realities of war from the transcendent meanings attached to it (the words "sacrifice" and "sacred" share an etymology, and both rely on the existence of transcendent, absolute truths for their power and authority). Thus, urging us to reconsider the meanings we assign to the deaths of soldiers in combat, Christian theologian Kelly Denton-Borhaug critiques the relationship between US war culture and Christian concepts of redemptive sacrifice. References to combat deaths as "necessary" draw from Christian interpretations of Christ's sacrificial death, a premise that makes war appear religiously sanctioned and morally authorized: "Just as the sacrifice of Jesus is declared theologically necessary for Christian salvation, so the mechanism of sacrifice explains, rationalizes and transcendentalizes the necessity of Just War" (*U.S. War-Culture*, 119–20). Noting the ubiquity of sacrificial discourse in US political rhetoric post-9/11, Denton-Borhaug points to its effects on the American citizenry: "Consistent and repetitive use of sacrificial language within the larger discourse of the 'war on terror' let loose into the wider culture a kind of power to shape the mood, motivation and response of the general public. This public disposition acquiesced to a paternal authority that would act on its behalf and was mystified by a shield of religious sanctity" (67–68). In the politics of war making, the "sacrificial deaths" of soldiers are used to prolong conflicts, creating an ontological state of war in which perpetual war is normalized and justified as obligatory.[34] According to this logic, "staying the course" repays the debt we owe dead soldiers—even if it leads to more dead soldiers. But as Denton-Borhaug insists, the death of soldiers is a "tragedy, a consequence of the failure of politics for which all citizens are responsible and accountable" (243). To honor fallen soldiers in this way is to confront our complicity and accountability as citizens—to disturb the complacency that marks Americans' response to ongoing wars.

Years after his return home, Luttrell is plagued by nightmares. "I always wake up in tears," he writes, "and it will always haunt me . . . it's never going to go away" (266). Grief, love, pride, regret, and survivor's guilt fuel the emotional economy at work here, compelling us—persuading us—to take sides. Luttrell's shared emotional pain narrows the breach that separates warrior and civilian. These moments of vulnerability and exposure, especially by a man who claims an "unspoken invincibility" (9), assume the aura of a confessional. Like sacred biography, the memoir's confessional mode works to "evangelize hearers or readers into a specific community of faith, to inspire the faith of existing members, and to reinforce the faith of doubtful or waning members" (Gilmour 74). Such personal disclosure is not just about unburdening the self of painful memories but is also a way of strengthening bonds between speaker and listener (or writer and reader) and thus building trust. The war memoir's potential to "evangelize" readers in this way is rarely acknowledged by its critics or proponents, yet it contributes to the genre's soft power.

Luttrell deploys this power by asserting his unassailable truths: believing in the absolute righteousness of his cause, Luttrell claims the authority of a religious evangelist who, bearing witness to a sacred experience, cannot be refuted through evidence, opposing viewpoints, or reason. Similarly, countering Luttrell's "truths" with accusations of zealotry or absolutism does little to dissuade acolytes who share his vision. In Latin, remember, faith (*fides*) means "trust." If the speaker is deemed credible, "truth" becomes a matter of faith, and only credibility distinguishes the evangelist from the charlatan.[35]

In a speech to West Point graduates, admiral Mike Mullen warned that to maintain the people's trust, service members must remain an apolitical, "neutral instrument of the state." At the same time, he acknowledged the gulf that separates combat veterans from the citizens they serve, admitting, "I fear they do not comprehend the full weight of the burden we carry or the price we pay when we return from battle" (qtd. in Shanker 21). Luttrell and O'Brien both carry this burden, but their narratives suggest different ways of coping with the loss, grief, and guilt of the survivor. Neither is apolitical, as each deploys a politics of credibility that can sway readers' judgments and responses. O'Brien returns home with "Nothing to savor with your eyes or heart" (*If I Die* 206). He does not reassure us that lives sacrificed or lies told were necessary means toward worthwhile ends; instead, he exposes the unreliability, impermanence, and constructedness of all authority and truth claims. But acknowledging the "unreality" or instability of a construct is not to deny its power or effectiveness in shaping subjectivity. Luttrell's story of unsullied heroism, unwavering conviction, and absolute faith wields a persuasive power that is difficult to resist, for made privy to personal experiences of such magnitude, how does one respond but with reverent and acquiescent silence? Luttrell's credibility invokes our own, luring us back to the certainty that, as New York mayor Rudy Giuliani declared on October 2, 2001, "We are right and they are wrong. It's as simple as that."[36]

OPERATION "IRAQI FREEDOM"

Autobiography is only to be trusted when it reveals something disgraceful.

—George Orwell, "Benefit of Clergy"

One way to gauge the extent to which a war story feeds into preconceived expectations and desires is to read readers' reviews posted online. According to many of these, war stories should be "realistic," "exciting," "honest," and, oddly enough, "uplifting." That is, for some readers, war stories should inspire confidence in our military and model martial virtues of courage, patriotism, and honor. A war story is "uplifting" if, like Luttrell, our protagonist prevails over challenges and restores our faith in humanity (the humanity of "our side"). This kind of story fulfills readers' craving for what Daniel Mendelsohn calls "the trauma-and-redemption memoir." But that is not the kind of war story readers get with John Crawford's *The Last True Story I'll Ever Tell* or Michael Anthony's *Mass Casualties: A Young Medic's True Story of Death, Deception, and Dishonor in Iraq*. As one poster warns about Crawford's memoir, "If you want an uplifting story of battle go elsewhere."[37] Both Crawford and Anthony avoid all the typical motifs of the genre: "the noble example, the test of courage, the battle as initiation" (Wesley 2). What we get are bitter accounts of the mismanagement and futility of the war in Iraq, a condemnation that is equally damning to their leaders as to the authors themselves. Both leverage their credibility as veterans who served in active combat zones, and neither is shy about using their power as storytellers to speak their truths. As Anthony says about his memoir, "I gave them more truth than they'll want. If ignorance is bliss, then the truth is a bitch" ("Interview").

These soldiers reflect a generational attitude quite distinct from that of the Luttrells and Kyles in the US military. They do not join because they believe in the cause or even believe what the government claims as justification; they have not bought into America's myths of innocence. They are more characteristic of the service members Evan Wright describes in *Generation Kill*. "The first generation of young Americans since Vietnam to be sent into an open-ended conflict," he writes, "entered Iraq predisposed toward the idea that the Big Lie is as central to American governance as taxation . . . in a way, they almost expect to be lied to" (6). At the same time, both Anthony and Crawford are savvy enough to understand that readers seek "truth" in their war stories—or at least, stories told *as if they were true*.

Thus the titles of both memoirs proclaim their veracity, each promising readers a "true story." Crawford's title playfully asserts and subverts his credibility, for if this story is the only "true" one he will ever tell, then every war story he has told since is a lie. There are, after all, risks involved in exposing ugly truths about his own, the military's, and the government's mishandling of the war in a context where readers want "uplifting" war stories. Rightly anticipating a negative reception (some readers' online posts reject Crawford's criticisms as mere "whining," "weakness," or "selfishness"), Crawford implies that he will henceforth resort to fiction. The title can also be read ironically: Crawford may be mocking the tendency in today's competitive market to proclaim a book the "only true account" of some significant event. As a self-described "accidental" soldier, Crawford cannot build credibility by asserting moral authority as a patriotic warrior who is "ready to die for his country." Crawford admits at the outset that he did not enlist in the Florida National Guard for love of God or country. His motivation was financial: he needed to pay for college. But three credits away from graduation and newly married, he is called to serve in Iraq. Acknowledging his distrust of the justifications given for the invasion, he nevertheless reports for duty: "I have heard veterans from other wars claim they never understood the reasons for the conflict they were dropped into. This was not the case with me. I had studied foreign policy and cultures in college. I knew my history and politics. I recognized the importance of Middle Eastern oil to European and Asian powers. This was a war I didn't believe in, but no one had asked my opinion. I had signed a contract, reaped the benefits of a cheap college education, and now it was time to pay it back" (8). Here war is simply a contractual agreement in the bona fide business of multinational capitalism.

Despite the irony implicit in his title, Crawford signals his authenticity in the opening pages. He distinguishes himself from "reporters and retired generals" whose war stories "can sound like glory and heroism" by pointing out that while they carried pens as they walked, he "carried a machine gun" (xiii). Downplaying what war stories can accomplish (they "won't bring back anyone's son or brother or wife"), he wants his book to "simply make people aware . . . of *what war is really like*" (xiv; emphasis mine). Crawford also subverts the "innocence to experience" war story convention by claiming that his is not a story of innocence lost but of "innocence stolen, of lies and blackness" (xix). While he admits in the preface that he feels "a kind of hatred" of something that he "cannot even grasp or imagine" (xi), he never explicitly identifies what that "something" is; instead, the voice that speaks throughout most of the memoir seems more apathetic than impassioned, less interested in self-reflection or philosophical musings than in the day-to-day banality of his war: petty squabbles, incompetence, and boredom characterize much of his extended tour of duty. These are momentarily suspended by glimpses of horror: "blood-soaked Iraqi men," hands tied behind their backs, one crying, the other "drenched in blood and chunks of meat" (pieces of other passengers in the car they were riding when hit by an American soldier's Browning Mark II fifty-caliber machine gun; 139); a dying Iraqi in the back seat looks at Crawford, and a gaping hole in his head has scattered "brain fragments and shards of bone" throughout. Such scenes remind readers that this memoir is, after all, a "true war story."

We should note, however, that memoirists create personas to suit their rhetorical aims; their autobiographical voice reflects a compilation of selectively revealing personal disclosures as well as invented aspects of their character. Crawford's self-creation is strategic: the aloofness and ironic distance he performs also contribute to his credibility, as he comes across as too self-absorbed and cynical to serve as an advocate for any political ideology. This unsentimental, irreverent, and self-incriminating persona casually exposes incompetence, broken promises, and misconduct—his personal memories serving as testimony and accusation. Crawford's cynicism masks an agenda: countering the sterile, "uplifting" political fictions that characterize "official" accounts of the Iraq War.

As a member of the military's elite forces, Luttrell mirrors the image of a disciplined, professional American warrior wielding the latest in the high-tech machinery of death. But the twenty-first-century version of American war making that Crawford experiences exposes the underside of this enterprise. In particular, he casts a harsh light on the unjust treatment endured by soldiers serving with the Florida National Guard. Crawford's descriptions of the conditions that he and his fellow soldiers are subject to have a political edge: he calls out politicians who proclaim their "support for the troops" while cutting funding for soldiers, noting the subpar equipment and Vietnam-era weapons the guard were afforded. "Modern warfare my ass," he writes. "There I was with a light machine gun, no air cover, no heavy weapons, no naval gunfire. Infantry against tank, fucking World War II shit" (11). He notices that while regular units are equipped with body armor that "would stop a round from an AK-47, the ones we wore were antiquated relics from Vietnam that did little more than make us sweat" (23). Crawford and his unit are continuously told they are going home, only to have their stay extended again as army regulars complete their tour and go home: "When the Third Infantry Division was sent home, our National Guard unit was passed around the armed forces like a virus: the 108th Airborne, First Marine Expeditionary, 101st Airborne, and finally the Armored Division" (xii). They were "forgotten, unnoticed," he explains, "the shadows of the shock-and-awe troops that Americans saw in television" (xii, 23). At one point, Crawford tells us, "the government even declared that we had been pulled out of Baghdad and brought home, although all around us the capital of our enemy seethed" (xii). While leaders

claim "mission accomplished" in public ceremonies, scarce supplies lead the
men in his unit to scavenge—for example, "commandeering civilian vehicles"
when their Humvees break down (23). Their "night-vision devices were useless
without the swing arm to mount them." "retooled Vietnam-era rifles" began
"falling apart," and their "boots had no soles on them" (23).

Crawford's criticisms are borne out by several news reports, including a
2004 *New York Times* piece about national guardsmen complaining that they
were being sent into combat with inadequate protection, aging equipment,
and insufficiently armored trucks. Defense secretary Donald H. Rumsfeld's
response further kindled suspicions among many national guard and reserve
troops that they were not receiving the same equipment, support, or treatment as their professional active-duty counterparts: "You go to war with the
army you have, not the army you might want or wish to have at a later time,"
Rumsfeld replied (Schmitt). *Mother Jones* reported in 2003 that a survey by
Stars and Stripes revealed that "over one-third of soldiers rate their morale as
low, or very low," and that the suicide rate among soldiers in Iraq was three
times higher than the usual rate. UPI reported, "The National Guard and
Army Reserve soldiers['] living conditions are so substandard, and the medical
care so poor, that many of them believe the Army is trying push them out
with reduced benefits for their ailments. . . . The soldiers said professional
active-duty personnel are getting better treatment while troops who serve
in the National Guard or Army Reserve are left to wallow in medical hold."[38]
After media coverage highlighted these problems, the Bush administration
blamed the messenger, claiming that the media was biased. President Bush,
who had been touting "good progress in Iraq," remarked, "There's a sense that
the people in America aren't getting the truth. . . . sometimes you just have
to go over the heads of the filter and speak directly to the people" (qtd. in
Bumiller, "Trying to Bypass"). In the administration's view, "getting the truth"
means reporting uplifting stories (America building schools and bringing
freedom to the Iraqis). In Crawford's view, you can tell his war story is true
"because it makes your stomach turn" (210).

Crawford's attitudes toward Iraqis, the war, and the military shift between
apathy and disdain, amusement and disgust. Yet Crawford reveals cracks
in his coolly indifferent persona with his descriptions of the homeless and
hungry boy who adopts him and the sweet respite he experiences in his brief
visits with a beautiful nineteen-year-old woman names Leena. In measured
tone, Crawford evokes in readers an emotional connection to these Iraqi
civilians. He first sees Leena wearing a "white and blue robe . . . accented

by a white head scarf. At nineteen or twenty, she was strikingly beautiful"
(104). She speaks English with a "slight British accent," having studied at the
university before the war made it too dangerous for her to attend class. They
would "talk about the music she liked, school, what America was like," and
Crawford looks forward to their brief meetings, even though he is married.
When he later tells us that her house was razed as punishment for befriending
him, Crawford offers little commentary. We are left to ponder her fate and
its effect on him, and to judge his actions. While Crawford's visits assuaged
his loneliness, they also compromised Leena's reputation in a conservative
culture and ultimately exposed her to untold dangers. His lack of emotional
response or moral judgment is self-incriminating: his relationship with Leena
is an implicit critique of America's own relationship with Iraq, one shaped
by self-interest and blissful disregard.

Crawford also befriends an Iraqi shop owner, Whalee, who welcomes him
into his tiny auto parts shop. During patrols, Crawford enjoys his visits with
Whalee, who would listen to his vintage radio and "babble about politics,
war, and love" (148). This Iraqi, who had fought against Iran as a noncommissioned officer, is protective of the young American soldiers, warning them to
stay away from certain areas and sometimes providing them with a meal of
kabobs and rice. Crawford ends this chapter with a brief summary of what
happens when American soldiers who do not know Whalee patrol the area:
they order Whalee out of his store, a heated argument ensues, and Whalee's
"head was crashed through the same window that he had once shot looters
from" (151). Here again Crawford avoids explicit critique or commentary, but
we are given a glimpse of the precariousness of Iraqi life under occupation:
civilians fall victim to both their own people and to the invading forces.

The self-incriminating image of American soldiers that Crawford sometimes culls is not one you will see in recruitment posters. Americans in
Crawford's story are often selfish, stupid, childish, entitled, and reckless. In
one scene, Crawford and his buddy Mitchell steal an old motorcycle from
an Iraqi man, because, Mitchell explains, "Dude, I wanna drive this thing"
(159). They get it started and make fools of themselves before a group of Iraqi
civilians, Mitchell whooping with joy and Crawford cackling (160). He tells
us that the "Iraqis loved to watch us whenever we acted like Americans.
From barbaric to decadent without even touching civilization was how Oscar
Wilde described us, and it was what everyone expected" (160). But the tone
soon shifts from wry to serious, as their joy ride leads them into danger.
With the bike now stalling as darkness descends, they turn into a street

"with no streetlamps or shops, no other cars on the road, only a high wall on the right, and on the left windows and rooftops of Iraqi houses loomed over us like vultures" (161). The Iraqis they see now appear "out of the dark like wraiths reaching out to us. Their eyes were wet with hatred, and I found myself repeating over and over, 'Don't fucking stall. . . . Please don't stall" (161–62). In these few pages, readers get two different points of view: Iraqis who regard Americans as reckless juveniles, and Iraqis who regard American soldiers as despised occupiers.

The title of Michael Anthony's memoir also leverages credibility, both as an account by "a young medic" and with the promise of a "true story." The book's publisher, Karen Cooper of F+W Media, has said that while they rarely publish books on war, Anthony's "searing honesty and intensity" compelled them to acquire his memoir. If, as Orwell quipped, "autobiography is only to be trusted when it reveals something disgraceful," then Anthony's memoir qualifies as trustworthy, for he discloses plenty of disgraceful behavior. Reviewers of the memoir have offered the usual disclaimers, denying that Anthony's work is concerned with politics and focusing on its veracity and authenticity. Even historian Howard Zinn, certainly no stranger to polemics, endorsed Anthony's memoir with the claim that it is "not about the politics of Iraq. Instead it takes us deep inside the war, inside and outside the operating room, the barracks, the talk of the soldiers, the feeling of the situation." In an interview, Anthony himself denied any political intent, saying that the book is "totally non-political" and reaffirming its credibility as a "true" story about "what really goes on behind the scenes" ("Interview"). Anthony, who became addicted to Vicodin during his tour, admits that his recovery was only made worse by the prevalence of romanticized versions of the war. As a result, he wanted "to share true war stories—the stuff behind the scenes, real stuff, real people" (Tuttle). Anthony's portrayal of "real people" devastates the idealized figures we encounter in both "uplifting" war stories and government propaganda.

Anthony's service as an operating room medic in Iraq from 2006 to 2007 brings him in constant contact with bodies injured, maimed, and killed by war. Short on staff and space but "not short on patients," he performs surgeries in a small operating room with beds placed "only a few feet apart" (6). We learn early on that Anthony chose to serve as an OR medic only because he wanted "whichever job had the highest bonus and the biggest kicker for school" (7). Like Crawford, Anthony sees enlistment as a means to an end, but unlike Crawford, he hails from a proud military family and grew up believing in the ideals of military service. He "grew up watching military movies and playing GI Joe in my backyard" (60). Only seventeen years old when he signed up, the memoir begins three years later with Anthony's admission that the enlistment bonus "money is gone" and he "would give back every cent to not be where I am" (7). This illusion-to-disillusion trajectory follows the conventions of the war memoir, but in Anthony's case, disillusion stems not from combat trauma but from the behavior of his fellow soldiers and commanding officers: the promiscuity, infidelities, drug use, and incompetence he witnesses. The few scenes that deal with combat are made only more senseless by the absurdity, ineffectiveness, and hypocrisy of the war effort. Having gone into the military a credulous seventeen-year-old, within a few days of his deployment Anthony admits that "military life hasn't been all I thought it would be" (17).

Throughout his memoir, however, Anthony treads a fine line between blatant disgust and dispassionate observation, each posture serving a different rhetorical purpose. First, by suggesting that he once believed in military honor, he fosters identification and trust in those readers who share this vision. Since his disgust stems not from a predisposition or bias against the military but from the depth of his disappointment, his account of "disgraceful" conduct seems authentic. However, Anthony strategically pulls the reins on his judgments and condemnations by repositioning himself as an objective observer. Thus he sometimes plays it coy with readers. For example, consider this passage in which he simultaneously undercuts and endorses naive trust in the American military: "I pictured men and women shoulders back and heads held high, living their lives by virtuous ideals and proud to wear the uniform of their country—maybe I'm not that naïve" (17). This idealistic vision is interrupted by the suggestion that he probably is not that naïve, yet he reverts to this naïve point of view in the lines that follow: "I saw a military marching, flying the American flag, singing the national anthem, and defeating all our enemies without losing a single man." He both distances himself from this naive view and yet clings to it, ending the passage by reaffirming the value of such a stance: "But I think there's something behind that, that in the end it's right and it works, and we can trust that—we have to be able to trust that" (17). Anthony seems to align himself with this collective "we" who trust this glorious image of America's military—only to shatter it in the pages that follow.

It is not long before the effort to hold on to this credulous point of view dissipates into disgust, as Anthony's unit includes "people in their thirties, married with children, all of them having affairs. One was a heroin addict;

the other has slept with eleven men in the past three months. One guy tried to kill himself and another kidnapped a drug dealer. Alcoholics, chain smokers, compulsive gamblers—who am I to judge?" (65). Yet in this passage he again plays both sides, appearing to walk back his criticism with the question "who am I to judge?" In another scene two wounded patients are brought into the OR: one an American soldier, the other an Iraqi insurgent. Anthony suggests the irony of the situation, and by extension, the war itself: "Only minutes earlier both had been trying to kill one another, now they're lying next to each other" looking "so fragile and vulnerable" (42–43). He imagines the families and friends of both victims "praying for the death of the other, saying as long as their son 'didn't die in vain' it would be okay" (42). Anthony then pivots to describing his partner during the surgery, his friend Crade, who "worships Satan" (43), a distraction that sidelines commentary on whether the men may indeed be dying "in vain."

Over the course of his tour, the commanding officer's mismanagement of their schedules forces Anthony to consistently work without adequate sleep. He comes to rely on sleeping pills, and sleep deprivation only intensifies Anthony's oscillation between despair and indifference. When he gives in to the former, his eyes tear up and he thinks about why he is fighting this war and about "all the people we've killed" (48). Yet on other nights, he admits, "the only thing I can feel is nothing. I think about the war and feel nothing. I think about life and death, mine and everyone else's, and I feel nothing. . . . I tell myself it doesn't matter if I live or die, nothing matters—I like it when I feel nothing" (48). When one of the female soldiers finally takes their complaints against an inept and volatile staff sergeant up the chain of command, Anthony finally expresses respect for a fellow soldier: "All it took for me to respect someone in the military was for that person to refuse a direct order" (68). He admires this small act of resistance in a context where he feels "powerless," "weak," "not a man," a "sprocket in the machine of the Army" (51).

Anthony's critique is strategic—by turns recanting, disavowing, or distracting readers in a kind of narrative sleight of hand. His apparent forthrightness establishes his credibility, and he certainly delivers on the promise of scandalous revelations—soldiers cheating on their wives and husbands or having "alcohol, and even cocaine and heroin, shipped to them," or the male doctor who "examines" a female soldier by "caressing her breasts and asking her to get naked" (149). He asserts that they are not the heroes civilians think they are, that some are "criminals," "molesters," or "people doing anything they can to help themselves" (153). Yet on the critical issues regarding the war—its legitimacy, effectiveness, purpose, or meaning—Anthony consistently defers. When a national guardsman describes how his one-year tour was abruptly "extended for another six months" after he had already boarded a plane home, Anthony does not "want to hear what he has to say" (130). He offers no opinion on the "stop loss" policy that allowed for such extended deployments. On another occasion Anthony describes the colonel standing before hundreds of military commanders to proclaim that a new hospital is "now officially open and ready for business" (136). Anthony tells us that the colonel "is lying to everyone," yet he remains silent: "I know I should say something, but I can't. Who would I talk to?" When the newly arrived command sergeant major gives a speech thanking the soldiers for making this achievement possible, Anthony acknowledges that this too is a sham, yet he ends this section with the statement: "He's another one I'll try to give the benefit of the doubt" (137). These efforts to preserve or restore his naive trust only increase his feeling of powerlessness.

Ironically, the only time that Anthony takes a stand (even asking his brother to contact the press and disobeying a direct order) is when he refuses an anthrax vaccination. It is in this small act of defiance that Anthony tries to regain his personal sovereignty. This act also expresses his most unmitigated skepticism: incredulous of the military's claims that the vaccine is harmless or for his own protection, Anthony is no longer willing to give them "the benefit of the doubt." He stages a "rebellion" with other soldiers, angry that "the U.S. Army can do whatever they want to [them]" (162). No longer "seesawing back and forth in [his] mind," Anthony finds comfort in finally knowing "the answer": their purpose as soldiers is to fight for the virtues that America stands for: "liberty and freedom" (169). But even this moment of moral clarity and purpose is undermined by the entry's final lines: lying in bed, he imagines going to jail and fighting to the death if an inmate tries to rape him: "I don't die from a mortar attack or a terrorist . . . instead I die fighting for what . . . an ideal . . . a belief . . . is it worth it . . . ? Is anything worth it?" (170).

In *The Art of Time in Memoir*, Sven Birkerts contends, "Memoir begins not with event but with the intuition of meaning—with the mysterious fact that life can sometimes step free from the chaos of contingency and become story" (3–4). Anthony's ambivalence suggests that his memoir stems from the opposite intuition: that there is no meaning to be had, no escape from the "chaos of contingency." By structuring the memoir chronologically, twelve chapters marking each month of his tour in Iraq, Anthony imposes the only "order" possible on his experiences. Throughout the memoir, his narrative voice is inconsistent, fluctuating between naive credulity and paralyzing skepticism. He admits, "I wish I could just forget everything and go back to thinking that everyone in the military is an American hero. I wish I still had someone to look up to" (208). Although toward the end of his tour Anthony again seems to affirm the value of military service ("The goddamn Army made me a man" 232), he ultimately shatters any lingering hope that the military's credibility will be restored in both Anthony's and the reader's eyes.

But perhaps Anthony has been deceiving us throughout, disguising his "politics" within the generic conventions of a "coming of age" war story, one that appeals to our expectations: an "honest" "authentic" account of one naive, idealistic young soldier grappling with the absurdity and horror of war (the numerous blurbs included on the dust jacket suggest as much: a "gut-wrenching journey . . . into manhood"; a "raw, vivid look at the realities" of war; "a riveting account of life within the pitch of battle"; "the TRUTH"). I would suggest that Anthony's ambivalent voice is a ruse, a way to get readers to trust him, while all the while satirizing—and thus subverting—the conventions of the generic war story. As Ronald Paulson explains, the satirist has "to be on his guard and hide his satires beneath the sheep's clothing of a commonly accepted form" (5). Read as satire, Anthony's memoir builds on vital distinctions between the romanticized, flawless heroes depicted in "uplifting" war stories ("men and women shoulders back and heads held high, living their lives by virtuous ideals") and the flawed, petty, dysfunctional human beings Anthony describes. Beneath the "sheep's clothing" that is this "young medic's true story" is a powerful indictment; his ambivalent subjectivity is strategic, as it works to expose and mock his own and his reader's credulity. As satire, Anthony's need to believe in a childish veneration of the military mirrors our own, his absurd "rebellion" is fraught with self-parody, and his own credibility as a "truth teller" is fatally compromised. Exploiting the *Bildungsroman* as a form suited to the war story (idealistic young man goes to war and gains wisdom and maturity), Anthony subverts these expectations. Left no wiser or better for his experience of war, Anthony instead reminds us that true folly lies in confusing myth with reality. He thus ends his memoir with the news that one of the soldiers he served with—his friend Crade—had taken his own life after returning home. Here the true cost of deception and dishonor are revealed, and only then does the heart of Anthony's critique register unequivocally.

As the memoirs discussed in this chapter suggest, veterans can be unreliable allies in efforts to control discourse. As trusted witnesses and participants in the nation's wars, they have the power of persuasion, influencing attitudes toward the military, modeling forms of political subjectivation, and subverting or endorsing authority. But, as Nye acknowledges, "All power depends on context—who relates to whom under what circumstances—but soft power depends more than hard power upon the existence of willing interpreters and receivers" (*Soft Power* 16). Veterans' stories challenge, negotiate, and reflect ways of telling and seeing, forging new connections and rupturing others, mining and disrupting our expectations as readers and exposing the shaky foundations that uphold many of our most uplifting fictions. Soldiers and veterans in America are the messengers we trust, sometimes at our peril.

Chapter 4

"SOLDIERS OF CONVICTION"
Duty, Dissent, and the Immigrant Soldier

The first US service member killed in the Iraq war, on March 21, 2003, was marine lance corporal José Gutiérrez, twenty-seven, an undocumented immigrant from Guatemala and one of the "Green Card Marines" who enlisted in 2003. Gutiérrez was one of over thirty-seven thousand immigrant soldiers deployed to the Iraq War as "Green Card Marines," along with almost twenty thousand foreign nationals who served in the reserves and inactive national guard. As a teen, Gutiérrez made the two-thousand-mile journey from Guatemala by "train hopping" about fourteen freight trains, crossing the border without documentation. He traveled alone, as his parents had died during Guatemala's civil war—a conflict abetted by the United States.[1] Granted asylum as an unaccompanied minor, he dreamed of becoming a US citizen, and enlisting in the US Marines offered him a fast track to achieving that dream. Deployed as part of initial invasion of Iraq on March 19, 2003, Gutiérrez was killed in a tank battle two days later. The US government awarded Gutiérrez American citizenship posthumously.

Like the young Gutiérrez, Jose Segovia Benitez also crossed the US border illegally as a child, and like Gutiérrez, was deployed with the marines as part of the initial Iraq invasion in 2003. Benitez, however, survived two tours of combat duty, a bomb blast, and a traumatic brain injury. Back in the States, he was classified by the Department of Veterans Affairs (VA) as 70 percent disabled for traumatic brain injury and post-traumatic stress disorder. He struggled—like thousands of other returning soldiers—to adapt to civilian life. After run-ins with the law, a felony drug conviction landed him in an Immigration and Customs Enforcement (ICE) detention center. A week later, in October 2019, he was deported to El Salvador, the country he left when he was just three years old. A similar story unfolds in the case of Miguel Perez-Montes, who came to the United States legally as a child and became a permanent legal resident when he was eleven. He enlisted in the US Army and served two tours of duty in Afghanistan, where he suffered a brain injury.

As a paratrooper and private first class in Afghanistan in 2002 and 2003, he began suffering from "severe" symptoms of post-traumatic stress disorder (PTSD) and was discharged in 2004. The VA diagnosed him with PTSD related to his service, but he turned to drugs and alcohol to self-medicate, which in 2010 landed him in jail for a felony drug charge. After his application for citizenship was denied because of the drug conviction, he was remanded to ICE custody and deported to Mexico, a country he had not lived in since he was eight years old.

These are just three out of the many thousands of Latino immigrants—some documented, others not—who have served in the US military. Their stories do not make it into history books, and their names rarely grace the covers of published memoirs. Many never made it home, others never felt at home to begin with—perceived as "illegals" or "aliens" with uncertain status and precarious means. A 2016 report by the American Civil Liberties Union (ACLU), "Discharged, Then Discarded," found that most deported veterans were in the United States legally and sustained physical wounds and emotional trauma in conflicts as far back as the war in Vietnam. Once they returned from service, however, they were subject to draconian immigration laws that reclassified many minor offenses as deportable crimes and deported.[2] Ironically, deported veterans are legally allowed to return to the United States after they die; as veterans, they are entitled to burial in a national cemetery and a military funeral. As deported US Navy vet Juan Valadez remarks, "They'll take you back once it's not no good to you anymore."[3] Although foreign-born Latinos have traditionally viewed military service as an honorable path to citizenship, their status is always subject to the vagaries of American politics and national mood swings. In today's political climate, immigrant veterans and active-duty personnel are in a precarious predicament. On the one hand, the uniform gains them legitimacy as representatives of the military (and, by extension, America). On the other, the slightest infraction or misstep can quickly elide that status, turning them into suspect outsiders and foreigners. Their precarity is even more salient at a time when early discharges and even deportations of immigrant service members are on the rise. This is especially problematic for Latinos, whose long history as "perpetual foreigners" in America continues to shape how even native-born Latino citizens are perceived, regardless of what their birth certificates or naturalization papers affirm.[4]

My aim in this chapter is to reflect on these issues through the lens of two immigrant Latino veterans' memoirs, Robert Mencia's *From Here to Insanity*

(Vietnam War) and Camilo Mejía's *Road from ar Ramadi* (Iraq War). I begin with a brief overview of recent changes in policies related to nonnative military personnel, particularly documented and undocumented Latino veterans. My readings then explore how these veteran-writers negotiate and reconcile their identities as American soldiers, Latinos, and political subjects. I hope to build on my conviction that veterans' memoirs can evoke meaningful connections across national borders and social realities, providing an important counternarrative against demonizing myths about our "others" and reimagining the concept of the citizen-soldier. Mencia's and Mejía's attitudes toward the uses of American military power are informed by their "outsider" status and by events in their native countries (El Salvador and Nicaragua, respectively). Situated at the intersection where personal beliefs, national identity, and moral agency intersect, their memoirs offer an alter/native vision of symbolic citizenship (notions of belonging and political recognition). They demonstrate the diverse ways that immigrant soldiers' shared memories can contribute to figurations of American national identity and politics. In the struggle to define the national self, memory is a territory to be conquered and held, a space where certain stories are validated or recuperated, while others are marginalized or silenced altogether. Using the memoir as a space for alter/native subjectivities, Mencia and Mejía suggest the interrelational, perspectival, and permeable nature of cultural memory, and, just as importantly, claim their hard-earned right to speak.

I aim to suggest that Mencia's and Mejía's memoirs articulate a more fluid understanding of citizenship and belonging, modeling a transnational subjectivity that imagines the "nation not as a closed chapter but as one endlessly in flux, endlessly in relation" (Dimock 2). In this sense, their war stories do not "belong" exclusively to an American context, but in relation to other contexts, other ways of telling and seeing. To approach these memoirs through a transnational perspective "is to encounter various and complex dynamics of exchange and transformation; dynamics which breach across a wide array of borders between as well as within cultural formations formerly perceived in a national paradigm" (Bieger 16). It is to understand citizenship not just as a system of rights and duties or as a form of national belonging and recognition—but as a frame for producing cultural memory. The Oath of Allegiance itself articulates an identity remade through erasure and severance from the past, citizenship disconnected not only from a history of US imperialism and militarization that can fuel immigration but also from class and racial stratifications that continue to mark the status of raced political subjects within US borders. Thus citizenship as a military recruitment tool can honor and integrate Latinos into the nation, but it can also work to erase the social, racial, and class pressures placed on many Latinos to enlist in the first place (Amaya). As Toby Miller argues, citizenship "is a means of transformation ready for definition and disposal in dispersed ways at dispersed sites. . . . It produces a 'disposition' on (the citizen's part) not to accept the imposition of a particular form of government passively, but to embrace it actively as a collective expression of themselves" (12). This "disposition" is evident in Mencia's and Mejía's disruptions of the rigid conceptual boundaries that precondition political and social exclusion as well as wars. Their perspective as both immigrants and US soldiers underscores the multiple social and political realities informing military service and the embodied experience of citizenship. Their memoirs, I argue, can help us recognize immigrant veterans as a political collectivity with distinctive, though not homogeneous, interests and needs—and to envision a more supple, complex, and dissonant understanding of citizenship.

In my view, the instrumentalization of citizenship as a recruitment tool can efface the relationship between domestic conditions and the history of colonial and imperial projects abroad. For Latinos, citizenship often involves both internal border-making processes (racializing discourses) and external violations of national borders (US exercise of military and political power abroad). Mexicans and Puerto Ricans, for example, were the first Latinos granted citizenship as a result of US expansionism. After the Mexican-American War (1846–48), the Treaty of Guadalupe Hidalgo "assimilated" Mexicans living in ceded territories, granting citizenship to residents of New Mexico, Nevada, Colorado, California, Texas, and Arizona. This triggered considerable angst about the racial composition of the "new" American nation—for, as senator John C. Calhoun (South Carolina) passionately argued after the treaty's ratification, "We have never dreamt of incorporating into our Union any but the Caucasian race. . . . I protest against such a union as that! Ours, sirs, is the Government of a white race. The greatest misfortunes of Spanish America are to be traced to the fatal error of placing these colored races on an equality with the white race. That error destroyed the social arrangement which formed the basis of society" (qtd. in Nieto-Phillips 53). This argument, that the incorporation of nonwhite peoples would destroy "the social arrangement which formed the basis of society," may seem anachronistic, but it informs political rhetoric and nativist discourses to this day. Before the United States entered World War I, president Woodrow Wilson signed the Jones-Shafroth Act, granting statutory citizenship to the inhabitants of Puerto Rico, a nation ceded to the United States in 1898 as a result of the Spanish-American War.[5] Two months later, Wilson's compulsory military service act conscripted twenty thousand Puerto Ricans. Coincidentally, right after the Spanish-American War, the War Department also began restricting the role of African Americans in the military.[6]

DYING TO BE A CITIZEN: MILITARY SERVICE AND THE FICKLE POLITICS OF IMMIGRATION

During the Civil War, well over 40 percent of Union Army soldiers were immigrants and sons of immigrants (Doyle 159). Almost 500,000 immigrants served during World War I, and over 300,000 in World War II. In 2019, about 530,000 US veterans were foreign-born, and currently about 65,000 active-duty service members are immigrants (Zong and Batalova). Since the Civil War, special provisions have made military service a reliable way for immigrants to earn citizenship in the United States. For example, about a quarter million immigrant service members became naturalized citizens during World War I, and more than 100,000 were granted citizenship during World War II. Congress extended the Immigration and Naturalization Act of 1952, which expedited naturalization for foreign-born service members, to Korean War era personnel in 1961 and to Vietnam-era personnel in 1968 (Goring). Between 2001 and 2015, 109,321 immigrant service members were naturalized (Batalova), and by 2015, over 120 immigrant soldiers killed in combat during the Afghanistan and Iraq Wars were naturalized posthumously. In fact, four of the first coalition soldiers to die in Iraq in 2003 were noncitizen Latinos who earned citizenship posthumously.[7]

Immigrants and noncitizens make significant contributions to America's war efforts: a study conducted by the Center for Naval Analyses for the Office of the Secretary of Defense concludes that noncitizens bring valuable "cultural and language skills that are of strategic importance to military operations outside the United States" (McIntosh et al. 2). They also have lower attrition rates than their native-born counterparts and "generally have a stronger attachment to serving the United States, which they now consider to be 'their country'" (McIntosh et al. 31). As I noted in chapter 1, immigrants often regard military service as way to demonstrate loyalty, earn respect, and prove their worth as Americans. Recognizing their importance, especially during wartime, when the military needs able bodies, the US government consistently offers noncitizens a carrot: a fast track to citizenship through wartime service.

Yet despite their service, many of these veterans remain vulnerable to the quirks of US immigration policy and public opinion, two interrelated and capricious forces. Since 9/11, John F. Kennedy's "nation of immigrants" has been in the mood to curtail immigration, slash funding for refugee programs, deny immigrants a green card if they or their family members have ever received public assistance, and even challenge the Fourteenth Amendment's guarantee of birthright citizenship (Auvil). While only 7 percent of Americans considered immigration a pressing issue in 2008, in January 2018, 15 percent saw it as America's most important problem, second only to dissatisfaction with government (Newport). Anti-immigrant narratives have fueled these shifts and fueled implementation of hardline policies (family separations, zero tolerance, "denaturalization task forces") as well as less conspicuous changes. For example, in 2018 US Customs and Immigration Services deleted the line "America's promise as a nation of immigrants" from its mission statement.[8] These wider trends have significant implications for immigrant service members.

In recent years, long-standing military practices regarding immigrant service members are also shifting. The Military Accessions Vital to the National Interest (MAVNI) program launched by the Defense Department in 2009 offered expedited citizenship to noncitizens who joined the military with needed language skills or medical training. The program also shielded Deferred Action for Childhood Arrivals (DACA) program service members from deportation, and in 2020 approximately 800 DACA recipients ("Dreamers") were serving through MAVNI. The Trump administration's termination of DACA left thousands of applicants in legal limbo, no longer able to join the military even after extensive background checks, despite the US Army struggling to meet its recruitment goals, and subject to deportations. While the Supreme Court ruled in June 2020 that "Dreamers" in the military could continue serving without fear of deportation, the ruling would allow an administration to petition the court again. Since MAVNI has been suspended, enlistees are left with few options and the threat of deportation. The Trump administration also shuttered naturalization offices at all US Army basic training sites (Nelsen). Another policy change was announced by the Department of Defense in October 2017 that further increases scrutiny of immigrant enlistees.[9] Immigrant soldiers are now more likely to see their attempts at citizenship rejected than foreign-born civilians, according to recent US Citizenship and Immigration Services data (USCIS). The report showed that in the wake of the Trump administration's stricter immigration policies on service members, citizenship applications plummeted and denials were on the rise (Copp, "Immigrant Soldiers"). In the first quarter of fiscal year 2019, USCIS reported a 79 percent drop in applications by immigrant service members. In response to this data, retired US Army major general Paul Eaton, a senior adviser to VoteVets. org, remarked, "To have this turnaround, where they are actually taking a back seat to the civilian population[,] strikes me as a bizarre turn of events" (qtd. in Copp, "Immigrant Soldiers"). New regulations extended the waiting period for military green-card holders to become naturalized citizens, and most recently the army stopped enlisting some immigrants who are legal permanent residents and mandating lengthy delays for others. In 2019, Jennie Pasquarella, the ACLU's director of immigrants' rights, presented written testimony to Congress noting that "since 2017, the Trump administration has also sought to unwind U.S. history to not only exclude noncitizens from the ranks of our military, but also to thwart the naturalization of the men and women presently serving our country at home and abroad." The Associated Press reports that immigrant military members are being discharged, and some told they are a "security risk" because they have relatives abroad or incomplete background checks. Immigration attorneys contend that many of those are labeled "uncharacterized discharges," which means they are neither honorably nor dishonorably discharged. Thus, they are not protected from deportation even after serving combat tours in Iraq or Afghanistan. According to *Military Times*, there has also been a rise in the denial rate for veterans requesting deportation protections for their spouses and dependents: "Among active duty service members the spike in 2017 from the year before was 33 percent, and among veterans, 29 percent" (Copp, "More Veterans"). Active-duty soldiers now live with the fear that their family will be deported while they are deployed.[10]

These policy changes are occurring against a backdrop of rekindled anti-immigrant sentiment. Many political leaders, including President Trump, have deployed stigmatizing rhetoric that brands many immigrants—asylum seekers, refugees, resident aliens, and undocumented immigrants—potential terrorists, criminals, or freeloaders. Immigration-related media spectacles bolster these negative stereotypes, most often in news stories about Latino immigrants. US news stories about immigration almost exclusively frame immigration in a threatening manner (as a cultural, economic, or criminal threat) and disproportionately and inaccurately focus on Latino immigrants (Haynes et al.). They draw on what Leo Chavez calls the "Latino Threat Narrative," which posits that Latinos are somehow "different" from previous immigrant groups and are unwilling or incapable of assimilating (5). These portrayals reify preexisting racial hierarchies, legitimizing claims about the innate inferiority, criminality, or ineptitude of target others, and contributing to more hostile attitudes toward immigration and greater support for punitive immigration policy.[11] Criminalizing frameworks also affect how the military perceives immigrant recruits, their levels of inclusion within the ranks, and whether higher-ups endorse citizenship privileges for foreign-born service members. Latinos in the military must effectively navigate what Ana Ramos-Zayas calls "the politics of worthiness" to compensate for their ethnic identity, trying to prove that they are assets and not liabilities. On those occasions when Latino contributions to America's military are officially recognized, during Hispanic Heritage celebrations, for example, Latino veterans serve as standard-bearers for America's "melting pot" ideology: they are characters in an immigrant assimilation story, patriotic "new Americans" proudly spreading democracy and freedom in the hinterlands. As Lorena Oropeza points out, this version of the national story excludes "Latinos who have questioned US foreign policy or war aims" and "leaves no room for voices of dissent or even for those voices expressing conflicting emotions about the cost of war" ("Fighting on Two Fronts").

This omission is especially troubling at a time when foreign-born service members are facing a two-pronged assault on their rights and dignity: on the legal front, their hard-won path to citizenship is in jeopardy, as even decorated Iraq and Afghanistan combat veterans are threatened with deportation. On the social front, they are subject to exclusionary and alienating rhetoric, a hostile climate for anyone dealing with the aftereffects of war and needing more than ever to feel included and supported on the home front. While these factors can affect all immigrants, negative stereotypes, exclusionary practices, and stigmatizing political discourses have plagued Latinos for generations and continue to inform attitudes against the largest minority group in the United States.[12] Thus while many soldiers and veterans increasingly play visible roles in the public sphere as citizens—participating in political campaigns and movements or expressing dissident views through blogs, memoirs, or veterans' groups, immigrants serving in the military are more likely to remain silent. They are constrained by a double bind, one created by their contractual obligations to the military, and the other by their ambivalent status as "ethnics" or immigrants. Unlike native-born Americans, immigrant veterans and soldiers who criticize any aspect of US war policy are not seen merely as troublemakers or misfits; their "otherness" makes them more likely to be denounced as ungrateful, disloyal, and even treasonous. In their case, "thank you for your service" can quickly turn into "go back where you came from."

I should note that while it is true that military service has historically been a reliable way to earn citizenship, not all immigrant recruits are motivated by personal interests alone. For example, in *The Cause of All Nations: An International History of the American Civil War,* historian Don H. Doyle shows that many immigrants were "soldiers of conviction" who, having experienced tyranny, dictatorship, war, or oppressive colonial rule in their home countries, saw the American Civil War as part of a broader human struggle for liberty, equality, and democracy (160). Similarly, during World War I, members of the Seventy-Seventh Infantry Division, nicknamed the "Melting Pot Division," were all immigrants or children of immigrants who "had only recently been subjected to the pogroms of Russia" or escaped religious persecution, famine, poverty, or political turmoil at home.[13] Memoirs and oral histories of World War II suggest that experiences such as these, which are often the impetus for mass migrations, leave their traces; they can awaken in affected groups a heightened political consciousness. In his memoir *One German Dead*, World War II veteran Jose Yglesias, the son of Cuban immigrants, explains that he volunteered to serve, despite a 3A deferment, because he "believed in the war, in the New Deal, in socialism and the brotherhood of man" (6). Research suggests that home-country political conditions and experiences can affect immigrants' political behavior in their adopted society, propelling them to be more engaged politically and to "militate within existing political structures for economic and social mobility" (Roach 26). Immigrants and the children of immigrants may apply their political knowledge to new political experiences in the United States, a process known as "translation" (Finifter and Finifter), or advocate for change in their home countries through US political institutions (Boswell and Curtis). This evidence suggests that immigrants who find themselves in contexts that allow political expression tend to mobilize politically, even when they are not fully endowed with political rights in their host countries.

While many immigrants may be motivated to enlist in the military for strategic reasons (obtaining citizenship or proving their loyalty), others are driven by altruistic, transnational aims: they may be "soldiers of conviction" who, recognizing the price paid for political failures, apathy, or corruption, are doubly committed to defending the rights, liberties, and just treatment of threatened groups or nations. Most are historically invisible, as seldom do war memorials and histories include perspectives by Latino or immigrant service members. These soldiers are peripheral in memoirs by White soldiers and mention of their contribution is minimal relative to their actual numbers in combat units (Gibson 469). Yet Latino soldiers have earned numerous commendations and medals fighting America's wars, including sixty Medals of Honor to date (over 20 percent of all Medal of Honor recipients are immigrants). Theirs is part of the American story—though they are often at odds with dominant images of steely-eyed White heroes or Latino immigrants as "freeloaders" and "wetbacks."

As a genre, the memoir is especially responsive to and reflective of cultural changes and political upheavals, offering important insights into the impact such events have on individuals, especially on members of marginalized or racialized groups. Mejía's and Mencia's memoirs respond to political and social turmoil sparked by significant events during their service years: the Vietnam War and 9/11, respectively. In responding to these events, each brings a perspective lacking from most accounts of the Vietnam and Iraq Wars—a perspective filtered through political events in their native countries. Given the history of US military interventions throughout Central America, this perspective is bound to differ significantly from mainstream or official versions of the American war story, particularly in its judgments about the military's role as a key institution of power as well as what Vietnamese writer Yen Le Espiritu calls the US "rescue and liberation" myth. These memoirs remind us that soldiers fight not only against a designated enemy but also against a history that precedes them into battle: the history of US military interventions informs not just how current wars are judged by an international community, allies, or the civilians whom troops are sent to "liberate"—but also how veterans judge their own actions and define concepts such as "honor" and "duty."

ANOTHER 17TH PARALLEL: VIETNAM, EL SALVADOR, AND ROBERT MENCIA'S LONG JOURNEY HOME

These are not your grandfather's stories, censored and full of glory. . . . If you are looking for heroes or drum beating jingoism, you have the wrong book.

—Brennan Morton, *Dying for Strangers*

Mencia's war memoir *From Here to Insanity: An Immigrant Becomes a Citizen by Way of the Vietnam Draft* does not pretend to be apolitical. There are no disclaimers, no conciliatory platitudes to blunt the force of his viewpoints. From the opening pages of his preface, "The Reluctant Citizen," Mencia is clear about what he believed in 1969 when he became a naturalized citizen, how he felt about the Vietnam War and US military interventions more broadly, and how he feels fifty years later about the Trump administration. He tells us that he was born and raised in what President Trump has called a "shithole country," El Salvador, and admits that even though he "didn't like the idea of becoming an American" he agreed to take the Oath of Allegiance and become a citizen because it offered a ten-day break from a war that had worn him "down to the bone physically and mentally" (4–5). In the photo on his naturalization certificate, Mencia wears jungle fatigues, the only clothes he had with him when he was sworn in. He points out that native-born Americans "never took the same oath of allegiance" and had no clue what it was like to commit to support and defend a way of life that includes "a purely 'white' version of democracy that excludes people of color" (6). This perspective on citizenship and its obligations, and Mencia's views on America's use of military force in Central America and Vietnam, are not ones many Americans want to hear. Mencia served honorably for eight years (once in combat duty at the height of the Vietnam War) and still bears the physical and emotional wounds of his service: exposed to Agent Orange, Mencia's body is mapped with "splotches" to this day (5); raped by two GIs when he tried to stop their assault on a Vietnamese girl who cleaned the barracks, he underwent years of treatment for PTSD and MST (military sexual trauma). Yet, Mencia's blunt criticisms of US policies, cultural prejudices, and military actions are unlikely to garner this Vietnam veteran a long overdue hero's welcome. This also makes his memoir an unlikely candidate for a commercial press.

In fact, Mencia self-published his memoir, and although that might disqualify his story in the eyes of some scholars, it also frees him from the profit and editorial constraints imposed by commercial publishers.[14] Mencia's motivation for writing the memoir, he says, was a desire to bridge the gap between his contemporaries who avoided or resisted the Vietnam War and those who "with much apprehension answered the call, fought in it, and fifty plus years later still suffer the ravages of an almost total devastation of our identity and emotional well-being."[15] But reliving these painful events during the writing left him "spent and in need of much counseling." Mencia admits he had nothing left for marketing or promoting his work to a publisher, and thus opted for a venue that "that required money and nothing else."

The relationship between writer and publisher is always shaped by a power dynamic, but as studies suggest, this relationship is further complicated by race and ethnicity. In his study of Vietnam War narratives, for example, James William Gibson notes that by 1985, only one memoir and two oral histories focused on Black soldiers' war experiences, and no book-length works by Latinos had been published. Further, these soldiers are most often peripheral figures in memoirs by White soldiers, and mention of their contribution is minimal relative to their actual numbers in combat units. This absence persists to this day. Mainstream publishers may inadvertently reify certain cultural preconceptions, promoting those minority writers who fulfill certain expectations, for example, as representatives of the "Black experience" in America or of the "Hispanic community."[16] In the case of Latino veterans, this can affect which war stories are published and included in Veterans Day Hispanic heritage commemorations, the latter often tacit endorsements of American wars rather than genuine engagements with the complex history of Latino veterans in US society. Mejía's memoir shows how this complex history is informed both by US military interventions abroad and by internal border-making and immigration politics.

As the youngest of thirteen children living in an impoverished country, the twelve-year-old Mencia was sent by his mother to live with an older sister in the United States. His mother joined him within two years, and the self-actualized, dignified woman he knew would be transformed into "a Spanish-speaking immigrant, low on the totem pole, compelled to work in a sewing sweatshop" (37). He contrasts their arrival as immigrants granted visas and green cards with which to attend school and work with the current conditions facing Salvadorians and other Central Americans who trek thousands of miles on land only to be rejected or denigrated, and admits that for him, "leaving the rest of my family, friends, school, country and culture behind signified an irreplaceable sense of loss" (36). Mencia credits his childhood in El Salvador for fostering a keen awareness of the dignity and resilience of many who endure abject poverty, a conviction that honor must be earned, and "concepts like loyalty and chivalry" to guide him through difficult times. His mother modeled self-sacrifice and generosity, taking him into neighboring villages each month with supplies she gathered for the poor and always treating everyone "with respect and honor" (32). Mencia's elementary school in El Salvador had partnerships with US ministries, and the kids jokingly called the missionaries they sent to the region, "*gringos en vacaciones*" (US Whites on vacation). He observed the air of superiority they carried, talking down to people they considered illiterate "*indios*" (natives; 33). Rather than trying to learn and understand their ways, "they would argue endlessly that we shouldn't call ourselves Americans, as only U.S. citizens were," oblivious to the fact that the United States is only one part of a hemisphere that includes North, Central, and South "America" (33, 38). These experiences led Mejía to reject a "narrow view of the world" and "to develop diverse spheres of friends" rather than sink into "a homogeneous philosophical pool of intolerant and single-minded people" (32, 35).

El Salvadorians are the second-largest immigrant group from Latin America after Mexicans, and their reasons for migrating not only involve domestic issues but are also related to US foreign policies and interventions. Reflecting on this past, Mencia comments on the effects of US involvement in El Salvador's internal affairs. He notes that "iterations of governments that have been installed at the behest of the U.S. in the 1980s" and the establishment of "an unsustainable peace" after El Salvador's Civil War left warriors on both sides of the conflict with a 40 percent unemployment rate (3). "Whereas millions of dollars were provided to the government to fight the uprising, no money was allocated after the treaty to provide jobs or social assistance to the fighter who had known no other way of life for the previous 12 years" (26–27). The "rampant crime and economic instability" that would plague El Salvador for a generation left nearly one million people displaced within El Salvador or living as refugees or unauthorized aliens, "treated as second-class citizens living in the shadows and abused by landlords, employers and any U.S. citizen who seeks to take advantage of their underclass status" (4).

Scholars have noted how this history entwines communities in both the United States and El Salvador. For example, in the years following the civil war, El Salvador implemented US neoliberal policies imposed by the US Agency for International Development and by the International Monetary Fund and World Bank in exchange for loans. These contributed to a "dramatic decline in social spending, especially on education, and led to the privatization of institutions including national banks and public services" (Menjívar and Cervantes). The civil war left a militarized society in its wake, "creating fertile recruitment ground for drug cartels and various organized-crime groups" and prompting many young Salvadorians to join gangs, which offered the financial and social resources systematically denied to them by their government (Menjívar and Cervantes). This exacerbated social unrest, poverty, crime, and migration—the latter prompting deportations of Salvadorans from the United States starting in the 1980s and increasing in the years since.[17]

The 17th parallel, which set the boundary between North and South Vietnam, also marks El Salvador's location on a map. The country shares with Vietnam not only this geographical demarcation but also its complicated relationship with American military and political might. Just as the United States supported a series of unpopular, corrupt, or inept leaders in South Vietnam, during El Salvador's Civil War, the United States supported what was arguably an oligarchic military regime against a guerrilla insurgency (the Farabundo Martí National Liberation Front, or FMLN).[18] Vastly outnumbered and outgunned, the FMLN nevertheless managed to grind the regime into a stalemate in 1989, which eventually led to a peace agreement and the political integration of FMLN members.[19] Mencia points out that "President Reagan provided $50 million in aid and American Special Forces to train the military, never mind that they were the ones behind the killing of thousands of civilians such as my childhood friend Ernesto, a professor at the university, four U.S. Army special forces soldiers, four American nuns and Archbishop Oscar Romero" (26). These events would inform Mencia's feelings of solidarity with disempowered peoples and shape his view of duty and honor as a US soldier sent to fight in Vietnam. They would also inspire his antiwar and social justice activism before and after his deployment.

During his teens growing up in Los Angeles, Mencia identified with the Black Panthers, Students for a Democratic Society, the antiwar movement, and respected clerics "such as Martin Luther King Jr., who opposed the war from the pulpits" (5). He believed, like his father before him, that Americans were imperialists "who wanted to take over the world" (5). His views were also shaped by his mother, who had visited New Orleans in the 1950s and returned to El Salvador "dismayed at how whites treated black people" (23). In a small act of resistance, she had "pointedly and illegally sat in the back of the bus reserved for 'colored people'" despite her white complexion (23). Today, a successful businessman and grandfather to US-born Americans, Mencia still sees vestiges of the racism and bigotry that he deplored: "We had fought a war to release Black Americans from the bonds of slavery," yet after one hundred and fifty years "cops still fire at will in our communities of color," "we're still segregated," and the current administration is focused on building walls, denigrating immigrants, and ripping "children away from their parents" (6). The sense that he betrayed his convictions also lingers, first because he served in the Vietnam War, then because he accepted US citizenship, which in his view made him complicit in "the imperialistic oppression of that small patch of soil" that, like his native country, El Salvador, "also lies exactly on the 17th parallel, but on the opposite side of the world" (6).

Although he was not a citizen of the United States, Mencia registered at the age of fifteen "out of ignorance" and was drafted as soon as he turned eighteen (71). A recruiter gave him a "choice of assignment" if he extended his contract, so Mencia opted for what he thought would be a "three-year tour in Germany" (75). Instead, he was immediately deployed to Vietnam as soon as he graduated from advanced individual training in 1968. Mencia's own father "had fought on horseback as a Captain Major in the Honduran cavalry and never compromised his principles, even when sentenced to seven years of house arrest for refusing to support the dictator in power" (40). Despite Mencia's father's refusal to emigrate to the United States ("I will give the imperialists my dead bones, he said. But I will not give them the fruits of my labor"), he nevertheless insisted that Mencia report to duty in Vietnam: "Son, I have never liked the borders carved by the imperialists on the backs of natives and slaves, but you chose to live in that country. You owe it your life if need be" (40). This sense of duty and honor is not bounded or defined by legal status or national allegiances. Mencia describes his journey to Travis Air Force Base, where his uniform attracted mockery at the airport "by anti-war protestors, regular people who in the end proved to be right about the politics that got us into the war, but wrong for demonizing individual soldiers" (88). He would later bond with other draftees, most of whom also opposed the war, as did "most junior officers" (104). During his deployment, Mencia felt the sting of demonization he first experienced as a new immigrant, but this time from fellow soldiers who "made derogatory remarks about everyone who was not white or what they considered 'real Americans'" (89). He was also quickly disabused of attitudes toward the Vietnamese, which had been instilled in them during training.

Seeing his "enemy" in person, Mencia realizes that many Viet Cong are even younger than he is and concludes "that if we had to come 10,000 miles to kill children, the folks back home were right, and we should pack up and go home" (95). He is also dumbfounded by the careless waste of resources that characterizes the American way of making war. As he notes, "We threw everything we had at them . . . we dropped more bombs on the Vietnamese than we did in both European and Pacific theaters in World War II. . . . But in the end they won the war" (95). Within days of his arrival in Vietnam, for example, "sappers" (Viet Cong units specialized in attacking airfields and other fortified locations) breached their perimeter, and his unit responded with a "mad minute mentality"—soldiers firing aimlessly into the night, choppers shooting "Gatling guns with six rotating barrels that can fire up to 6,000 rounds per minute," and all hell breaking loose (96). Yet despite their heavy artillery and expenditure of abundant resources, "the Vietnamese survived whatever we threw at them by going underground" (97). Mencia sees reflected in these conditions the asymmetrical power dynamic that characterizes relations between First and Third World nations: "The money wasted on the 100 meters between the bunkers . . . that single night would provide books for the entire population of my native El Salvador. Or build a new hospital. . . . What we debate endlessly and refuse to spend on a needed social or foreign aid program," he writes, "is wasted away in one second of war" (100).

Mencia also wonders at the careless waste of human lives, both American and Vietnamese. Within days of his arrival in Vietnam, for example, his convoy was ordered to deliver supplies to a "hot area." Expecting an ambush, he could not understand why a jeep was the lead vehicle rather than a truck "well-armed with dual M60s or larger guns" (105). He also wondered "why the convoy leader was riding there, nonchalantly, and totally exposed—almost advertising that he was in charge" (105). Within seconds of an attack, the lead jeep was hit with a rocket-propelled grenade, killing the driver and convoy leader immediately; his vehicle's driver was also instantly killed, along with his friend Stu, "who reached for the M60 and whose lifeless body fell against the passenger door" (107). Mencia notes that carelessly devised missions such as these caused countless unnecessary deaths. During the ambush, Mencia was forced to shoot and kill an enemy soldier, "a young child like myself," at close range. He discloses that this "boy solder's" death "would rule the rest of my life, and I would think about him hundreds of times per day 50 years later" (109). Over time, Mencia writes, he and his fellow soldiers would become increasingly demoralized, losing their motivation to fight. Search and destroy missions were avoided, and air support and artillery intensified, causing even more civilian deaths and environmental devastation (115). Mencia and the men he served with "slowly became old men and faded into the dark pages of history, not of the Vietnam War but of the American War" (111). Fifty years later, unable to remember the many names and faces of friends he lost in Vietnam, Mencia sees them all "blended into one person, symbolized by the boy whose name I never knew who I killed in the April 7 ambush" (127).

Mencia's empathy for the oppressed and exploited was nurtured by his upbringing and culture, but his own physical experience of disempowerment would bring these realities to bear on his body and psyche. He recounts a sexual assault that occurred during his service in Vietnam, a violation enacted against him that only deepened his feelings of solidarity and concern for those on the receiving end of violence and power. Heading back to his room after pulling guard duty, Mencia heard muffled cries coming from one of the rooms reserved for NCOs in the barracks. He saw two large soldiers he did not recognize raping a young Vietnamese girl. Assigned housekeeping duties, the girl "was no more than four feet six inches tall" and "obviously undernourished" (120). When Mencia told them to stop, they punched him in the stomach then beat and kicked him as they held him down and sodomized him. Mencia and the girl were left sobbing together in the corner of the room, holding each other, "two broken human beings from across the ocean having been born on the same parallel unable to stop the people who were supposedly her country's benefactors" (121). Their victimization stands in stark contrast to the myths of salvation, liberation, and "protection" that have sustained US proxy wars from Vietnam to Iraq, wars that devastate weaker nations in lieu of powerful ones. Mencia would blame himself for this brutal act, not only because he was unable to protect the girl ("What sense of protection would a 135-pound boy provide—a boy who had no chance against two 200-plus-pound rapists?") but also because he was aligned with the military raining destruction on her and her country (122). He dissociates himself further from his identity as an American and from the army that had put "so tender a girl, and boy for that matter, in a position that allowed this to happen" (122–23). Mencia is haunted by the memory of that day, yet, like many survivors of sexual assault, he never reported the attack or disclosed it to even those closest to him. He credits years of therapy as well as the "Me Too" movement with giving him "the impetus and courage to tell it as it was and explain my vulnerabilities."[20] Revealing these details publicly for the first time in his memoir brought "unbelievable sadness and grief" but also helped him "dispel its hold on my psyche and move forward."[21] But it took him over fifty years to arrive at this point, for like most male veterans who suffered sexual trauma in the military, he did not seek treatment until many years later. For example, at the C. W. Bill Young VA Medical Center in Bay Pines, Florida, the country's first residential facility for men suffering from military sexual trauma, most patients are veterans of the Vietnam and Korean conflicts and the average age of admission is fifty (Penn).

Most male victims of rape in the military, an estimated 81 percent, never report being attacked. Among those who do report, 64 percent were sexually assaulted at a military installation or aboard a military ship (Matthews et al.). Studies suggest that men develop PTSD from sexual assault at nearly twice the rate they do from combat (Penn). These victims are doubly stigmatized by a military ethos that prizes physical strength, power, and masculinity. Warrior culture also values stoicism, "which encourages a victim to keep his troubles to himself and stigmatizes him if he doesn't" (Penn). These victims are then ignored in most studies of military sexual assault, which tend to focus almost exclusively on female victims. Yet more males are sexually assaulted in the military than females. According to the Pentagon, thirty-eight military men are sexually assaulted every single day, nearly fourteen thousand in 2012 alone (Penn).

Mencia's traumatic experience would also dominate his "views about gender, sexuality, power and control." Many male victims question their own sexuality, as "straight men often question their own sexual orientation, while gay men may struggle to find intimacy in relationships because they don't trust other men (or their own judgment)" (Penn). They must also contend with myths, including the notion that perpetrators are gay men. In fact, most perpetrators are heterosexual men. As one VA psychologist reminds us, "It's not about the sex. It's about power and control" (Penn).[22] Feminist international relations researchers have exposed the inextricable connection between imperialism, militarism, and sexual violence. They have argued that rape is an act of violence that expresses and enacts a form of domination founded and sustained by other forms of unequal power.

Sexual assault is grounded in and enforces ideologies of supremacy, whether gendered (as in patriarchy) or political (as in the domination and conquest of groups or nations). This form of violence is the ultimate expression of the implicit connection between the personal and the political. As Carolyn Nordstrom argues, rape expresses an imbalance "that is as fundamental to the ontology of personal and social identity as it is political" (148). While the United States and other nations have begun to recognize war-related sex crimes as a breach of international law and human rights, most of the focus is still on female victims, despite the high rate of male victims. In 2016, Congress finally responded to this reality, including in the National Defense Authorization Act a requirement to improve prevention of and response to sexual assaults against male members of the US armed forces. According to a 2016 Veterans Affairs study on sexual trauma in the military, men who are exposed to combat are 3.41 times more likely to experience sexual assault than men who are not.[23] Veterans who are victims of military sexual assault are forced to carry the combined emotional burden of combat and sexual trauma throughout their lifetimes. Survivors of these two interrelated forms of violence afflict countless veterans, but they remain the most invisible casualties of war.

"NO GREATER FREEDOM": MEJÍA'S REBELLION

While on leave from Iraq, Camilo Mejía, an infantry squad leader, turned himself in to military authorities as a conscientious objector, refusing to redeploy. In May 2004, he was convicted of desertion by a military jury and sentenced to one year in a military prison. It is therefore not surprising that his memoir, *Road from ar Ramadi: The Private Rebellion of Staff Sergeant Camilo Mejía*, is dedicated "to the war resisters, to those facing the imperial powers of the earth," and "to the people of Iraq." His reference to "imperial powers" implicates the United States in a history of conquest that connects the invasion of Iraq with a colonialist, imperialist militarism rather than with its justificatory narratives of freedom and democratization. Mejía aligns his opposition with war resisters past and present, although, as he notes, when he refused to redeploy to Iraq in October 2003, "no combat veterans had taken a public stance against the war" and it was "a lonely path to walk" (xi). Although he was the first soldier to go AWOL and publicly protest the Iraq War, thousands would follow: in 2004, there were 2,450 deserters, then approximately 2,700 in 2005, and 3,300 in 2006.

But Mejía was more prepared than most to take an oppositional stance. Raised in Nicaragua and Costa Rica, he was no stranger to dissent: his parents were both political activists. His father, a popular troubadour, hosted a radio show in Nicaragua often satirizing the Anastasio Somoza regime, a corrupt military dictatorship "that ruled Nicaragua with great brutality and the official blessing of the U.S. government for nearly forty years" (3). Both of Mejía's parents became revolutionaries, actively supporting Nicaragua's left-wing Sandinista movement, which overthrew Somoza in 1979. Mejía was also no stranger to US military interventions claiming to support "freedom." The Reagan administration sent money, weapons, and operational support to a paramilitary group, the Contras, which sought to overthrow the Sandinista government; it referred to the right-wing rebel group as "freedom fighters" even after reports revealed systematic atrocities by Contra rebels—including torture, kidnapping, murder, and rape.[24] After the fall of the Sandinista government in 1990, Mejía lived in Costa Rica, then moved to Miami in 1994 when he was eighteen years old. He obtained resident status through his grandmother, a US citizen. Working dead-end, lowwage jobs, and with few prospects, Mejía joined the army the following year. Although he needed the financial stability and college tuition the army offered, Mejía had more complex motives: "The military held out the promise of helping me claim my place in the world," he writes. "It wasn't even that I wanted to be a U.S. citizen; I just wanted to be with a group of people with whom I shared something, to acquire a sense of belonging" (15). As I argued in chapter I, this desire to achieve a sense of belonging and shared purpose has long been a powerful incentive for members of marginalized groups in the United States.

During his three years in active-duty service with the Fourth Infantry Division in Fort Hood, Texas, and Fort Benning, Georgia, Mejía's performance earned him the army's Good Conduct Medal and certificates of achievement, despite his being known as "a bit of a rebel" for his critical remarks. At the end of his initial term, he opted to serve out the remaining five years with the Florida National Guard, expecting to be activated in response to a natural disaster or posthurricane relief effort.[25] Instead, just two months before the end of his eight-year term, Mejía's Florida National Guard unit was deployed in support of Operation Iraqi Freedom and his contract extended to 2031. Although by the time he refused to redeploy Mejía had completed his eight years with the army and the national guard, a stop-loss measure extended soldiers' active-duty service beyond their initial obligation. Intended as a short-term policy to keep soldiers beyond their initial contract end date and thus maintain troop levels, the stop-loss program increased desertions (Fantina). One of the stop-loss orders issued by the Department of Defense also suspended the normal regulation limiting a noncitizen's service, which would have made extending Mejía's tour illegal.[26]

Mejía's memoir takes us from his early life in Nicaragua to his military service in Iraq and subsequent court martial and imprisonment. He recounts his struggle during the writing process, as he tried to reclaim painful memories that he had locked away. Before his deployment his aversion to war was exclusive to the war in Iraq, but it was also "grounded in political reasons" (22). Mejía felt that the motives for the war had more to do with geopolitical power and oil than with bringing democracy to the Iraqi people or defending the United States (23). He sympathized with the antiwar demonstrators and knew that there was no proven connection between Saddam Hussein and the September 11 terror attacks. Yet he did not openly express his doubts at first, fearing he would be labeled a coward and knowing that his views "could be construed as unpatriotic and treasonous" (23). He would come to regret his silent acquiescence. Writing the memoir helped him begin his healing process but also registered a refusal to be silenced again: "I knew that somehow I had to turn my words into weapons, that speaking out was now my only way to fight" (223). Mejía expresses the hope that his memoir will serve as "a tool of activism" (xx). In the wake of its publication, he has continued to speak out in interviews, community centers, churches, and alternative high schools and has donated copies of the book to school libraries. Amnesty International named him the Iraq war's first "prisoner of conscience," and in 2007 Mejía was elected chairman of the board of directors of Iraq Veterans Against the War.

In his introduction, Mejía points out that many service members would come to oppose the occupation of Iraq for a variety of reasons, not always "purely political" or even "purely antiwar" (xxii). Instead, many would share his view that "unsound practices" were costing unnecessary American and Iraqi civilian deaths; some would refuse to participate in what he calls a "morally indefensible war"; others, like army specialist Suzanne Swift, would have different reasons. In 2006, Swift refused a second deployment in Iraq "with the same supervisors who had forced her into a sexual relationship in exchange for not sending her on senseless, suicidal missions, a practice known as 'command rape'" (xxiii). Mejía argues that "the many struggles waged by servicemen and servicewomen against their mission and leadership are part of a painful process of realization that something has gone awfully wrong" (xxiv). Speaking out, Mejía contends, is a way for GIs "to reclaim our love for humanity and our dedication to justice" (xxvi). His own refusal to return to Iraq, he explains, was not just fear of "physical death" but of "the many deaths of the soul every time you kill a human being. Whether we squeeze the trigger, give the order, or simply stand idle in the face of senseless missions that result in the spilling of innocent blood, it doesn't make a difference. We die, little by little, each time someone gets killed, until there is no soul left, and the body becomes a corpse, breathing and warm but devoid of humanity" (213). Mejía's description of this kind of spiritual death expresses what psychologists have identified as "moral injury": the lasting emotional, psychological, social, behavioral, and spiritual effects of acts that violate a service member's core moral values and expectations of self or others (Litz et al.).[27]

Mejía recounts his growing awareness that the Iraq War was not only poorly planned and justified but also dangerously ineffective. From the outset, everything about the Iraq invasion "seemed rushed and unprepared" (37). When his platoon landed in Baghdad, there was no unit waiting for them, "no orders, no place to sleep, not even food or water" (37). He writes, "My

lieutenant and I had to go out the next morning, in a borrowed Humvee, to
try to find another unit nearby that had extra water and MREs (meals ready
to eat)" (37). Like Crawford's *The Last True Story I'll Ever Tell*, Mejía's memoir
describes the second-class status of the Florida National Guard during the
war, noting, for example, that they were issued Vietnam-era flak vests that
"could not stop a bullet even if the enemy threw it at us by hand" (137) and
that their Humvees "were not close to being properly armored; they didn't
even have doors" (69). At the beginning of his tour, Mejía patrolled a series
of destitute towns, where most Iraqis simply wanted to "take a closer look at
their latest invaders" (39). The US occupation still being in its initial stages,
the Iraqis did "not appear to be angry with us; for the most part they would
smile and wave, gently tapping the top of their heads in a gesture we later
learned meant thank you" (39). This would change as civilian deaths increased
and occupation hardened soldiers' attitudes toward Iraqis.

Ordered to assist in running a prisoner-of-war camp, Mejía's platoon
leader informs the men, "They said we should not call this a POW camp, but
rather a *detainee* camp," speaking "the word 'detainee' in a sarcastic tone" (41).
The reason for this distinction is that the facility does not "meet the proper
requirements of a POW camp" (42)—not only because of the shortage of
medical personnel or living conditions but also because of the ways that the
prisoners are treated by "spooks" (a term "used in the Army to refer to people
who work undercover and whose affiliation is unknown"; 44). Spooks wear no
uniform—they may be Special Forces, Delta Force soldiers, Navy SEALS, CIA,
NSA, or private contractors. Mejía also notices fires burning in metal barrels,
one inside the "detainee" facility, and another outside for US soldiers: he learns
that both of these contain a "toxic mixture of fuel and human excrement"
(43).[28] He witnesses the abusive treatment of detainees and the racist hostility
some soldiers express toward Iraqi civilians. He describes the interrogations
of Iraqis picked up for reasons that are often unclear or absurd (getting off
a bus before a checkpoint; owning a gun in a country where a majority are
armed). Mejía watches as naked, handcuffed, and hooded Iraqis are asked
a series of questions to which there seem to be no "correct" answers, and as
interrogators grow increasingly angry and resort to shouting insults and
threats. Yet most interrogations end the same way: detainees are ordered to
put their clothes back on, and are classified as noncombatants and released,
with "nothing in the way of an apology" (46). Mejía also observes how some
detainees classified as "combatants" are questioned. When a fellow soldier
asks what classifies them as combatants, the answer is simply, "The spooks

decide" (47). He is informed that the "spooks" get these men to talk through sleep deprivation. Mejía is taken aback by the casual cruelties he witnesses. The lieutenant who accompanies him on their "training" talks to them as if they "were tourists and he was our tour guide" (53). At one point a hooded, handcuffed prisoner is sobbing quietly. A staff sergeant puts a nine-millimeter pistol to the man's temple, pulls the pistol's receiver back "as if loading a bullet into the chamber," and orders him to be quiet (54–55). The terrorized man, thinking he was about to be executed, let out "long anguished sobs and his entire body started to tremble uncontrollably" (54). Ordered again to be quiet, the pistol at his head, the man stops wailing and the lieutenant turns to Mejía, smiling with satisfaction. "You see?" he says. "You can communicate with them; you just have to know how" (55). Mejía "was completely against the way the prisoners in the camp were being treated" but was "afraid of speaking up for them and appearing soft and weak as a squad leader" or being charged with insubordination (55). He tries to justify his silence, but admits, "To this day I cannot find a single good answer as to why I stood idly by during the abuse of those prisoners except . . . my own cowardice" (56).

During his combat duty in al Ramadi, Mejía grows increasingly frustrated with some commanders who repeatedly send his squad out on "senseless missions"—intent on earning their combat medals even at the risk of not only Iraqi civilian but also American lives. On one occasion, they are sent back to a spot where an ambush had occurred earlier that day. Arriving after midnight, they are ordered to set up a traffic control point and detain and search any vehicles. By 3 a.m. the soldiers know that they are inviting another ambush by staying in one place so long, but the commander insists that they remain. As they finally drive back to their base, the soldiers are indeed ambushed as insurgents shoot at them from buildings along the road back. Following standard operating procedure (SOP) for a moving ambush, Mejía orders his men to "return fire and keep moving" (69). Relieved that despite the hail of bullets coming from buildings on both sides of the road the soldiers make it back to base, Mejía is reprimanded by the captain and first sergeant because his men did not stay and fight, despite receiving fire from "a ghost enemy of unknown capability but with evident advantage" (75). Mejía argues that such a decision, given the conditions, would have been not only suicidal but also against SOP. He is told that he had sent the "wrong message" to the enemy: "By getting away . . . you let them know that we are afraid. It was a victory for them" (76). Mejía was then admonished again because his men celebrated their survival back at the base. They had "sent the wrong message to other soldiers in the unit" (82).

Mejía's interactions with Iraqis further reinforced his belief that "our occupation was wrong" (84). Because of his concern for Iraqis' welfare, he was often ridiculed and earned the nickname "the humanitarian" (120). He was also conscious of the subtle and not so subtle racism he observed, both against Iraqis (often referred to by derogatory terms such as "ragheads" or "Hajjis") but also against US troops of color. He notes, for example, that the Puerto Rico National Guard were "royally screwed from the beginning" (183): "Their units had been sent to Florida at the request of Florida's governor . . . to pull security on the ports and airports while we were deployed to the Middle East. But once they arrived, they were immediately . . . sent to war" (183). During Mejía's training in Jordan, "Alpha Company's executive officer, a white man, had taken digital pictures of Puerto Rican personnel and a couple of black troops and pinned them to silhouettes for target practice" (183). The officer "was merely transferred to an administrative position, probably more for his own safety than anything else" (183). In another case a White soldier accidentally discharged his weapon and the bullet ricocheted and hit another soldier (luckily wearing a vest and not injured). Mejía explains that a "similar mistake had resulted in the serious reprimand of two Latin noncommissioned officers in our platoon. Not only did the white soldier escape reprimand, he was awarded a Purple Heart" (183–84). Mejía found the "racist attitude toward cultural differences" common throughout his deployment, to the point that an old Iraqi man asked him "why Americans treat Iraqis like dogs" (131).

Eight years was the maximum time a non-US citizen could lawfully serve in the armed forces (189). Given that Mejía's green card was about to expire while he was still serving in Iraq, there was a possibility that he could return to the States only to be deported. But when he brought this to the attention of his commanding officers, he was told, "Don't worry sergeant, you'll be a hero and a citizen when you get back home" (189). On leave for two weeks in Miami, he tries going through the chain of command, requesting to be discharged because he is no longer legally bound to the military. The captain refuses to sign his discharge documents, telling him, "Not only do I think your request is disrespectful, I think of it more as cowardice" (212). With each subsequent attempt to be released from service, he is urged to apply for citizenship, as that would allow the army to extend his deployment further. "I didn't want to appear unpatriotic, but I had started to wonder why they were so hell-bent on making me a citizen. . . . Now everything seemed to center on my becoming a citizen" (198–99). Even the Florida National Guard civilian employee with whom he'd spoken while in Iraq had said, "You have to be discharged from the military immediately" (208). Yet once he makes the request again in person, she responds, "Oh, no, no, no, no. . . . I meant when your unit returns from Iraq, then I can discharge you" (209). Then, "You know sergeant . . . it really strikes me as odd that you have been in the military longer than eight years and have not yet become a U.S. citizen" (210). He is told he must return to Iraq and only then can he be discharged. "I had never thought about citizenship much," he responds, "but I don't think that not being a US citizen makes me a bad person" (210).

Mejía attended a family support group service, and a Fox News reporter asked to interview him. Avoiding any moral or political commentary, he expressed concerns about low troop morale, inadequate logistical support, and an unclear mission, clearly not what the reporter wanted to hear, as "the story never aired" (223). He later declared his refusal to return to the Iraq in a press conference. "I went to Iraq and was an instrument of violence," Mejía said, "and now I have decided to become an instrument of peace" (qtd. in Finer). After his public declaration he surrendered to military authorities on March 15, 2004. Media outlets ran stories on his surrender, including interviews with some members of his unit who disapproved of his actions; not one soldier in his squad or his platoon was among those interviewed, "though they all lived in the Miami area" (247).

During Mejía's trial, the military judge did not allow his defense team to call expert witnesses. He was also denied the opportunity to present his allegations of prisoner abuse and other war crimes as the basis for his refusal to redeploy to Iraq. Service members representing the military were also brought into the courtroom, not only limiting seats available to Mejía's supporters but also serving as a powerful visual sign of opposition from fellow soldiers. All pretrial motions were struck down, evidence regarding violations of military and international law were ignored, and the entire case rested on Mejía's refusal to board a plane back to Iraq (Fantina 196). Even the fact that a treaty between Costa Rica and the United States (Mejía holds dual citizenship in Costa Rica and Nicaragua) stipulates that neither country may force citizens to serve in the other's military was refused as evidence. Minutes before his sentencing, Mejía addressed the jury, noting that it was easier to blame individual soldiers for abuses or flaws rather than acknowledging systems problems: "We're all on trial. everybody here in uniform, everybody in this country. . . . If we really want to look at ourselves as a military, and we really want to keep our pride and honor as a military, then we have to start from the top" (295). After just twenty minutes of deliberation, and despite overwhelming evidence, Mejía was sentenced: he would forfeit a year's salary, be imprisoned for twelve months, and be discharged from the service with a bad conduct discharge (298). After his sentencing, even as he faced a year in prison, Mejía writes, "I gained my freedom. I understood then that freedom is not something physical, but a condition of the mind and of the heart. On that day I learned that there is no greater freedom than the freedom to follow one's conscience. That day I was free, in a way I had never been before" (300). The word "freedom" has served as a battle cry for many wars, but Mejía here alludes to a freedom that is not about national sovereignty, for "there is no greater freedom than the freedom to follow one's conscience" (300).

   Current scholarship on citizenship suggests a move away from its conceptualization as a disembodied set of rights and toward one that calls attention to the dynamic and dialogical processes of political claim making (Chatterjee). Citizenship in this sense is not passive consent to conditions imposed by a state or allegiance to fixed formulations of identity, but an ongoing process of meaning making and becoming that is explicitly disruptive to entrenched power. As immigrants from countries that have experienced political turmoil and violent internal conflicts, and as combat veterans who must negotiate competing moral claims, Mejía and Mencia push at the narrow parameters that typically define citizenship, duty, and honor. They identify with the embodied experience of the governed and recognize the effects of unmitigated power on those at the receiving end of military force. Both claim a form of allegiance untethered from homogenized models of American identity, models that normalize social and political boundaries and in turn legitimize asymmetrical power relations and structural inequalities. In doing so, their memoirs participate in an alter/native discursive arena, or what Nancy Fraser calls a "subaltern counterpublic" that can promote more inclusive forms of participatory citizenship. While concurrent with official public spheres, these discursive fields reflect the dynamic interrelations that create publics—whether in the form of "public opinion" or in the constitution of political subjects. Fraser contends that the preconditions that organize political life in the official public sphere are themselves premised on "socioeconomic and sociosexual structures that generate systemic inequalities." Her formulation of counterpublics points to unruly spaces "where subordinated social groups invent and circulate counter discourses to formulate oppositional interpretations of their identities, interests, and needs" (Fraser 123).[29] Veterans' stories participate in this dynamic struggle over meaning, interpretation, and history.

For those veterans like Mencia and Mejía who reside in the gaps between dual identities—foreign/national, subjugator/subjected—memory is a series of skirmishes fought at the margins of a public sphere that devalues or ignores their experiences. While public memorials work to transform personal loss into collective mourning, there will be no such recognition for those whose war stories do not speak of "our" greatness. Their "truths" do not fit into tidy narratives, and instead contradict and complement them. What we learn from their war stories calls into question our most cherished illusions, tells us what we do not want to hear. But that is what war stories have always done—exposed contradictions between our national myths and our lived realities, demanded that we reckon with our duty as citizens. Mencia's and Mejía's memoirs are indeed painful counternarratives. Reading them is like tearing scabs off old wounds: it hurts but hastens the process of healing.

Chapter 5

SILENCE AMID THE DIN OF WAR
The Politics and Poetics of Audibility in Brian Turner's *My Life as a Foreign Country*

Was it not noticeable at the end of the war that men
returned from the battlefield grown silent, not richer,
but poorer in communicable experience?
—Walter Benjamin, "The Storyteller"

"Without the loudspeaker, we would never have conquered Germany," Hitler wrote in 1938 (qtd. in Attali 87). The loudspeaker, the airwaves, and now the Internet are vehicles for communicating worldviews. They are ways of making power manifest—of speaking to and for others, exerting influence, intervening and interjecting, commandeering language and sound. As a political metaphor, making noise is akin to occupying and conquering territory: a way of monopolizing space, overwhelming competing voices and drowning out criticism. Politics in this sense is a matter of frequency and volume, of presence, of occupying a space that would otherwise be filled by another. It can serve as a strategy of suppression, a way of keeping the majority silent, a filibustering imperative: the drone of endless chatter exhausting others into acquiescent silence. Such strategic noisemaking is not restricted to control of media and other audio communication forms. It has its equivalent in literary styles that eschew the whispers of intimation, innuendo, and subtlety in favor of the hyperbolic, jarring, and strident. Writers use such techniques to shake readers up: shocking, riling, arousing them from a passive or conventional posture, dinning the audience into hearing the writer's message across distances created by ideological differences, making their vision apparent. This synesthetic appeal, in which *sound* is used to stimulate *sight* (seeing past "blind spots"), relies on vision as a conceptual metaphor for understanding. Hearing, in this sense, breaches the divide between writer and reader, sensory and cognitive, and is key in conveying the writer's vision.[1]

I invoke these aural metaphors to initiate consideration of literary noise/silence as rhetorical devices that can activate readers' perceptual faculties. Focusing on Brian Turner's Iraq war memoir about his service as an infantry team leader with the Third Stryker Brigade, *My Life as a Foreign Country*, this chapter considers some of the ways that inaudibility, both metaphorical and literal, can invoke reflection and judgment, convey trauma, or register complicity. I aim to suggest that silence can work as a defamiliarizing strategy to sharpen vision or enhance awareness. "Defamiliarization" is the English translation of the term *ostranenie* ("making strange") that describes an artistic technique aimed at enhancing an audience's perception by forcing them to see something familiar in a new way.[2] In particular, I argue that Turner's evocation of things silent or muted—hooded prisoners, ghostly figures, dead or broken bodies—as well as his forays into memory and imagination, summon active listening as a bridge to understanding. Silence cues readers to pause, and to look and listen more carefully. Just as we strain to hear a soft voice—leaning closer or tuning out competing sounds, Turner beckons us to discern what is hushed, silenced, or repressed amid the din of war.

Critics have addressed the uses of silence in literature and art in diverse ways. As Janet Perez notes, many have become increasingly aware "of the multivalent aesthetic dimensions of silence, and of the complexities of its causes, its uses, and its messages" (116). Some point to distinctions between "the absence of sound when no communication is going on, and silence which is part of communication" (Saville-Troike 4). They theorize silence as one of the forms that a speech act may take, "to question, promise, deny, warn, threaten, insult, request, or command" (6). Others focus on the political implications of silencing, or, as Cheryl Glenn explains, on the recognition that "the meaning of silence depends on a power differential that exists in every rhetorical situation: who can speak, who must remain silent, who listens, and what those listeners can do" (9). Michelle Cliff, for example, notes "the alliance between speechlessness and powerlessness; that the former maintains the latter; that the powerful are dedicated to the investiture of speechlessness on the powerless" (121). Feminist critics have called attention to the gendered and racialized aspects of silence, with some women of color posing the problem as not "merely the absence of speaking voices" but the absence of "hearing ears" (Ratcliffe 85). Hearing is thus not simply a physiological act but also a receptive mode that engages the listener in a relationship. In contrast, silence can also serve as an oppositional force, a strategic form of communication with the potential to disrupt, rather than enforce, power. As

Kennan Ferguson argues, "Silence can serve as resistance to any institution that requires verbal participation (as do virtually all)" (49). The refusal to take an oath, to recant, to self-incriminate, and to pledge allegiance are all forms of resistance through silence.

Silence can also serve as a metaphorical repudiation or rejection of language, authority, or inauthenticity. In "The Aesthetics of Silence," Susan Sontag describes silence as "an ideal plenitude to which the audience can add nothing, analogous to the aesthetic relation to nature" (191). The metaphorical silence to which she alludes—the blank canvas, the empty page—plays a mediating role, invoking its opposite: "If only because the art-work exists in a world furnished with many other things, the artist who creates silence or emptiness must produce something dialectical: a full void, an enriching emptiness, a resonating or eloquent silence. Silence remains, inescapably, a form of speech (in many instances, of complaint or indictment) and an element in a dialogue" (187). Thus, rather than a cessation of expression, silence initiates an interaction, a hermeneutical process, since "somebody's silence opens up an array of possibilities for interpreting that silence, for imputing speech to it" (191). Silence counters a culture of noise—meaningless chatter in an age of inauthenticity, of speech that is "false, inane, ignoble, weightless." Not speaking invites listening, or at least it creates the possibility of "feeling more fully one's physical presence in a given space." Sontag also posits silence as a metaphor for a "cleansed, non-interfering vision" (191). In this case, language "points to its own transcendence in silence" (192). Silence always depends on the presence of sound elsewhere, she argues, for "one must acknowledge a surrounding environment of sound or language in order to recognize silence" (187).

Despite its many rhetorical and aesthetic uses, however, silence is rarely associated with war or its literature. On the contrary, war is noisy—it invades the auditory landscape.[3] Readers are sure to encounter lots of noise in accounts of war: the onomatopoeic sounds of bombs exploding or fighter jets overhead, heavy machinery grinding over land, civilians screaming, and what Turner describes as "the fucks and goddamns and Jesus Christs of the wounded."[4] In Turner's second book of poetry, *Phantom Noise*, the title poem alludes to the "noise" of war as something that lingers in the body's memory, like the persistent "ringing hum" of tinnitus, a "rifled symphonic" singing a "bullet-borne language." This is the din of war that makes us recoil, cringe in horror. In this setting, silence can surprise, evoke suspicion, heighten perception. War also produces another kind of noise: pundits gushing over sensational graphics of smart bombs hitting their targets, loud political speeches invoking fear and hate, dissenting voices clamoring to be heard over megaphones and microphones, shouting matches about policy or strategy, filibusters in the halls of Congress. These comprise what Jodi Berland identifies as the "discourses of power effected by technology, technological processes, mediated social relationships" (41). This is the noise that serves as intermediary of war, or, as Barry Truax puts it, the "alienating force that loosens the contact the listener has with the environment, and an irritant that works against effective communication" (94). In war making, power makes its presence known through noise.

Whereas the absence of sound can stimulate our visionary faculty, noise can overpower our senses and interfere with our capacity to hear clearly; this is the kind of "noise" that confounds or threatens communication, disrupts our ability to understand the messages transmitted. In this way, noise obscures vision, short-circuits understanding. The audible articulations and byproducts of war intrude, disturb, and command. In the literature of war these intrusions alert readers to the integral relationship between sound and forms of communication, control, surveillance, and oppression. Turner's moments of silence or inaudibility in this setting confound this relationship; they can elicit receptivity and response. Readers are not only prompted to try harder to hear but also to comprehend that which is figuratively out of earshot and out of sight. This is an ethical call, a technique that situates readers as witnesses to the events unfolding before them rather than as passive spectators: active listening becomes a call to see, and more specifically—to *recognize*. The etymology of the word "recognition" itself suggests a call to "know again, recall to mind." This implies an act of seeing something anew, acknowledging what was previously unknown, unfamiliar, nebulous.

This kind of recognition stems, in part, from *active listening*. Scholars argue for the importance of active listening in forging connections across cultural and ideological differences, for as Pat Gehrke reminds us, "those which can be placed out of sight, to whom we can avoid listening, can be excluded from our ethical concerns far more easily" (4). Paula S. Tompkins connects what she calls "rhetorical listening" to vision, as we are asked to "recognize those who are present, while also being attentive to traces of the relational connections of Others whose presence is obscured or absent" (69). In her view, "Moral sensitivity informed by a practice of rhetorical listening helps create a space for the possibility of ethical action" (77). This implies "a kind of listening that takes as its purpose a response to greater obligations" (3). Listening with an awareness of "greater obligations" implicates the reader in the events described; it entails not just a cognitive process but also a practice in the ethical constitution of the subject. The term "rhetorical listening," Krista Ratcliffe proposes, is a trope for interpretive invention that signifies "a stance of openness that a person may choose to assume in relation to any person, text, or culture" (17). Such listening may help us interpret and "ultimately judge differently in that perhaps we can *hear* things we cannot *see*" (25). My approach draws on Ratcliffe's latter point but reverses it to suggest that Turner uses silence to help us *see* or envision things we cannot *hear*.

THE POLITICS AND POETICS OF SILENCE

Don't look for meaning in the words. Listen to the silences.

—Samuel Beckett, *The Unnamable*

Turner's rhetorical use of soundlessness is evident from the outset, as he begins his narrative with the disembodied view of "a drone aircraft plying the darkness" from thirty-two thousand feet. Usually associated with the destructive power of American military drone strikes, here the war machine is a silent, detached observer—a machine that does not feel, does not judge—only transmits the image of what it sees: Turner's wife sleeping below, then countries touching countries, "cumulus scattered above them, their shapes authored by sunlight on the ground beneath" (ix). Like lines on a map, artificial barriers are created by those who generate the loudest noise: discourses that define, differentiate, and separate, or bombs that kill, maim, and silence. But in the absence of such noise, there is a natural coexistence ("authored by sunlight"). This soundless observing suggests the possibility of transcending, if only momentarily, the artificial divisions constructed through language, but also the limits of time and space, inviting us into the realm of imagination. Vision is here not only literal but figurative, suggesting the possibility of contiguity and connection. In this state of pure vision, unencumbered by noise, language no longer serves to differentiate us from them, friends and enemies, or even the dead from the living, as "scorch marks on the asphalt where transport trucks were left to burn" in Iraq coincide with the "eucalyptus trees" of Turner's childhood, where his "dead Uncle Paul steals oranges in the night groves there . . . while fresh earth covers the newly dead on the other side of the highway" (x).

With this opening, in which vision prevails, Turner initiates a journey that will take us not only to the imagistic, boundless space of memory but also toward a vision that sees beyond the politics of the moment, beyond the borders etched on maps though war and conflict, labels, accusations, and other noise. But Turner's opening silence signals not only the absence of sound but also its displacement: readers need to look elsewhere for what is missing or absent, consider where noise thrives, negates, or supplants. For Turner's use of the drone as a metaphor for an expanded, godlike vision also resonates: the drone is, after all, not omniscient; it suggests not only boundlessness but also boundaries between those who wield this instrument of power and those who are its targets. While we witness what Turner describes, we are also implicated in a surveillance practiced in our name: America's increasing use of drones in striking targets has claimed the lives of countless Iraqi civilians, its grim silence leaving death and destruction in its wake. These unmanned aerial vehicles, like those who monitor their shadowy images on computer screens hundreds of miles away, do not hear the cries of the dying below, cannot discern the details of a life unrecognized. Theirs is sight devoid of vision, incapable of hearing.[5]

Turner's brief prologue therefore suggests two complementary figurations of silence. In one sense, the drone is simply the receiver and transmitter of visual signals; it reflects a nonjudgmental and unfiltered receptivity that creates a space for "listening and hearing as a generative action of perception" to challenge, augment, and expand what we see (Voegelin 12). This receptivity allows the observer a "big picture" view—one in which the past and the present are "compressed into the demarcations in the map below" (x). But it also conveys an oblique silence: Turner's readers are keenly aware of the role that drones play in contemporary American warfare. They know that the absence of noise is precisely what makes drones so deadly; they strike without warning, and despite their surveillance capacity they are unable to discern whatever subtle visual differences may distinguish the jihadist from the doting father.[6] This aspect of silence suggests a space "either beyond words or conventionally delimited as left out of what we talk about" (Winter 4). In this figuration, silence is politically enforced and even ritualized; it is part of the framing of distant wars for local public consumption, that which remains unacknowledged (etymologically "unknown") or strategically left unspoken. This is the silence that deflects and defers, a silence of complicity or imperviousness. The subjectivity implied through the drone's point of view is on the one hand seeking "necessary intelligence," fulfilling its role as an instrument of surveillance; on the other, Turner shifts this perspective from a drone monitoring "heat signatures in the landscape" to his personal search to understand "all that I have done," then again to an incriminating "all that *we* have done" (x; emphasis mine).

It is thus fitting that toward end of his prologue, Turner hears owls calling "out for water" from the gravestones of the Iraqi "newly dead" (x). This image recurs throughout the memoir, and it signals an ethical call that goes unheeded by the living—a figurative "droning" that fades into the background despite its urgency (the fact that "fresh dark earth covers the newly dead" suggests that the killing and dying continue). Again, in the scene immediately following, the occlusion of ambient noise hones perception: as his sergeant explains how to "label and keep track of the dead" after an ambush, Turner's "eyes wander over the grassy field" toward "the early morning light [that] illuminates the translucent nature of the grass in its subtle gesture toward infinity" (3). Tuning out the sound of his sergeant's voice and the banter of his fellow soldiers, Turner connects this transitory moment to a timeless cycle of nature (the sunlight illuminating the grass). This state of heightened perception stirs Turner's consciousness, and he begins to "hear" through his mind's eye the dead from wars past calling out "with hoarse voices, quietly, asking for a drink of water. A small sip, they say. Just a sip of water" (3). These voices are "hoarse" from their repeated efforts to be heard by the living, their lifeless bodies craving water as a source of renewed life.

Turner hears these whispered pleas throughout his tour in Iraq, yet the war continues unabated. It thus dawns on him that human beings inhabit a "landscape of ghosts," not only in Iraq, but anywhere that war has left its "harvest of death" behind.[7] At one point, he compares this vision to the way photographers talk about the presence of the dead on the battlefield at Gettysburg, whose "shadows fall among the leaves of grass and the stalks of purple thistleweed" (25). But this image of dead soldiers extends beyond any specific war, as Turner's shadows haunt battlefields across time and space. The trenches of the Somme. The beachhead at Anzac Cove. Along the Chickahominy River. Vicksburg. Cold Harbor. A spot by the Tigris "the more recent dead from the strafed and bombed Highway 1—some glancing across a mist of smoke in silence" (25). The dead cannot speak, but their presence signals Turner's awakening consciousness: he (and we as readers) are implicated in a futile cycle of war and death.

Aware of his increasing isolation and disconnection from civilian life and human relationships, Turner seeks connection through silent intercourse with nature. At one point, he steps outside his tent "to get a breath of air and quiet." In these moments, he experiences "a distinct sense of the past and the future being erased at the horizon's edge" as "the circumference of the world retracts" (7). During this interlude, in which nature creates a space for introspection, Turner quiets his mind, finding comfort in silent solitude. The image of the world "retracting" suggests a withdrawal from the temporal preoccupations that characterize human activity. Apprehension about his role as one in a line of soldiers and even his loneliness in the aftermath of a divorce fade into a silent communion with the natural world, a communion that contrasts with our incessant preoccupation with what is ultimately ephemeral. Alone later that night he reads Marcus Aurelius's *Meditations* and again reflects on connections across time and space, realizing that he is, as Aurelius noted centuries before, one of the many "leaves that the wind drives earthward" (7). His quiet contemplation of the natural world has given him a temporary respite from the noise and bustle of human-created alienation and strife, reminding him of a cyclical process of renewal. Silence here opens a space for observation, receptivity, and even transcendence from the temporal, the transitory, suggesting the possibility of continuity and regeneration.

Echoing transcendentalism's appeal for humans to rekindle, in Emerson's words, "an original relation to the universe" (3), poet Wendell Berry describes silent intercourse with nature as a gift that quiets the mind so that we can see "the larger circle of all creatures, passing in and out of life, who move also in a dance, to a music so subtle and vast that no ear hears it except in fragments" (*What Are People For?*). Berry contends that in these instances, "one's inner voices become audible." He thus instructs poets to "be quiet" and "accept what comes from silence" ("How to Be a Poet"). But he also acknowledges that these are transitory moments inevitability followed by a return, "from the order of nature" to "the order—and the disorder—of humanity" ("What Are People For?"). Turner seems to confirm this movement from silence to noise, from an escape to a reimmersion in human conflict. Following his silent interaction with the natural world, he begins his next chapter with a description of soldiers preparing to head into battle. However, Turner's silent interludes leave traces on his consciousness, for as Berry suggests, following moments of quiet solitude with nature, "one responds more clearly to other lives. . . . [and enters] more fully . . . into the communion of all creatures" ("What Are People For?"). Thus as Turner awaits the order to roll out, he recalls these words: "Facing us in the field of battle are teachers, fathers and sons/grandsons, grandfathers, wives' brothers; mothers' brothers/and fathers of wives" (8).[8] This recognition of the humanity he shares with those he is soon to confront in battle registers only momentarily, as sound interrupts and he is called back to a world defined by duty and obligation, back to the "circle of the human," where, in Berry's words, "we are weary with striving, and are without rest" ("What Are People For?"). Sound once again intrudes on Turner, as the soldiers are ordered to "lock and load our weapons, mount up and move out" (8).

Ideas about what defines a nation's symbolic boundaries are inseparable from its stories about war. Passed on from one generation to another, these inform collective and personal memories and forge connections across time. Turner's memoir recognizes this slippery slope from the "I" to the "we"—the ways each of us is shaped by the stories that bind us to family and national history. In this sense, Turner's memoir is what Stephanie Patterson calls "a book of inheritances. . . . about legacies. . . . about duty" (22). This "inheritance" includes the war stories he grew up hearing and reenacting: Turner as an eleven-year old wearing his father's "old National Guard uniform" (38); or as a thirteen-year-old amateur actor playing a soldier in a movie made with his friends, all "dressed in green army fatigues" with "fake bloodstains on their uniforms and . . . fake blood smeared onto their faces" (47–48). As Turner explains his decision to join the military, the call to duty stems not from a patriotic desire to serve on behalf of a cause ("the war on terror") but from a bequest that joins him to a family of soldiers. Turner feels obligated to join the ranks of those who came before him, relatives who served as well as heroes he read about as a child. Joining the military grants him access to a landscape defined by sound: "If I hadn't . . . it would have meant that between me and the people I revered there were explosions I couldn't hear, curses and shouting and laughter, engines thrumming, Hueys and Blackhawks . . . surgeons calling for scalpels and sutures and more blood" (56).

While the men he knows rarely speak of combat, opting instead to describe scenery while "circling the things not talked about" (45), Turner has been initiated into a fraternity maintained by secrets, omissions, and a "liturgical silence" that marks the sacred; he understood the "themes of loss, mourning, sacrifice and redemption" that characterize the stories of war (Winter 4). Thus, when Ray, a friend of Turner's father, teaches Turner to play the horn, Turner writes, "I won't ask him about his time as a mortar man in Vietnam. And Ray won't talk about the burned grass. . . . He won't tell me about the bugle he found beside a Vietnamese soldier who stared at him with his dead eyes" (46). Although Turner notes that his grandfather was as "a man of historical silence" (100), his example speaks volumes, bestowing the legacy of soldiering that Turner will continue. Turner admits that he "would've been ashamed in the years to come if I hadn't, even if it didn't make sense, even if nobody I cared about ever thought about it, even if all the veterans in my family never said a word, or even if they did, saying, It's cool, Brian, it doesn't mean a thing, believe me, the uniform doesn't make the man, or anything along those lines" (56). Turner will later find that to some extent, the uniform does "make the man," as he will lose his personal identity to the objectified "look" of those who will see only his uniform, just as he will be trained to see potential "enemies" in all the Iraqis he encounters.[9]

Throughout his tour of duty Turner will appear to others not as an individual but "as a foreign country." He is also a character, Sergeant Turner, defined in this case by his rank. In one scene, for example, Turner is charged with guarding a group of Iraqi prisoners. One of the captured men catches Turner's eye, and they stare at each other, their silent communication comprising "one moment in history's vast archive of the unrecorded" (23). He realizes, "We both live in pens made of wire. I carry an M4, have a boot knife strapped to my flak vest and the American flag silently listening in from the uniform on my shoulder. He's in his man dress, wearing sandals and shivering in the damp cold" (23–24). The flag "silently listening" is a reminder of the legacy Turner carries, the duty to which he is bound through blood and nationality.

Later, he notices that two of the prisoners are kept separate from the others, either because they are "high value" or more likely, he thinks, because "they have been forgotten within the vast machinery of war" (27). They are "caged in a tiny side room" reminiscent of "a jail cell in the American West, circa 1870"—a "ghost-town cell" (27). Looking at them, he "can barely make out the forms shivering shoulder to shoulder, squatting down, hunched, a couple of pieces of soaked cardboard the only thing between them and the cold concrete" (27). These figures, obscured and silent, are barely perceptible as human beings. Yet, he "can feel their eyes through the darkness. Looking at me. Chiseling into memory the anonymity of the uniform. They can barely distinguish me as a man, either" (27). Ironically, the "either" here suggests that this reductive gaze mirrors his own. A mutual misrecognition—whereby neither side can discern the other's humanity—is another legacy of war. This impaired vision lingers in soldiers' memories, yet it is often left unspoken, like the stories Turner's Uncle Jon would not speak: of interrogation cells in Vietnam, for instance, stories of how "he questioned the prisoners in their blue suits, how they huddled in the cages at the zoo, how they begged" (46).

Turner's attempts to "hear with his mind's eye" momentarily disrupt this dominant framework of war, these rigid "us" versus "them" polarities. Listening in this sense is not merely a physical act but a relationship with another, the invocation of moral consciousness. To listen in this way is "to adopt an attitude of decoding what is obscure, blurred, or mute, in order to make available to consciousness the underside of meaning" (Barthes 249). Describing preparations for a night raid, Turner momentarily mutes the sound of his soldiers' banter to listen for what is left unspoken: "They don't talk about the people who live in the target house. . . . They don't talk about the men eating dinner in that house now, the children who run in through the front door, the sound of their laughter as they turn and run upstairs, their mother calling to them from another room" (67). Visualizing the other as an active presence, Turner reminds us that the collective memory of war drowns out the "noisy alterity" of competing voices.[10] In his memoir, memory "is conceived as no longer located solely within the experience of a particular individual but as exceeding the personal, traversing subjects and temporalities" (Cetinic 287). Listening for what has been omitted, silenced, or repressed complicates meaning, for surely, "America, vast and laid out from one ocean to another[,] is not a large enough space to contain the war each soldier brings home" (173).

"Soldiers are citizens of death's gray land," wrote World War I veteran-poet Siegfried Sassoon, an image that aptly reflects Turner's struggle to understand an inscrutable landscape. Throughout the memoir, dreams serve as a trope for this experience of ambiguity, this "gray land" without discernible meaning or purpose. Following his stare-down with one of the prisoners, for example, Turner tries to decipher a dream that begins when a mortar explodes and its "sound waves reverberate outward from the blast" (28). Stuck in slow motion, he sees a camel behind him, nudging him forward, "whispering something, its voice at the twin thresholds of human hearing, low and ethereal all at once, a voice whispered from enormous lungs . . . a guide to the landscape of dream, a creature I need to know, I think, as I continue to move the way sand is carried over the surface of the earth by wind, away from detonations and the waves rippling outward, away from the soldiers sprinting in slow motion to overhead cover, away" (29). Here again Turner strains to hear, trying to understand a meaning that seems just below the surface of cognition. But he is awakened once again by war's sonic intrusions, left unmoored in a world that appears even more unreal and illusory than the world of his dreams. He hears "the outgoing booms" of mortar rounds, and listens "for the missiles spinning over the rooftops of the city . . . the velocity of metal given an irrevocable intention" (30). Indeterminacy is replaced by the unwavering certitude of a missile.

Noise interrupts thought, disables perception; it penetrates, occupies, and overwhelms the body. In these instances, the reader is thrust back into the acoustic turmoil of war, into a language that requires no translation, suffers no semantic ambiguities: the sound of mortars—the "outgoing booms of their cannons" (30); "the reports of M4 carbines and squad automatic weapons" (59); the "sound of the detonations, the crack and airy breath of it all" (15); the machine gunners firing quick bursts in pairs, "*pop-pop, pop-pop, pop-pop*" (59); "the sound of that helicopter riding over the waters. The low thwap-thwap-thwap-thwap of the rotorblades spinning—one of the sounds of death, the machine gun's prelude" (163). A bomb exploding nearby speaks with a "metallic elocution" (59) that registers on the brain "as a type of conversation. The extension of an idea expressed in the physical language of shrapnel" (15). This "physical language" has no use for the abstract, the conceptual, or the imaginary; it communicates with the precision of a hammer to the head.

The sonic language of war leaves its imprint not only on the physical body but also on the psyche of those who hear it. Investigating the effects of the Iraq War's "belliphonic landscape" on military and civilian personnel, J. Martin Daughtry explores "the spectrum of sounds produced by armed combat" (3). Drawing from interviews, blogs by American soldiers, news videos, and other sources, Daughtry suggests an inherent link between sound and violence, arguing that war's sonic episodes should be understood as "disturbance events introducing forced change in a system" (169). In his view, war's noisiness invades and "conquers" the body (208), resulting in an "inexorable process of sensory impoverishment" (205). This sonic battlefield, Daughtry argues, is a "shadow war of the senses" that potentially creates not only a "trauma zone" (i.e., "the innermost zone of wartime audition," where sounds produce physiological damage) but also an "ethical vacuum" (211). Of special interest here is the contrast Daughtry draws between American soldiers' "situational awareness" (the imperative that they be hyperaware of their environment) and the sensory deprivation imposed on Iraqi detainees: "Situational awareness was precisely the affordance that the US military and intelligence services wanted to deny the large population of Iraqi men who were detained for questioning over the course of the war. The standard technology for achieving this purpose, the hood, was the [advanced combat helmet's] affective opposite: it was designed to close off the sensory world rather than open it up, disorient the wearer rather than orient him within his environment, and create an embodied state not of security but of vulnerability" (206). We know that sound can be weaponized, turned into an *instrument* of power. But most relevant here is the suggestion that audibility "opens up" the world and is thus a *prerogative* of power. What serves as a means of self-preservation and knowledge on the one hand (the imperative to hear) becomes a weapon of deprivation and dehumanization on the other (the injunction against hearing).

This contrast is best exemplified by two scenes Turner describes, each of which creates an "ethical vacuum." During a night raid targeting what they believe is an Iraqi insurgent's home, Turner's description highlights the effects of extreme "situational awareness." As he runs toward the house, Turner's body is in a state of hyper-alertness: "Adrenaline mutes the world around me until all I can hear is the sound of my own breathing, gear jostling on my flak vest, the dull clanging of ammunition strapped to my chest, impossibly loud, so loud I think the dogs will bark." (22). In this state, Turner's ethical consciousness collapses into solipsism, as the internal movements of the body, normally drowned out by ambient sound, shut out the world beyond the self. Oriented only by the weapon that ensures his self-preservation, the "M4 pointing the way forward," Turner's "tunnel vision" comes at the cost of his peripheral vision, for "as the world funnels in toward the door" (22), he no longer sees the wider picture. This moment suggests a figurative shrinking of his circle of obligation, a temporary occlusion of an external reference point, or what critic Stephen Darwall calls a "scheme of accountability" that can form the basis of morality.

Turner's audio hypersensitivity in this case stems from privilege, both because it reflects an agentic subjectivity (this is, after all, *his* narrative) and a vantage point (he is part of an occupying force). But the opposite is true for those deprived of the right to choose when, what, or whether to hear. Elaine Scarry has described the annihilating power of torture, as intense pain contracts and ultimately dissolves the victim's consciousness. During this process of disintegrating perception, "the created world of thought and feeling, all the psychological and mental content that constitutes both one's self and one's world, and that gives rise to and is in turn made possible by language, ceases to exist" (30). Similarly, the mind-numbing effects of both sensory deprivation and sensory overload can be used to disorient or break down consciousness. The body's sensory powers are used against the prisoner, "a means of turning the body back in on itself, forcing the body to feed on the body: the eyes are only access points for scorching light, the ears for brutal noises" (48). This makes sound an important interrogation technique, one used by the US military to systematically "harass, discipline, and in some cases 'break' detainees" and "drown out" their inner thoughts (Cusick). Turner alludes to this in his poetry, specifically in "The Discotheque," which refers to the metal container where some prisoners were interrogated. Transporting blindfolded prisoners, Turner notes how their heads "slumped in resignation," yet he admits he "didn't feel a thing," longing only for some much-needed sleep. After he turns the prisoners in to the MPs, he watches as they are taken to the metal container, but Turner will hear only the sound of loud guitar music coming from "distorted speakers," never hear "the screaming . . . the breaking of men." Loud music muffles the sounds that would otherwise disturb sleep and provoke empathetic response.

In his memoir, Turner revisits such scenes, yet again leaves out direct commentary or judgment. Overhearing "loud music reverberating from the prisoner containment areas," the area referred to as "kennels"—he first reads the sign above the entry, "Discotheque," literally: "I thought the pogues were drinking chai and kicking back listening to music in their self-styled chill spot" (74). But he soon realizes that he is actually "listening to the interrogator's craft" (75). For inside those metal boxes music blared night and day as sleep-deprived men "were being broken down and changed forever" (74). Recounting this scene, he says simply, "I never fully appreciated [what] the depth of the cold . . . could offer a man's body, the hypothermic value of intelligence. Or the need for sanitary gloves, a rectal thermometer" (74). Here Turner's silence is what Jay Winter describes as "political" or strategic in that it suspends or truncates "open conflict over the meaning and/or justification of violence" (5). Unable or unwilling to explain, justify, or openly condemn the use of these items in this context, Turner withholds judgment. The reader is left to imagine horrors left unspoken. We are also left to wonder whether this silence reflects Turner's own ethical grappling with what he has seen or if it is a silence imposed on him by the uniform that defines him. As Gary Baines argues, silences can be group or collective responses that are "proscribed and enforced, socially conditioned and sanctioned, or voluntarily embraced" (79). Turner's silences can involve a degree of agency, or none at all.

In another scene, the soldiers raid a house of suspected insurgents, terrorizing its inhabitants. Turner watches the sergeant yelling at the silent prisoners, sandbags over their heads so they cannot see their tormentor as he screams repeatedly, "All you gotta do is tell. Tell us what you know" (17). Flex cuffs bind the men's wrists as they kneel in an animal stall, "one of them sobbing to himself" (17). Hours later the higher-ups notify the soldiers that they've raided the wrong site, and the soldiers will remove the hoods and apologize, "mount their vehicles and roll out." Turner doesn't comment on this absurd miscommunication, does not accuse, opine, or condemn its effects. In both instances noted above, he remains speechless in the aftermath of events that probably occurred numerous times throughout the war—the "enhanced interrogation" of Iraqis, the breakdowns of communication that cost countless lives, the empty gestures and enforced silences that follow. In my view, these silences invite speculation; they are strategic interruptions during which the writer reneges on his implicit promise to tell, to reveal, to expose. In relinquishing his authorial power, so to speak, Turner creates an awkward epistemological void, an aporia that the reader is compelled to resolve through inference, intuition, or interpretation. I would add that such silences also suggest not only his but our own complicity in these acts. For while most Americans have heard news reports and seen visual evidence of such practices, these too, like the hoarse pleas of Turner's imaginary owls, have not altered the nation's moral landscape.[11]

In the context of traumatic events or recollections, silence expresses a rupture in continuity. Shoshana Felman reminds us that trauma can be spoken only in a language that disrupts linear flow and the notion of authority or mastery: "Testimony [of trauma] seems to be composed of bits and pieces of a memory that has been overwhelmed by occurrences that have not settled into understanding or remembrance, acts that cannot be constructed as knowledge nor assimilated into full cognition, events in excess of our frames of reference" (Felman and Laub5). Turner's silences often stage an ontology of trauma, of what cannot be spoken. For example, following the suicide of one of the men, words fail his fellow soldiers. They silently pack up the dead man's belongings, and Turner imagines the platoon leader "trying to formulate the words and sentences for an impossible letter home, words meant to convey our own loss within the platoon and to console a family" (83). He implies the ineffectiveness of such expressions, the inability to achieve their intended meanings. Any attempt to break the grip of grief and loss with empty gestures or words seems futile, an intrusion on the senses. Turner imagines those who will deliver the message to the family as they stand at their front doorstep, then hears "the sound of the doorbell ringing inside, too shrill, I think, too bright" (83).

Upon Turner's return home, the sounds of celebration and Americana fill his memories: a parade, a colonel giving a speech he can barely hear "even over the loudspeakers" "one bromide at a time" (157). The brigade listens, motionless, as the "colonel drifted further and further away on a speech of heroes and sacrifice and nation-building" (158). After the obligatory parades and speeches, Turner feels that he is "witnessing the erasure of a kind of set design, the dismantling of a stage treatment" as the "landscape pulls the vestiges of war under and replaces them with a monument" (159). Silence will prevail—but this time not as a space for listening but as an act of forgetting. Yet Turner will be haunted by memories of death, visions of suicide: a veteran stepping "away from the chair and the rope does its work. Pills swallowed with whiskey or coconut rum. . . . A pistol or rifle barrel positioned inside the cavity of the mouth" (165). And like voices no one listens to, "high-altitude drones continue their nightly patrols out of earshot above" (165).

It is important to note the political implications suggested by Turner's role as both an *eyewitness* and one who *bears witness*. As a participant in the war—a soldier who was there and thus saw its destructive effects on the bodies of enemies, civilians, and his fellow soldiers, Turner must attend to some element of historical accuracy in his memoir. At the same time, he is also attendant to the importance of reflection and judgment in the aftermath of his experiences. I draw here on the distinction between two voices inherent in the narrative structure of witnessing: eye-witnessing, which entails the soldiers' descriptions of the battlefield, and bearing witness, which involves evaluations of their war experiences. Kelly Oliver calls attention to the differential power relations that are implicit in the notion of recognition: oppression creates the need in the oppressed "to be recognized by their oppressor, the very people most likely not to recognize them. The internalization of stereotypes of inferiority and superiority leave the oppressed with the sense that they are lacking something that only their superior dominators have or can give them. The very notion of recognition . . . is, then, a symptom of the pathology of oppression itself" (189). The struggle for recognition is thus implicated in the very structures that perpetuate oppression, for if "recognition is conceived of as being conferred on others by the dominant group, then it merely repeats the dynamic of hierarchies, privilege and domination" (78), replicating a master-slave, subject-other/object hierarchy. Oliver argues that "witnessing has both the juridical connotations of seeing with one's own eyes and . . . political or ethical connotations of testifying to that which cannot be seen (bearing witness). It is this double meaning that makes the concept of witnessing such a powerful alternative to recognition in reconceiving subjectivity and thereby ethical relations" (80). In his poem "Illumination Rounds," Turner describes a dream sequence that affirms the ethical role of the veteran-poet as witness: he is shoveling graves for the dead in his backyard, in a futile effort to honor them, "if only with a coffin." Turner calls for an interrelational ethic of recognition that demystifies and thus rehumanizes:

We should invite them into our home.
We should learn their names, their history.
We should know these people
we bury in the earth.

In an e-mail interview about this scene, Turner asserts the need to widen the circle of responsibility, especially as Iraqi dead rarely make news in the United States. He poses the question, "What does it say about a nation that can wage war and yet know very little about [the enemy]?" (Bishop 304). Although he claims that the poem avoids the rant, "the rant is woven into it." This is Turner's version of the "loudspeaker"—but his poetic voice is a whisper that resounds. It demands more of us as readers and as human beings. Perhaps Turner's way of remembering and recording war represents his attempt to escape the solipsistic constructions of personal trauma by seeking threads of connections, affiliative bonds across boundaries of difference, a kind of universality born of shared humanity. This is suggested in his memoir when, on his way back to war after a brief leave, he writes, "I realized then that I carried a desire within me . . . toward the infinite, something circular, something repetitive, a tether cinched fast to something deep in the well of memory" (126). While language delimits this possibility, his text strains against its own limits, breaching and traversing spaces in the distance between hearing and cognition, the "I" and the "not-I."

Literary critic Peter Brooks has argued that a text's meaning resides in the dialogical relationship between "tellers and listeners" (260). Readers are "solicited not only to understand the story, but to complete it" (236). Turner's tapestry of sound and silence invites readers to fill in missing pieces and encounter what Brooks calls the "'horror,' the taint of knowledge gained" (236). Ultimately Turner's technique invokes the reader's role as witness, for to remain detached or acquiescent or to refuse to see is to be complicit. He has said that he hopes that his own explicit complicity as the grave digger in his poem "Illumination Rounds"—and by extension, his role in the war itself—might expose the unspoken complicity "within us all. I'm talking about torture," he writes. "I'm talking about a country that must be responsible for what it has done. I'm talking about the country I love. America." While his figurative rants, persistently woven into the fabric of his poems and memoir, may often be drowned out by the language and machinery of war, Turner's aesthetic still summons us, a voice grown hoarse but not silenced, *bearing witness.*

Chapter 6

BEGINNINGS
Stories That Need Telling

The gunner spit the windblown sand out of his
mouth. "Now, tell me again why we are here?" "Politics,"
the driver broke in. . . . It's politics, that's all."
    "Tell that to the five poor lads who won't be
returning with us."

—James Lewandowski, *Road Hunter in the Lands between the Rivers*

Toward the end of his Iraq war memoir *Kaboom: Enduring the Suck in a Savage Little War*, Matt Gallagher describes a group of soldiers gathered to watch the 2008 presidential election returns. Gallagher explains that while "soldiers' politics varied almost as much as those of the greater populace," the outcome of the election would affect not only their own future but also the "future of the nation we all treasured" (229). The men, some Black, some White, some Brown, Gallagher tells us, listened to president-elect Barack Obama's speech that night with a shared understanding that something momentous had occurred, and regardless of party affiliation or personal differences, it captured what they were fighting for. In a rare moment for Gallagher, who maintains an ironic, often witty tone throughout his memoir, he is unable to come up with a joke that can "temper the politically correct banality of the situation." Instead, listening to the president-elect affirm the "enduring power of our ideals: democracy, liberty, opportunity, and unyielding hope," Gallagher admits that he "got goose bumps" (230).

My intent in noting this scene is neither to idealize these soldiers—to interpret this scene as representative of blissful political consensus or harmony—nor to read it as Gallagher's paean to warrior brotherhood, his version of a group hug. Gallagher knows that this is just a moment, one that does not reflect the broader political affiliations or variances of the soldiers he served with. Different needs, desires, and circumstances brought these men to the battlefield, and these were not erased or forgotten because they wore the same uniform. Gallagher, for one, had not joined "the military for glory or for country" (4). A product of "modern white-collar contentment," he was a young man who simply had "read too many damn books about soldiers" (4). Yet the man who "got goose bumps" listening to a president's election night speech was a far cry from the prewar millennial who "yawned along with most of my peers as the president asked for our continued participation" in the economy after 9/11 (3). As a college student enrolled in the ROTC program, he was more interested in waging "war on sobriety" than in the American tanks already "screaming north across the sands of Iraq" (3). "I was drunk when we invaded Iraq," he admits, "safe and secure and carefree in my frat castle" (3). But for Gallagher, as for many combat veterans, the experience of war had broken through the self-centered, "me-first" bubble of complacent youth. While Gallagher tries to maintain the cool indifference that had characterized his prewar identity as a citizen, he admits, "Voting from a combat zone had been one of the proudest moments of my life" (230). Gallagher had made an investment, and now had a personal stake in the war and, by extension, in his country's politics.

I have argued throughout this book that the experience of war elicits bonds and obligations that inform veterans' memoirs and also their politics. For some, duty to country postwar takes the form of civic engagement, public service, or activism. For others, writing extends their deployment into the realm of memory, where they seek to salvage bits of knowledge or understanding that may render their experiences meaningful, or at least useful. Many veterans find it difficult to become "civilianized," as Michael Anthony calls the process of transitioning from a war zone. Anthony believes that writing saved his life, brought him "out of his funk" (*Civilianized* 190). Addicted to Vicodin, enraged by "all the bullshit" he had heard since coming home, drinking and smoking heavily to get through each day, Anthony considers suicide, but for "the thought of leaving an unfinished book"—the one inside him (181). Writing his memoir "was the perfect distraction," he remarks, as "a man can't kill himself with an unfinished book" (181). Thus he sets out on a new mission: writing "a true war story" (190). As he explains it, "Sometimes a soldier returns home and all he can do is share his story in the hopes that somehow . . . it helps another soldier make sense of things. . . . Sometimes just sharing is enough to make a difference" (191–92). This inducement to speak one's truths is what drives memoir as a genre and what lends war stories their credibility and power, for better or for worse. But as my readings in this study demonstrate, "truth," "realism," "accuracy," and "credibility" are all relative, dubious terms in the realm of memory and storytelling.

Yet despite this, stories serve as a critical mechanism of political influence at various levels, articulating both cultural and individual psychological processes; they are integrated into our personal constructs, providing a system of orientation for action. The prominence and legitimacy of political attitudes depend on which stories are most widely circulated and promoted at any given time. In this book, I considered some of the ways that veterans' memoirs *talk back* and also *with* prevailing cultural narratives, sometimes affirming what we think we know about war, and other times disrupting or revising our views. But with the increasing politicization of the military—with politicians using service members to score political points—veterans' stories are also ripe for exploitation and appropriation. They can be used as "evidence" of whatever "truth" someone wants to believe or promote. We have seen this in stories circulated by political leaders, who, using veterans as props in staged performances, only deepen the divide between military and civilian populations. Some feed into dueling narratives about which political party "supports the troops"; some situate veterans as sole keepers of knowledge about war; some cast civilians, the media, or anyone who protests a war as ignorant or treacherous. Veteran-writer Phil Klay decries this "patriotic correctness" that shuts down civilian debates about foreign policy while ceding authority to veterans or military leaders: "If I have authority to speak about our military policy it's because I'm a citizen responsible for participating in self-governance, not because I belonged to a warrior caste" ("Warrior"). Klay recognizes that it "can be comforting to reverse the feelings of hopelessness and futility that come with fighting seemingly interminable, strategically dubious wars by enforcing a hierarchy of citizenship that puts the veteran . . . on top, and everyone else far, far below" ("Warrior"). In his view, "The pageantry of military worship sucks energy away from the obligations of citizenship." Like many of the veteran-writers examined in this study, Klay sees it as his responsibility to "assume that our military policy is of direct concern to me, personally" ("Warrior").

I suggested at the outset of this book that every story's ending marks a beginning—a new insight, judgment, or perception that follows in its wake. While I explored a range of veterans' perspectives, both through published memoirs and through a glimpse at the diverse issues and concerns that have mobilized them as citizens, I realize that, as in any single volume, much has been left out. Clearly, there are many more stories that need telling in our rapidly changing cultural and military landscape. In particular, three recent significant developments in the history of the US military are reshaping its cultural politics and generating new stories: the reversal of "Don't ask, don't tell," the admission of women in combat roles, and the integration of transgender service members. These changes—as monumental as the desegregation of the military was to a prior generation—will produce new challenges, trials, and triumphs, the stuff of war memoirs past and present. Like many minority service members before them, LGBTQ and women combat soldiers are fighting battles on two fronts—performing their duties under the watchful, often skeptical eye of superiors and peers while navigating the vicissitudes of politics that affect military policy. Many of these veterans will shoulder new obligations as citizens postservice, for they will have experienced firsthand the effects of politics on their personal lives.

A 2018 Palm Center study estimated that approximately 14,700 transgender troops currently serve across active-duty and reserve units. The Trump administration's ban on transgender people serving in the military temporarily set back years of efforts aimed at ending discriminatory policies against LGBTQ individuals; the ban sought to enforce "standards associated with . . . biological sex" and prohibit service members from seeking "transition to another gender." One of president Joe Biden's first acts as president was to rescind this ban, but it is difficult to gauge the ban's impact on would-be soldiers and on the morale of active-duty personnel. To date there are few published veterans' memoirs that can speak to the personal effects of government policies on the lives and careers of LGBTQ service members. For example, the University of Wisconsin Press has a special series devoted to gay and lesbian autobiographies, but only one of their published memoirs is by a veteran, Bronson Lemer's *The Last Deployment: How a Gay, Hammer-Swinging Twentysomething Survived a Year in Iraq* (2011). In my own search for LGBTQ military memoirs that could inform this study, I found that among the few published memoirs available, most did not coincide with my focus on "war stories." That is, they included reference to their military experiences, but this was incidental to the crux of their narratives. Monica Helms, who cofounded the Transgender American Veterans Association in 2003 and designed the "Transgender Pride Flag," served as a navy submariner in the 1970s, but her memoir, *More Than a Flag*, published in 2019, focuses on her experiences transitioning as a transgender female rather than on her military life. Pete Buttigieg's prominence as an openly gay political leader was certainly relevant to my book's general topic, but his memoir *Shortest Way Home: One Mayor's*

Challenge and a Model for America's Future (2020) is not a "war memoir" but an
account of his life growing up and his rise in politics.

LGBTQ veterans are an emergent and potentially vocal political force.
Those who are finally telling their stories are paving the way for others.
Vietnam War veteran Larry Sanders, who served in combat during the Tet
Offensive, only recently self-published his memoir *INCOMING! Memories of
a Combat Medic: Growing Up Poor, Getting Drafted to Vietnam, Coming Home and
Coming Out* (2019). Throughout his tour as a medic in Vietnam, he hid his
sexuality, leaving him alienated from many of the men he served with and
struggling with shame. Drafted into the war, Sanders could have answered
"yes" to the question on the registration form "Do you identify as a homosexual
or ever had sexual feelings for persons of the same sex?" But he feared the
repercussions of such an admission: would he be "singled out in this group
of unknown young men?" Would they call his parents and say, "Do you know
your son is a homosexual?" (54). While checking "yes" on the form would have
spared him a year in a combat zone, he chose to lie—even if it meant he might
die in Vietnam. Sanders understood that in his day, "coming out" made him
a potential target of harassment and even violence.

Transgender individuals today face similar threats, with trans women of
color being especially vulnerable. Human Rights Campaign, which tracks
these crimes, reported that by mid-2020, at least forty-four transgender
individuals had been murdered; the majority were Black and Latinx transgender women. This heightened threat, along with discrimination; bullying;
rejection by family, friends, and community; harassment by police; and
ill treatment in the health care system, all contribute to a high suicide
rate among transgender persons in the United States: 41 percent attempt
suicide at least once in their life (Clements-Nolle et al. 51). These stories
often go unreported. Active duty soldiers and veterans are not unaffected
by these crimes. For example, twenty-one-year-old army private Barry
Winchell was bludgeoned to death with a baseball bat by two fellow soldiers as he slept in his barracks at Fort Campbell for dating a transgender
woman. His death and the ensuing trials were seen as a clear indictment
of Congress' "Don't ask, don't tell" policy. Winchell's brutal beating death
led president Bill Clinton to concede that the measure he signed into law
in 1993 to protect lesbian and gay soldiers had been a failure. An investigation by Servicemembers Legal Defense Network found that Winchell
had been the target of constant antigay harassment in the months leading
up to his murder.

More recently, Kristen Beck's willingness to tell her story, *Warrior Princess: A U.S. Navy Seal's Journey to Coming out Transgender,* stemmed from her desire to "reach out to all of the younger generation" so they might be spared some of the emotional pain she experienced while struggling to hide her true self. As a Navy SEAL, Kristen (then identified by his biological gender as Chris) served multiple combat tours and earned both a Purple Heart and a Bronze Star. "I knew I was a girl in third grade," Kristen admits, yet as Chris she would marry twice and serve as a SEAL for twenty years, trying to "turn off my gender problem by being Superman" (144). In the latter role, she writes, "I was usually on my own, alone as a bearded local warlord doing my job" (144). Kristen points out the irony of this position: "It was weird that I could grow a beard and trick [the Taliban] into thinking I was one of them—and really *I'm an Amazon woman in disguise as a U.S. military guy in disguise as a Pashtun!*" (146). For Kristen, coming out as trans and writing a memoir was her form of political activism: she knew there were "many people out there with similar problems. They have no mentors and sometimes no hope" (139). Often ignored in debates about transgender service members is the unique contributions they can make: as a former Navy SEAL, Chris was often called on to speak at Pentagon events regarding cyber warfare; as Kristen, she notes, "I can probably think about irregular and unconventional warfare, innovation and many things much more creatively than any other SEAL team member can! I have a perspective and point of view that most military or government officials will never have" (162). Further, while politicians often cite "troop morale" as a reason to reject LGBTQ service members, Kristen shares many of the supportive letters she received from her fellow SEALS after coming out. This offers a more complex image of SEALS than the ones popularized in movies and recruitment posters and bodes well for a more inclusive future military.

The lifting of restrictions on women in combat will also inform the politics of memoir, as more female veterans feel empowered to tell their own stories. In 2012, two lawsuits contesting limits on women in combat were filed. One of the plaintiffs in the ACLU lawsuit was Mary Jennings Hegar, whose memoir I discussed in my introduction to this book. Writing a memoir was just the beginning of Hegar's postdeployment activism. She would continue to fight for women's right to compete for combat and special ops positions, both through the lawsuit and by authoring numerous informative essays and opinion pieces. While secretary of defense Ash Carter formally lifted the ban in 2015, and the first gender-integrated infantry basic training cycle began in 2017 (with eighteen female graduates in the inaugural class), women remain a significant minority of combat arms in military occupational specialties. Although female-authored war memoirs remain relatively limited, their perspectives will increasingly inform the political landscape of America's twenty-first-century wars. I hope my approach in this book invites future scholarship as more female combat vets "talk back" to the military establishment, politicians, and fellow soldiers. In 2020, there were about 231 female marines serving in combat arms quarters; female officers are best represented in artillery and combat engineer fields, enlisted women in infantry, assault amphibious vehicles, and artillery (Moore). The absurdity of not acknowledging women's combat roles dating back to at least the Civil War (when women such as Frances Clayton, Sarah Emma Edmonds, and Mollie Bean, disguised as men, fought for the Union and Confederate Armies) became especially obvious after 9/11, as women service members actively supported ground combat and special forces units through the Lioness program, female engagement teams, and cultural support teams. As Iraq War veteran-memoirist Kayla Williams argues, "To me it wasn't so much a real change, it was the policy catching up with reality. . . . It was driven by what has been happening already" (qtd. in Beynon). Williams also remains politically and civically engaged postservice; for example, she served as senior fellow and director of the Military, Veterans and Society Program at the Center for a New American Security, a national security think tank, and is currently serving in the Office of Public and Intergovernmental Affairs and the Department of Veterans Affairs.

Anuradha Bhagwati served in the marine corps "during a time when it was criminal to come out of the closet." As an officer, she knew marines who were hiding their sexuality but could "not talk about it with anyone in uniform." In *Unbecoming: A Memoir of Disobedience*, Bhagwati finally talks about it, offering rare insights gleaned at the intersection of race, gender, sexuality, and ethnic identity. As a vocal woman of color in "the fiercest old boys' club in America," the marine corps, this daughter of Indian immigrants faced challenges on various fronts. She describes herself as "Brown, female, and queer," as someone who is "fundamentally different in a way that made powerful people uncomfortable" (201). During her service, she endured racist discrimination and even sexual violence, but her military service also empowered her to speak: "The Marine Corps opened me to a world of people I'd never have otherwise known. . . . I was a better person for it, and prepared to be a better activist because of it" (201). Postservice, Bhagwati works to bring equality issues she cares about to a national platform: "opening combat assignments to women, ending sexual and domestic violence, improving women veterans health care"

(201). She cofounded the Service Women's Action Network (SWAN) to "provide a safe space for all women veterans and not to divide our community by party politics" (202). SWAN members are "outspoken and unapologetic" about issues that other veterans organizations have "tiptoed around," such as the "rights of queer Americans to serve, or the wide prevalence of sexual violence in uniform" (209). Bhagwati was also a lead plaintiff in the ACLU's lawsuit challenging the military's ban on women serving in combat. In 2009, SWAN members were invited to testify before the House Committee on Veterans Affairs. Bhagwati describes these veterans as "possibly the most diverse group of women the national security world had ever seen: Brown, Black, white, straight and queer, buzz cuts and ponytails" (203). As an ex-marine, she had earned credibility and "some cover" when telling the stories that needed telling—stories about sexual violence, discrimination, and using your voice to advocate for change.

Psychologist Edward Tick contends that in all traditional societies, returned warriors were seen as "keepers of dark wisdom for their cultures" (34). In contemporary America, warriors' accounts of their experiences are crucial guideposts in the disorienting political and social landscape that serves as backdrop to our postmodern wars. Unmoored and confused by the sundry scandals and misdeeds that have shaken the foundations of America's institutions, we are polarized and wary; the old myths of kinship or shared purpose seem either irrelevant or unrecognizable, the latter deployed by politicians bent on contracting rather than expanding our "borders of belonging."[1] Even the most fundamental processes of our democracy—a presidential election and subsequent transfer of power—has been called into question, with thousands of Americans denying the legitimacy of President Biden's win and violently storming the Capitol.

In these turbulent and disenchanted times, the longings that compel belief—in a god, nation, or myth—lead us to seek stories that can fill the void, that can revitalize and redeem. We seek heroes to restore order in a broken world, and war stories often provide those—for it is in personal encounters with death or overwhelming trials that the hero—or heroine—is born. This desire coincides with many service members' self-image: studies suggest that many see themselves as more moral than the civilian population they serve, a judgment that can inspire civic duty and engagement in the nation's political processes.[2] Conversely, it can also inspire an inflated sense of moral righteousness, deepening the military/civilian divide and threatening a long-standing pecking order: the subordinate role of the American military to its civilian leadership. How veterans navigate and respond to these cultural currents will be critical in shaping judgments about the sacrifices future soldiers are asked to make in our name. The best veteran-memoirists can challenge readers' own allegiances and preconceptions, fostering a more ambivalent, tentative, and open-ended view of our individual and collective selves. At their best, they tell stories that serve as antidotes against collective amnesia and are thus the nation's line of defense against the impulse to mythologize, glorify, or negate the realities of war. This is indeed a powerful political act. When the prospect of yet another war is again before us, self-proclaimed patriots, politicians, and opportunists will clamor to take center stage. Let us hope that more of our soldiers and veterans will be armed with their stories.

NOTES

INTRODUCTION: PLAUSIBLE DENIABILITY

1 Throughout this book, I use "soldier" as shorthand for members of the armed forces who have served in combat zones. I realize this ignores differences among branches of the military; for example, Navy SEALs are members of the navy and thus "sailors" and "marines" are not "soldiers."

2 Critics repeat this disclaimer. For example, in his review of contemporary war literature for the *New Yorker*, George Packer concludes, "In the literature by veterans, there are virtually no politics or polemics." In a scathing rebuke, veteran-author Roy Scranton refutes the assertion that these works are apolitical: "Packer makes the specious assumption that ignoring the causes, background, and motivating forces for a war represents an absence of politics, rather than seeing it for what it is, which is a kind of politics—namely, a politics of forgetting that actively elides the question of what US soldiers were fighting for and the bigger problem of who they were killing, in favor of the more narrow and manageable question of 'what it was like.'" See Scranton, "Trauma Hero."

3 See Kitromilides for an insightful analysis of this autobiographical practice, which gives memoir writers "a vantage point through which to pass judgment—through self-criticism—on the human condition" (6). This ability connects personal narrative to political agency and constitutes "two sides of the same relation, that between the self and society." I borrow the term to suggest this link between personal disclosure and public critique while signaling the memoirist's ability to simultaneously reveal, disclose, confess—and disavow, devise, deflect, disguise.

4 Although fiction dominated the literary marketplace during the twentieth century, memoir has become the genre of choice for America's twenty-first-century readership. Total sales in memoirs increased more than 400 percent between 2004 and 2008 (Yagoda 7). In 2014, memoirs saw another 12 percent spike in sales, outselling even popular non-fiction genres such as self-help, religious, and health/fitness books. See Jim Milliot, "The Hottest (and Coldest) Book Categories of 2014," *Publisher's Weekly*, Jan. 23, 2015, https://www.publishersweekly.com/pw/by-topic/industry-news/bookselling/article/65387-the-hot-and-cold-categories-of-2014.html. Thomas Larson notes that 80 percent of all *New York Times'* nonfiction paperback bestsellers in 2007 (twelve of fifteen) were either memoirs or autobiographies ("Age of Memoirs"). The genre's resurgence coincides with the popularity of other subjective platforms for self-exposure, including reality TV, blogging, vlogs, online chat rooms, and YouTube videos.

5 In her analysis of the military memoir's global production, Kleinreesink calls attention to another factor in the genre's extended reach: "The military memoir that was carefully selected for its literary qualities by a renowned publisher is nowadays supplemented by self-published books that are affordable to almost any soldier wishing to publish his or her stories in book form" (3). The military memoir has gone mainstream, or, as she puts it, "war stories are hot" (4).

6 Social media and other online forums provide veterans with more access to information and venues through which to express themselves politically and mobilize others. Daily or weekly posts retain the details of experiences and can later form the basis of published memoirs. As Morton Ender points out, "American soldiers in Iraq and Afghanistan . . . participated in the most communicated war in U.S. history" (104).

7 This is surprising given the increasing scholarly interest in veterans and military studies generally. Some examples of academic book series devoted to publishing in this area include Warfare and Culture (NYU Press), Cultural History of Modern War (Manchester Press), American Military Experience (U of Missouri P), Military Studies (Yale UP), Military

History (Oxford UP), War Culture (Rutgers UP), and the University of Massachusetts Press book series Veterans.

8   Along with fiction, film, and blogs, I exclude accounts written by journalists, regardless of how "embedded" with soldiers. Soldier memoirists are not journalists, and in fact, some consider their accounts necessary correctives to misconceptions and false narratives perpetuated by the media.

9   Castner notes that the Iraq War generated far more works of fiction than the Afghanistan War: "If World War II is the Good War, Korea the Forgotten War, Vietnam the Bad War, and Iraq the New Bad War, then Afghanistan, it would seem, is the Lonely War. Or maybe the Ignored War. It is, at least, the Undescribed War."

10 Indian Country is also the title of a 1987 novel by Philip Caputo, one of the veteran-writers featured in this study.

11 As Shaheen shows, American pop culture reduces the diverse Islamic world to images of "bearded mullahs, shady sheikhs, terrorist bombers, and harem belly dancers." Such images, Shaheen argues, have dangerous and cumulative effects.

12 For studies of this corporeal-political aspect of soldiers' war experiences see Achter; Bulmer and David; Dyvik and Greenwood.

13 Academic research shows that the risk of sexual harassment and assault against women is higher in the military than in civil society, partly because it is a male-dominated culture: "The victimization rates of military servicewomen are around 28 percent in their lifetime versus 13 percent in comparable civilian studies" (Lee 46–47).

14 Feminist scholarship has exposed "biology as ideology" in medical and cultural constructions of women's bodies. For a historical overview of hysteria ("the wandering uterus" theory) see Bronfen.

15 Penguin published a young adult version of Hegar's memoir Fly Like a Girl: One Woman's Dramatic Fight in Afghanistan and on the Home Front in 2020.

16 Andrea Huyssen argues that modernism associated "inferior literature" with the "subjective, emotional, passive, and female." In this binary, "genuine, authentic literature" was defined as "objective, ironic . . . in control" and male (46).

17 Mid-twentieth-century American confessional poets such as Silvia Plath, W. D. Snodgrass, Anne Sexton, and Robert Lowell used their craft to share dark secrets and painful memories, their poems expressing fierce emotions.

18 A Dartmouth University study found that even when a politician's lies are exposed, Americans' judgments remain aligned with their political affiliations. Fact-checking President Trump's statements, the study concluded, exposed his lies but did not measurably alter support for him. See Nyhan et al.

    Similarly, an earlier study found that countering lies with facts did not change people's minds if the corrective information ran counter to their predispositions; in several cases "corrections actually strengthened misperceptions among the most strongly committed subjects." See Nyhan and Reifler. Also see Farsetta.

19 In his short story "The Things They Carried," O'Brien conveys both the literal and symbolic weight soldiers bear: in addition to heavy equipment and supplies, the soldiers "carried all the emotional baggage of men who might die. Grief, terror, love, longing—these were intangibles, but the intangibles had their own mass and specific gravity, they had tangible weight" (21).

20 For an overview of this research, see P. Miller. For analyses of the relationship between emotion and politics, see Goodwin et al. 1–24; Gould 155–75. For a collection of essays highlighting the multiple ways emotions shape politics, see Thompson and Hoggett. For examples of how emotions mobilize constituencies and fuel beliefs, see G. Marcus and Demertzis.

21 In his overview of Vietnam War literature, veteran-scholar Tobey Herzog contends that despite their differences, veterans' stories all share an emotional effect: "a fundamental

sympathy for combat soldiers as fallible human beings living within the crucible of war" (*Vietnam War Stories* 3).

22 Luttrell's book is the only cowritten account included in this study, and unlike the other memoirs, aesthetic value was not a primary concern. This memoir was a bestseller turned into a feature film with a mass marketing and international distribution network reaching millions of viewers. It reinforced certain political assumptions and attitudes enough to get Luttrell invited to speak at the 2016 GOP convention nominating Donald Trump. Since my interest is in the politics of military memoirs, I thought it important to include Luttrell's influential voice.

I avoided coauthored texts because there is no way to determine the extent of a cowriter's influence on the veteran-writer's politics or narrative choices. Unfortunately, this limited my inclusion of several female veterans' memoirs, such as Kayla Williams' *Love My Rifle More Than You: Young and Female in the U.S. Army* (2006); Jessica Lynch's *I Am a Soldier, Too* (2003); Theresa Larson's *Warrior: A Memoir* (2016); and Janis Karpinski's *One Woman's Army: The Commanding General of Abu Ghraib Tells Her Story* (2005), all coauthored by men.

23 Consider the crucial role that America's slave narratives played in evoking sympathy and supporting the abolitionist cause. These first-person accounts were often edited to elicit the most powerful emotional responses and support an antislavery position, compromising veracity to achieve political aims. Similarly, "Indian captivity narratives," such as Mary Rowlandson's or Hannah Dustin's, were heavily edited then circulated by religious leaders to affirm the demonic nature of "savages" and model Christian notions of redemptive suffering.

24 Coincidentally, "post-truth" was selected as Oxford Dictionary's 2016 word of the year.

25 In General Petraeus's words, "Soldiers and Marines are expected to be nation builders as well as warriors" (XLVI). US Army/Marine Corps, Counterinsurgency Field Manual, 3–24, 2007, https://www.fas.org/irp/doddir/army/fm3-24.pdf.

CHAPTER 1: PROTESTORS, PATRIOTS, AND CULTURE WARRIORS

1 See Dickson and Allen for an in-depth study of these events.

2 For a history of Vietnam Veterans Against the War (VVAW), see Hunt.

3 Popular memory of the Vietnam War privileges the notion that there was always broad opposition to the war, but this is shaped more by postwar myths than facts. John Zaller's content analysis of news magazine coverage of the Vietnam War, for example, found much stronger prowar than antiwar attitudes from 1964 to 1968. It was not until 1968 that the antiwar message gained steam.

4 Psychiatrist Robert Jay Lifton describes the effects of the "John Wayne Syndrome" on Vietnam-era GIs.

5 See Vera and Gordon.

6 President Johnson implied as much, claiming in his 1965 speech at Johns Hopkins University, "To withdraw from one battlefield only means to prepare for the next. We must stay in Southeast Asia—as we did in Europe—in the words of the Bible: 'Hitherto shalt thou come, but no further.'"

7 Many Americans may now view this line of thinking as uninformed, naive, and simplistic—and it was. For one thing, it assumed that all "dominoes"—all Asian countries in the region—were the same, all subject to similar external pressures and effects. Yet a revised version of this metaphor frames the US approach to the "war on terror." As Robert Scheer observes, "The 'war on terror' is turning out to be nothing more than a recycled formulation of the dangerously dumb 'domino theory.'"

8 For an analysis of the ways that images of crazed Vietnam veterans served to delegitimize their complaints, see Risquez.

9   Along with VVAW's founder, Jan Barry, Ehrhart published the first collection of Vietnam War poems, *Demilitarized Zones: Veterans After Vietnam* (1976).

10 An archival copy of this memo is available online. Helene Cooper, "African-Americans Are Highly Visible in the Military, but Almost Invisible at the Top," *New York Times*, May 25, 2020, https://www.nytimes.com/2020/05/25/us/politics/military-minorities-leadership.html.

11 Sociologist Aldon Morris also points to the politicizing effects of service, showing the links between veterans and the civil rights movement: "Black soldiers returning from the wars began urging their relatives and friends not to accept domination. In many instances black soldiers disobeyed the policy of bus segregation and refused to give up their seats long before Rosa Parks" (80).

12 Farrell features Adams along with other Black servicewomen who played a role in integrating the armed forces in her book *Standing Up against Hate*.

13 Christine Knauer points to the founding of the Committee Against Jim Crow in the Military Service and Training by Black vets as a pivotal step.

14 For an in-depth history of Red Summer and of Black veterans' responses, see Krugler.

15 In a letter to President Truman, Black World War II veteran Isaac Woodard, Jr., describes being dragged off a bus and beaten until blinded by police in Batesburg, South Carolina, just hours after being honorably discharged from the US Army.

16 The political attitudes of draft-age men strongly correlated with their vulnerability to the draft. Levels of support for the war as well as partisan attitudes were most affected among men with lower lottery numbers; the resulting shift in their political views endured decades after the war's end, even if they had never been called to serve. See Erikson and Stoker, 2011.

17 This sense of identification with black- or brown-skinned "enemies" still poses a moral dilemma for many soldiers of color. Iraq War veteran-poet Christopher Paul Wolfe admits, "As a black veteran, I find it hard to reconcile my pride in my service with a sense of complicity in upholding my country's legacy of white supremacy while deployed. I still remember the black and brown faces of Iraqis that I helped to round up, zip-tie and detain using tactics similar to stop and frisk, the use of which some courts in America have found to be unconstitutional. These experiences created a moral chasm with which I continue to grapple."

18 Digital copies of *A'Bout Face*, the newsletter distributed by members of Unsatisfied Black Soldiers and published by GI Press, are available online.

19 President Truman's 1948 Executive Order 9981 called for "equality of treatment and opportunity for all persons in the Armed Services," but lingering racial prejudices delayed its full implementation until 1954. According to testimonials by African American Korean War vets, the US military was still segregated throughout the Korean War.

20 For an overview of how changing definitions of ethnicity and shifting bureaucratic racial classifications complicated efforts to tabulate exact numbers of Latino service members, see Eschbach and Rivas-Rodriguez.

21 Between 250,000 and 500,000 Mexican Americans served in World War II, and twelve would earn the Congressional Medal of Honor. Part of this history is recounted in Dave Gutierrez's *Patriots from the Barrio*. Gutierrez grew up hearing stories about a cousin, Ramon, who had served honorably in World War II, earning a Silver Star and three Purple Hearts. Ramon was a source of pride in Gutierrez's family, inspiring the author to document the exploits of this all-Hispanic unit.

22 While I focus most attention on Mexican Americans due to their unique historical relation to the US-Mexico border, Puerto Ricans are US citizens who also face discrimination and exclusion, despite their contributions. For example, the Sixty-Fifth Infantry Regiment from Puerto Rico (the "Borinqueneers") served in both World War II and Korea. Congress finally recognized the unit with a Congressional Gold Medal in 2016.

23 The Treaty of Guadalupe-Hidalgo (February 2, 1848) ceded Mexican lands but guaranteed its Mexican residents full rights of US citizenship. Despite this legal status, Mexican American citizens are still often perceived as foreigners.

24 The organization included a clause in their founding documents denying membership to communists. See a detailed history of this group's founding and political tactics in Allsup.

25 Saul Schwartz argues that military service did not improve Mexican American veterans' economic standing, at least in the short run: in 1979 Chicano Vietnam War vets were earning less than their White counterparts and even less than nonveterans (568).

26 In one horrifying scene recounted by veteran-author Roy Benavidez, the seriously wounded, semiconscious Mexican American soldier realizes that he has been mistaken for a North Vietnamese casualty:

> "Just put him over here with the other three on the ground," said the voice belonging to the arms holding my legs.
>   The other three? "Oh, Christ, No!" my mind cried as realization dawned. Half of the blood I had just dumped over Southeast Asia belonged to the Yaqui Indian nation. More than once my native American features had been mistaken for Oriental. Now, by God, they were going to get me dumped with the enemy dead. (4)

27 Leal and Teigen argue that military service is especially useful in overcoming educational and resource disadvantages that can translate into less civic knowledge and involvement.

28 Many Black and Latino veterans still face economic hardship after serving their country. According to the National Coalition for Homeless Veterans, about 45 percent of all homeless veterans are African American or Latino, despite accounting for only 10.4 percent and 3.4 percent of the US veteran population, respectively. National Coalition for Homeless Veterans. "FAQ about Homeless Veterans." NCHV Report, 2019. http://nchv.org/index.php/news/media/backgroundandstatistics/.

29 Damigo is not the only connection between veterans and the Charlottesville rally. Representatives of the neo-Nazi group Vanguard America, founded by veteran Dillon Hopper, were also present (Linehan). James Alex Fields, Jr., the driver of the car that struck and killed Heyer, spent several months in the army but was released from active duty in 2015 for failing to meet training standards. He was never assigned to a unit outside of basic training and was "infatuated with the Nazis, with Adolf Hitler" long before his brief stint in the military (Keller).

30 The president's response also led to internal disagreements among VA officials torn between expressing condemnation and not criticizing the White House. See Rein.

31 About Face: Veterans Against the War, "TROOPS: Stand Down for Black Lives," May 29, 2020, https://medium.com/@VetsAboutFace/minnesota-national-guard-stand-down-for-black-lives-7596e1f0493b.

32 Kaleth O. Wright, Twitter, June 1, 2020, https://twitter.com/cmsaf18/status/1267572335239929862.

33 Paralyzed Veterans of America, the Wounded Warrior Project, and the National Association for Black Veterans, as well as other smaller, newer veterans organizations, spoke out in support of the protests.

34 Another group, Veterans Challenge Islamophobia (a campaign affiliated with Veterans for Peace), aims to "defend the values of religious freedom, equality, and individual rights." Their call to veterans can be found on the Veterans for Peace website: https://www.veteransforpeace.org/take-action/veterans-challenge-islamophobia.

35 New social movements tend to arise out of cultural and symbolic issues linked to identity and associated with "beliefs, symbols, values, and meanings related to sentiments

of belonging to a differentiated social group; with the members' image of themselves; and with new, socially constructed attributions about the meaning of everyday life" (Laraña et al. 7).

36 Among Latino eligible voters in 2016, about half (53 percent) of immigrants voted, compared with 46 percent of the US born. This pattern has persisted since 2000. See Budiman et al.

37 "Strategic Partnership Plan for 2002–2007," US Army Recruiting Command, Fort Knox, USAREC, 2001.

38 According to a Pew Research study, Latinos comprised 12 percent of all active-duty personnel in 2015, three times more than in 1980. Kim Parker, Anthony Cilluffo, and Renee Stepler, "6 Facts about the U.S. Military and Its Changing Demographics," April 13, 2017, https://www.pewresearch.org/fact-tank/2017/04/13/6-facts-about-the-u-s-military-and-its-changing-demographics/.

39 Referring to the caravan of Central Americans walking toward the US border seeking asylum, President Trump warned that soldiers could fire at anyone throwing rocks: "They want to throw rocks at our military, our military fights back. I say, consider it a rifle." The expectation that US Latino military personnel should fire on asylum seekers at our southern border poses a similar dilemma as the one Black service members faced after MLK's assassination or at the 1968 Democratic National Convention: some African American military personnel refused to turn their weapons on Black protestors, and some even refused to participate in riot control training. See Westheider, especially 74–75.

40 Leo Shane III, "Signs of White Supremacy, Extremism up Again in Poll of Active-Duty Troops," Feb. 6, 2020, https://www.militarytimes.com/news/pentagon-congress/2020/02/06/signs-of-white-supremacy-extremism-up-again-in-poll-of-active-duty-troops/.

41 In 2008 there were 149 militia groups in the Unite States, but by 2012, that number had risen to nearly six hundred. By 2019, the SPC's Annual report noted 940 active hate groups across the United States. According to an Anti-Defamation League report, 2018 was the "fourth-deadliest year on record for domestic extremist-related killings since 1970" in the United States.

42 Now known as About Face, IVAW's mission and resources are available on their archived website, https://www.ivaw.org. The quotations that follow are from the website.

43 Members of Vets for Freedom self-identified as "promission" rather than "prowar."

44 Brookings Institution, "Vital Statistics on Congress," Jan. 9, 2017, https://www.brookings.edu/wp-content/uploads/2017/01/vitalstats_ch1_full.pdf.

45 "The Problem: Public Trust in Congress Is Far Too Low," Without Honor, https://withhonor.org/purpose/.

46 "About," VoteVets.org, www.votevets.org/about.

47 For example, Black Veterans for Social Justice, originally founded in 1979, defines their mission as addressing the needs of a new generation of veterans, such as medical care, unemployment, legal advocacy, and reentry into civilian culture.

CHAPTER 2: THE FATE WORSE THAN DEATH

1 The importance of the other's gaze (real or imagined) in regulating behavior is implicit in Emmanuel Kant's political philosophy: he defines morality as "being fit to be seen" (Arendt, *Lectures* 49).

2 See, for example, seminal research by F. L. Ford, *Political Murder: From Tyrannicide to Terrorism*, Harvard UP, 1985; M. R. Gottfredson and T. Hirschi, *A General Theory of Crime*, Stanford UP, 1990; A. N. Groth, *Men Who Rape: The Psychology of the Offender*, Plenum, 1979; and Elaine Scarry, *The Body in Pain: The Making and Unmaking of the World*, Oxford UP, 1985.

3   In response, political scientists are increasingly incorporating insights from social and cognitive psychology into their analyses, offering empirical demonstrations of how systematic and predictable psychological processes affect political processes.

4   Also see Jean Bethke Elshtain, *Women and War*, U of Chicago P, 1995; Cynthia Enloe, *Bananas, Beaches and Bases: Making Feminist Sense of International Politics*, U of California P, 1990; Jan Jindy Pettman, *Worlding Women: A Feminist International Politics*, Routledge, 1996; Jill Steans, *Gender and International Relations: An Introduction*, Rutgers UP, 1998; Christine Sylvester, *Feminist Theory and International Relations in a Postmodern Era*, Cambridge UP, 1994.

5   Performing "manhood" is not about biology—it is about ideology. Thus, women in male-dominated societies (such as the military) are also expected to enact toughness, strength, and invulnerability if they are to achieve status or rank. Veteran memoirist Theresa Larson was warned by her colleagues that marines think of women in three ways: as "bitches, sluts, or pushovers" (*Warrior* 77). To a female soldier, being labeled a "pushover" may well be the worst insult of the three.

6   David Gelernter, "Another Vietnam?" *Weekly Standard*, Oct. 11, 2004, https://www.weeklystandard.com/Content/Public/Articles/000/000/004/713dawas.asp.

7   "Bush in Vietnam Warning over Iraq," *BBC News*, Aug. 22, 2007, https://news.bbc.co.uk/2/hi/middle_east/6958824.stm.

8   A University of Chicago National Opinion Research Center survey of thirty-four countries, released June 27, 2006, found that the United States ranked first in terms of overall national pride. See Marni Goldberg, "National Pride Survey," *Chicago Tribune News*, June 28, 2006.

9   Campaign address in Jersey City, May 25, 1912.

10 NBC *Today* show, February 19, 1998. In a 2014 piece in *Foreign Policy*, Micah Zenko points to the range of politicians—from Barack Obama and Hillary Clinton to Chris Christie, Jeb Bush, Marco Rubio, and Michelle Bachman—who have repeated this assertion, remarking, "This bipartisan group may not agree on much, but they are all proudly 'Indispensables.'" "The Myth of the Indispensables," *Foreign Policy*, Nov. 6, 2014.

11 The traditional peasant dress of the area worn by the Viet Cong became the guerrillas' trademark among US soldiers. It also served as object of disdain or ridicule. In 1971, reporter Tom Braden wrote, "It was Robert Kennedy who encouraged McNamara to leave behind him an objective record of the decision-making process which led his country from a game of bluff against a lot of little men in black pajamas to a devastating and terrible war." See Tom Braden, "An Odd Fact about the Vietnam 'Record,'" *Washington Post*, June 22, 1971, A19.

12 J. William Fulbright, "Vietnam: The Crucial Issue," *Progressive*, Feb. 1970, https://progressive.org/Archive/1970/feb/thecrucialissue.

13 "Nixon at the Brink over Viet Nam," *Time*, May 22, 1972, https://www.time.com/time/magazine/article/0,9171,879069,00.html.

14 "President George Bush Announcing War against Iraq," January 16, 1991, The History Place: Great Speeches Collection, https://www.historyplace.com/speeches/bush-war.htm.

15 Caputo served as a marine corps lieutenant with the 3rd Marine Regiment in the area around Danang from March 1965 through July 1966. At the age of twenty-three, Caputo faced court-martial charges that extended his one-year tour of duty.

16 Fighting our longest war yet, the conflicts in Iraq and Afghanistan, many of today's soldiers take a more ironic view of these inducements. For example, Colby Buzzell seems to wink at his reader when he claims that he did not join the army because he had been traumatized over 9/11 but because "it was not just another job, it was an adventure" (20).

17 Yet many critics might disagree. In his *Los Angeles Times* review, John Gregory Dunne calls *Rumor of War* "a dangerous and even subversive book." Terry Anderson of the *Denver*

Post calls it "an eloquent statement against war" (qtd. in https://www.philipcaputo.com /books-all/a-rumor-of-war/).

18   Mark A. Heberle, *A Trauma Artist: Tim O'Brien and the Fiction of Vietnam* U of Iowa P, 2001, 49.

19   Bertram Wyatt-Brown's notable scholarship contributed rare insights into the role of shame and honor, particularly the ideal of "Southern honor," in the American Civil War. Wyatt-Brown argues that in the antebellum South, honor reinforced hierarchical relationships, and the greatest dread imagined by adherents of honor was "fear of public humiliation" (viii). The ethics of honor were reflected in a social order that valued rituals of violence and shaming: charivari, dueling, and lynch law. Interestingly, while we tend to associate dueling with an atavistic premodern sensibility, military theorist Carl von Clausewitz (1780–1831) viewed all wars as "extended duels" to be regulated in accordance by the same honor codes (15).

20   For a history of the GI movement, see Carver et al.

CHAPTER 3: TRUSTING THE MESSENGER

1   For other critics defending the importance of credibility in international affairs see Harvey and Mitten; Weisger and Yarhi-Milo; Press; and McMahon.

2   See, for example, Judge Advocate General major Todd E. Pierce's analysis, "The Long Reach of Vietnam War Deceptions."

3   Peter Proctor argues that the Johnson administration's deceptions altered the opposition's strategy from "attacking military containment as a justification to attacking the administration's credibility" (ix). This strategy had important consequences, as the question of credibility "expanded to virtually every facet of the administration's prosecution of the war" (222).

4   Dempsey also points out that academics paid scant attention to the military during the 1970s—and military sociology consistently ranked last among sociological specialties after 1965 (3). This proved shortsighted, as the 1980s saw a "Vietnam-book-boom" (Wood 2).

5   Kleinreesink found that veteran authors with a traditional publisher are four times more likely to add truth claims to their books than self-publishers (213).

6   Transcript available at https://www.humbleisd.net/cms/lib/TX01001414/Centricity /Domain/5915/A%20Conversation%20with%20Tim.docx.

7   This postmodern emphasis on the contingency of truth is often erroneously reduced to the notion that truth does not exist, particularly in reading Michel Foucault's work as mere relativism. But as Sergei Prozorov argues, to recognize the contingency of all truth claims is not to reduce all truth to mere opinions, "which can be neither true nor false and whose contestation is therefore meaningless" (27). Foucault's understanding of truth discourses captures what I see as the political dilemma at the heart of O'Brien's narrative ethos: unlike authoritarian regimes, which assert their power on irrefutable truth claims (tradition, religion, ideology), democracies can exist only where truth is "the object of ceaseless contestation and problematization" and its deployment in politics can "produce unintended and unpredictable effects" (Prozorov 19). This "radical contingency" is how democracy is sustained but also how it is continuously threatened.

8   Lieutenant colonel John Paul Vann called leaders' deceptions during the Vietnam War "bright shining lies." See Sheehan 385.

9   The Gulf of Tonkin incidents in August 1964—when US destroyers presumably suffered two "unprovoked" attacks from North Vietnamese warships—allowed President Johnson to obtain approval from Congress for the use of force against Vietnam. Even at the time, evidence of a second attack was questionable; investigations and interviews with commanders and crew later showed that the second attack did not happen. See Prados.

10 Nye points to a recent international Pew poll showing that only 29 percent of people surveyed in thirty-three countries trust President Trump, ranking him as low as president Xi Jinping of China ("No, President Trump"). Similarly, a Gallup poll of people in 134 countries found that only 30 percent held a favorable view of the United States under Mr. Trump's leadership. This low level of credibility translates into a decline in America's soft power, Nye argues, evidenced in the British index, the Soft Power 30, showing America slipping from first place in 2016 to fifth place in 2019.

11 An American Press Institute survey found that only 6 percent of Americans express confidence in the news media. Tom Basile, "American Cynicism: In Nobody We Trust," Apr. 27, 2016, https://www.forbes.com/sites/thomasbasile/2016/04/27/in-nobody-we -trust-american-cynicism-in-the-digital-age/#7d81e37b7575.

A Pew Research study in 2015 shows rising distrust of our government. Pew Research Center, "Beyond Distrust: How Americans View Their Government," Nov. 23, 2015, https://www.people-press.org/2015/11/23/beyond-distrust-how-americans-view -their-government/.

A Gallup survey showed that eight in ten Americans trust the government only some of the time to never. See Basile's "American Cynicism."

12 This trend also shapes the ways that young people regard and access news sources. Marchi found that teens not only accessed news information through social media, blogs, and other online sites but also that their attitudes and behavior were more influenced by platforms that rely on opinion than on objective news.

13 See Arceneaux et al.; DeMarzo et al.

Countering lies with facts does not necessarily change people's minds if the corrective information runs counter to their predispositions; one study showed that "corrections actually strengthened misperceptions among the most strongly committed subjects" (Nyhan et al.).

Consider the "birther" movement, whose proponents (including Donald Trump) believed that Barack Obama was not born in the United States and thus was ineligible for the presidency. After President Obama released the legally binding "certification of live birth" in 2008, "birthers" countered that it was not an official document. His lawyers then presented certified copies of the long-form certificate in 2011, but "birthers" still discounted the evidence as forged, doctored, or invalid. A CNN/Opinion Research poll conducted after the certificate's release found that more than four in ten Republicans still believed Obama "probably" or "definitely" was not born in America.

14 Deception is not limited to obscure fringe groups or politicians: as reported by the *Columbia Journalism Review,* both CNN and *The New York Times* were used by the US military as unwitting coconspirators in spreading false information justifying the invasion of Iraq (Love). War correspondents also have a credibility problem. NBC News anchor Brian Williams reported that he was almost shot down in a helicopter when covering the invasion of Iraq in 2003, a lie that got him suspended. Bill O'Reilly would then blast Williams on his Fox News Show, blaming the "liberal media's" culture of deception and "distortions." O'Reilly himself would be called out in a *Mother Jones* article for his own deceptions and exaggerations, particularly that he has reported in many active war zones, a claim he used to buttress his credibility: "I've been there. That's really what separates me from most of these other bloviators." See David Corn and Daniel Schulman, "Bill O'Reilly Has His Own Brian Williams Problem" *Mother Jones,* Feb. 19, 2015, https://www .motherjones.com/politics/2015/02/bill-oreilly-brian-williams-falklands-war.

15 Oxford's Project on Computational Propaganda, which studies fake news and propaganda, found that military personnel are often targeted by political operatives both in the United States and abroad. During the 2016 presidential race, Russian trolls and others aligned with the Kremlin used Twitter and Facebook feeds to incorporate fake news into legitimate content consumed by veterans and active-duty personnel. These groups read

and shared articles mostly favoring Donald Trump and maligning Hillary Clinton, as well as pieces on right-wing political thought and politics. See Gallacher et al.

16   The erosion of Americans' trust in the media is evident in the following timeline: In the 1950s, the news media was one of America's most trusted institutions, with a 1956 American National Election Study finding that 66 percent of Americans thought newspapers were fair, a view that extended across party lines. In 1973, when the General Social Survey began regularly measuring confidence in various national institutions, only 15 percent of respondents had "hardly any" confidence in the press. By 2008, the GSS showed that the portion of Americans expressing "hardly any" confidence in the press had risen to 45 percent. By 2004, a *Chronicle of Higher Education* poll found that only 10 percent of Americans had "a great deal" of confidence in the national news media (Ladd).

17   For a study of the media's staged spectacles throughout the wars, see Kellner, "Media Propaganda."

18   A Pew Research survey found that trust in the military was at 78 percent, the highest rating among sixteen institutions tested, including the church or organized religion (48 percent), big business (19 percent), and Congress (12 percent) (Pew Research Center). A Gallup poll from June 4, 2006, reported confidence rates for the military, the Supreme Court, the presidency, and Congress at 73 percent, 40 percent, 33 percent, and 19 percent, respectively. The study found that nine in ten Americans (91 percent) say they are proud of soldiers serving in Iraq and Afghanistan.

19   Adrian R. Lewis, *The American Culture of War*, 2nd edition, Routledge, 2007, 4.

20   Similarly, antiwar veterans' groups that challenge dominant discourses receive less mainstream coverage, though they can sometimes influence cultural attitudes (Woehrle).

21   Brian Van Reet, "A Problematic Genre, the 'Kill Memoir,'" At War: Notes from the Front Lines, *New York Times*, July 16, 2013, https://atwar.blogs.nytimes.com/2013/07/16/a-problematic-genre-the-war-on-terror-kill-memoir/.

22   Examining the reception of Vietnam War fiction and film, for example, Jim Neilson argues that readers and viewers tended to judge these as "good or bad" based on their politics. The film *Platoon*, because it focuses on atrocities by Americans, was "generally shunned by people with a rightist bent," while Left-leaning viewers tended to appreciate the subversive politics of a novel like *Meditations in Green* and to write off *Fields of Fire* "as militarist and jingoist" (10).

23   Vice president Mike Pence speaking to troops on January 21, 2018, "Remarks by Vice President Mike Pence to Troops." *White House*, US Government, https://www.whitehouse.gov/briefings-statements/remarks-vice-president-mike-pence-troops/.

24   Incidentally, Kyle admitted he was hesitant to see the movie *Zero Dark Thirty* "because he'd heard that it was a lot of propaganda for the Obama administration" (Mooney, "Legend of Chris Kyle").

25   Separating fact from fiction in a *National Review* article, A. J. Delgado writes, "Out of the staggering $3 million that *American Sniper* collected in royalties for Kyle, only $52,000 actually went to the families of fallen servicemen. (Rather than 100 percent of the proceeds, as the public was led to believe, try 2 percent!)."

26   See "Gary Brozek," Conservative Book Club, https://www.conservativebookclub.com/profile/gary-brozek.

27   The plaque Irving received from his men for "exemplary service and heroism," however, is inscribed with a quote attributed not to a "real" soldier but to John J. Rambo—a fictional movie character played by an actor, Sylvester Stallone, who never served in the military. The plaque appears in *The Reaper*'s photo section.

28   In his 2013 article "The Legend of Chris Kyle," Mooney's physical description of Kyle combines all-American folksiness (blue jeans and baseball cap) with mythic "White Knight" stature: "6-foot-2, 230 pounds, and the muscles in his neck and shoulders and forearms made him seem even bigger, like a scruffy-bearded giant. When he greeted

me with a direct look in the eye and a firm handshake, his huge bear paw enveloped my hand. That day he had on boots, jeans, a black t-shirt, and a baseball cap." Mooney admiringly recounts how when two men attempted to steal Kyle's truck soon after his return home, Kyle had shot and killed them both. "Kyle wasn't unnerved or bothered," he writes. "Quite the opposite. He'd been feeling depressed since he left the service, struggling to adjust to civilian life. This was an exciting reminder of the action he missed."

29   Partisanship also shapes publishing decisions. Ian Kleinert, literary manager at Objective Entertainment, a multimedia Literary Management and Production Company, explains that in our polarized culture, "most veterans books currently are published by publishers that are known for more conservative content, because conservative media is the platform that seems most fitting for the story to be marketed on, and consumers of conservative media are identified as the target audience" (qtd. in Bussel). Kyle himself was a guest on various conservative talk shows, radio programs, and Fox News.

30   McIntosh notes that the film turns the story of real-life soldier Marc Lee into a cautionary tale against those who would be critical of the war. When Lee is killed in the film, Kyle's character remarks that Lee "paid the price" for not believing in the war. But, as McIntosh points out, the "real" Marc Lee died after stepping into the line of fire twice to save another soldier's life.

31   For critiques of the film from an opposing political perspective, see Soberon; C. Burke; Weigel.

32   The film version also performed well at the box office, raking in almost $38.5 million during its weekend premiere—the second-best opening of all time for the month of January, after *Cloverfield* ($40.1 million). See "Box Office: *Lone Survivor* No. 1 Friday," *Hollywood Reporter*, Nov. 11, 2014, https://www.hollywoodreporter.com/news/box-office -lone-survivor-no-670047.

33   G. W. Bush, "Address to a Joint Session of Congress and the American People," Sept. 20, 2001, https://voicesofdemocracy.umd.edu/bush-an-address-to-a-joint-session-of-congress -speech-text/.

34   Torgovnick shows how this argument circulates in discussions of the Iraq War: "When a politician or pundit uses the almost obligatory code words 'honoring the troops,' the phrase segues into the assertion that to make their deaths and sacrifices count we cannot 'cut and run'" (1839).

35   Retired air force lieutenant colonel William Astore warns that America's militarization is becoming a national religion: "We believe with missionary zeal in our military and seek to establish our 'faith' everywhere." Such pieties may also be influencing soldiers' self-image. A 2003 survey of military personnel found that "two-thirds said they think military members have higher moral standards than the nation they serve" (Trowbridge).

36   "Full Text: Giuliani Addresses United Nations." Oct. 1, 2001, transcript, *New York Times. com*, https://www.nytimes.com/2001/10/01/nyregion/full-text-giuliani-addresses-unit -ed-nations.html.

37   John Crawford, "The Last True Story I'll Ever Tell: An Accidental Soldier's Account of the War in Iraq," Goodreads, https://www.goodreads.com/book/show/894391.

38   Mark Benjamin, "Sick, Wounded U.S. Troops Held in Squalor," *UPI*, Oct. 17, 2003, https://www.upi.com/Odd_News/2003/10/17/Sick-wounded-US-troops-held-in-squalor /1418106641934 0/.

CHAPTER 4: "SOLDIERS OF CONVICTION"

1   See, for example, Robert Parry, "How Reagan Promoted Genocide," *Consortium News*, Feb. 21, 2013; Susanne Jonas, "Dangerous Liaisons: The U. S. in Guatemala." *Foreign Policy*, no. 103 (Summer 1996): 144–60.

2   Hector "Hex" Lopez founded the Unified US Deported Veterans Center across the border in Tijuana, Mexico. There are now several deported veterans rights organizations

in the Tijuana area, including the Deported Veterans Support House, also founded by a deported vet.

3   Valadez was brought to the United States from Mexico when he was twelve years old, enlisted in the Navy in 2000, and served honorably until 2004, including six months overseas during Operation Enduring Freedom. He was deported in 2009 on a marijuana charge. See Vakili et al.

4   In 2017, 14 percent of military personnel identified as Hispanic or Latino; at 21 percent the marine corps has the highest percentage of Latinos. See US Department of Defense (DoD).

5   Statutory citizenship was granted by Congress and thus not guaranteed or protected by the Constitution. Also noteworthy in this context is the US occupation of the Philippines after the Spanish American War, which led to yet another war as Filipino insurgents battled for control of the nation from what many saw as a new colonial ruler. The Filipino-American War (previously called the "Philippine Insurrection") led to the deaths of between 250,000 and 600,000 Filipinos. Incidentally, the top two countries of origin for foreign-born military personnel during the Iraq and Afghanistan Wars were the Philippines and Mexico. Filipinos comprised the largest percentage of the foreign born in the armed forces in February 2008 (22.8 percent). See Batalova.

6   As Franqui-Rivera points out, "All the prejudices used to explain segregation and the inferiority of African Americans were applied to the new territories" (10).

7   Marine lance corporal José Gutiérrez (killed March 21, 2003, and reported as the first US Army soldier killed) was a native of Guatemala; marine lance corporal Jesús Suarez del Solar (March 27, 2003) and corporal Jose Angel Garibay (March 28, 2003) were from Mexico; army private first class Diego Rincon (March 29, 2003) was from Colombia (Amaya 3–4).

8   Richard Gonzales, "America No Longer a 'Nation of Immigrants,' USCIS Says," NPR. org, Feb. 22, 2018, https://www.npr.org/sections/thetwo-way/2018/02/22/588097749 /america-no-longer-a-nation-of-immigrants-uscis-says.

9   The Obama administration increased scrutiny of MAVNI enlistees in 2016; further restrictions were added by the Trump administration in 2017 that effectively froze the program.

10 Iraq War veteran Tammy Duckworth proposed a bill in 2019 to require the secretary of homeland security to parole certain relatives of current and former members of the armed forces. "S. 2797—116th Congress: Military Family Parole in Place Act," https:// www.GovTrack.us (2019), Oct. 22, 2020, https://www.govtrack.us/congress/bills/116 /s2797.

11 The label "illegal immigrant" did not exist until the early twentieth century, when Congress began categorizing immigrants who were ineligible to enter the United States. See Ngai.

12 See Dovidio et al.

13 "The Immigrant Army: Immigrant Service Members in World War I," US Citizenship and Immigration Services (2017), last updated Mar, 5, 2020, https://www.uscis.gov/history -and-genealogy/our-history/immigrant-army-immigrant-service-members-world-war-i.

14 For a study of the racial politics of publishing, see Young, *Black Writers, White Publishers*. For analysis of the rise and role of self-publishing, see Dilevko and Dali. Self-published authors include Margaret Atwood, Willa Cather, W. E. B. Du Bois, Mark Twain, Walt Whitman, and Virginia Woolf.

15 Email correspondence with the author, Nov. 14, 2020.

16 The lack of diversity in the publishing industry workforce may also be relevant. The Diversity Baseline Survey found that in 2020, only 6 percent of the US publishing workforce identified as Latinx/Latino/Chicano, and 5 percent as Black/African American/ Afro Caribbean. The vast majority (78 percent) were cisgender women. See Maher.

17 The Reagan administration characterized Salvadorans as "economic migrants" and denied that the Salvadoran government had violated human rights. As a result, approval rates

for Salvadoran asylum cases were under 3 percent in 1984, compared to 60 percent for Iranians and 40 percent for Afghans fleeing the Soviet invasion. See Gzesh.

18   According to historian Joaquin M. Chavez, the FMLN "self-identified as Marxist-Leninists, but the insurgent leadership also included social democrats, radicalized Catholics, and eclectic intellectuals and activists" (1786).

19   The United States funded the expansion of El Salvador's armed forces during the civil war. Made up of about seven thousand in 1979, by 1983 "the army comprised 22,400 men, backed by the 11,000 men" of the militarized public security forces and about fifty thousand paramilitaries (McClintock 337).

20   Robert Mencia, "Author Interview," e-mail received by Myra Mendible Nov. 14, 2020.

21   Mencia e-mail.

22   Prior to the repeal of "Don't ask, don't tell" in 2011, male-on-male-rape victims could even be discharged for having engaged in homosexual conduct.

23   "Military Sexual Trauma in Recent Veterans," U.S Department of Veterans Affairs, accessed October 4, 2021, https://www.publichealth.va.gov/epidemiology/studies/new-generation/military-sexual-trauma-infographic.asp

24   See Dutcher; Brody. While the Reagan Doctrine's stated aim was to support "democratic reform," Grandin (2006) argues that Reagan's conservative advisors saw Central America as the place where the United States could "salvage" its foreign presence after Vietnam.

25   The Florida National Guard, incidentally, is not only the oldest militia in the continental United States (the first Florida militiamen were activated in 1565), it has served under four different flags. The Florida militia system began under Spanish—not English—law, and Spanish was the official language of the military in Florida for 250 years. For an intriguing and comprehensive history of the Florida National Guard, see Hawk.

26   Under army policy a soldier who is not a US citizen cannot reenlist if he or she will have in excess of eight years of federal military service at the expiration of the period for which they seek to reenlist. See Stahl.

27   "Moral injury" was first conceptualized by Vietnam War veteran and philosopher Camillo "Mac" Bica, and clinical psychiatrist Jonathan Shay. Iraq combat veteran and writer Tom Voss puts it this way: "The cool indifference of a commanding officer as he stands over a dying civilian; the capture and torture of men who are known to be innocent; the bomb that was planted purposefully to destroy human life: all can call into question our deeply held cultural belief that all people, deep down, are innately good" (xiv).

28   For a DoD report assessing the health effects of such practices, see "Military Deployment Periodic Occupational and Environmental Monitoring Summary (POEMS): Camp Bucca and Umm Qasr, Iraq, 2003–2011," 2013, https://usaphc.amedd.army.mil/PHC%20Resource%20Library/U_IRQ_Bucca%20and%20Umm%20Qasar%20POEMS%202003–2011.pdf.

29   Fraser acknowledges that subaltern counterpublics do not always promote inclusive, egalitarian forms of democratic engagement; in widening the field of discursive contestation, they can also serve antidemocratic and antiegalitarian movements.

CHAPTER 5: SILENCE AMID THE DIN OF WAR

1   Sight metaphors usually align the act of seeing with revelation and truth, but hearing also can connote revelation and cognition. Tibor Fabiny, for example, argues that unlike ancient religions, which used the eye as the source of revelation, the Bible repeatedly uses the ear as "the proper organ of religious understanding" and "faithful apprehension of God's word." An inability or unwillingness to hear, on the other hand, signals hard-heartedness or stubbornness caused by sin (190). See Fabiny. For a linguistic analysis of the metaphorical link between hearing and vision, see Dancygier and Sweetser 24–32.

2   The term was coined in 1917 by the Russian formalist Victor Shklovsky. As Uri Margolin explains, "Defamiliarization of that which is or has become familiar or taken for granted,

hence automatically perceived" can slow down "the process of reading and comprehending" (815).

3   J. Martin Daughtry's excellent study is one example of studies focusing on what Daughtry calls the "belliphonic landscape" of war. An ethnomusicology and sound studies professor at New York University, Daughtry explores sonic violence in the context of the Iraq War.

4   This is a line from Turner's poem "The Hurt Locker."

5   Under the Trump administration, US use of drone strikes in Yemen, Pakistan, Afghanistan, and Somalia increased. The Bureau of Investigative Journalism is an independent, not-for-profit organization that monitors US drone strikes and their civilian casualties using both military and local source data. See "Drone Warfare," Human Rights, Bureau of Investigative Journalism, https://www.thebureauinvestigates.com/projects/drone-war.

6   See, for example, the *New York Times* investigative report on the Iraqi family mistakenly killed by a US drone strike. In this case, they were sleeping in their homes when the strike occurred, killing all the members of the family except the father—who awoke next to his dead wife with the taste of blood in his mouth. Azmat Khan and Anand Gopal, "The Uncounted," *New York Times*, Nov. 16, 2017, https://www.nytimes.com/interactive/2017/11/16/magazine/uncounted-civilian-casualties-iraq-airstrikes.html.

7   Alexander Gardner used this image to describe the scene following the Battle of Gettysburg (July 1–July 3, 1863): "Through the shadowy vapors, it was, indeed, a 'harvest of death' that was presented; hundreds and thousands of torn Union and rebel soldiers—although many of the former were already interred—strewed the now quiet fighting ground, soaked by the rain, which for two days had drenched the country with its fitful showers." See *Gardner's Photographic Sketch Book of the Civil War*, Dover Press, 1959.

8   The warrior Arjuna speaks these words to Krishna before battle in *The Bhagavad-Gita*.

9   In his novel *The Yellow Birds*, Iraq War veteran-author Kevin Powers alludes to this loss of personal identity, as the main character, Bartle, realizes that in Iraq he is only "a uniform in a sea of numbers" (12). He mourns this loss of individuality: "Nothing made us special. Not living. Not dying" (14).

10 Schweighauser uses this term to describe sounds that seem alien or nonsensical for their nonconformity or difference, for example, immigrant accents, working-class crowds, "exotic" music, and cheap entertainment.

11 Ironically, Iraq's government, whether through coercion or choice, continues the legacy of silence: a section of Abu Ghraib prison has been refurbished and turned into a museum documenting Saddam Hussein's abuses, but there is no mention of the abuses committed there by American troops and contractors.

CHAPTER 6: BEGINNINGS

1   I borrow the term "borders of belonging" from Barbara Young Welke, whose scholarship examines the symbolic lines of exclusion and inclusion that have defined US citizenship. Welke calls attention to "fundamentally abled, racialized, and gendered borders of belonging," suggesting how changing meanings ascribed to aspects of identity, such as race, ethnic or national origin, or religion, designate who belongs in the nation and who does not (7).

2   A 2003 *Military Times* poll suggested that military personnel tend to see themselves as morally superior to civilians. Two-thirds said they think military members have higher moral standards than the nation they serve, and over 60 percent labeled the country's moral standards only fair or poor. In follow-up interviews, many said that the choice to serve demonstrates moral quality above most civilians. See Trowbridge.

WORKS CITED

Abrams, Elliott, and Andrew Bacevich. "A Symposium on Citizenship and Military Service." *Parameters*, vol. 31, Summer 2001, pp. 18–22.

Achter, Paul. "Unruly Bodies: The Rhetorical Domestication of Twenty-First-Century Veterans of War." *Quarterly Journal of Speech*, vol. 96, no. 1, 2010, pp. 46–68.

Addison, Joseph. "Number Fourteen." *The Freeholder: Or, Political Essays by the Right Honourable Joseph Addison. London: Printed for Jacob and Richard Tonson, 1758.* Elibron Classics, 2005.

Ahmed, Sara. "Affective Economies." *Social Text*, vol. 79, no. 22, 2004, pp. 117–139.

———. *The Cultural Politics of Emotion.* Routledge, 2004.

Allsup, Carl. *The American G.I. Forum: Origins and Evolution.* U of Texas P, 1982.

Altman, Neil. "Humiliation, Retaliation, and Violence." *Tikkun*, vol. 19, no. 1, 2004, pp. 16–59.

Amaya, Hector. "Dying American or the Violence of Citizenship: Latinos in Iraq." *Latino Studies*, vol. 5, no. 1, 2007, pp. 3–24.

Anthony, Michael. *Civilianized: A Young Veteran's Memoir.* Zest, 2016.

———. *Mass Casualties: A Young Medic's True Story of Death, Deception, and Dishonor in Iraq.* Adams Media, 2009.

Arceneaux, Kevin, et al. "Polarized Political Communication, Oppositional Media Hostility and Selective Exposure." *Journal of Politics*, vol. 74, no. 1, 2012, pp. 174–186.

Arendt, Hannah. *Lectures on Kant's Political Philosophy.* U of Chicago P, 1992.

———. "Lying in Politics." *Crises of the Republic.* Harcourt Brace, 1972.

Ashplant, Timothy G., et al., editors. *Commemorating War: The Politics of Memory.* Transaction, 2009.

Astore, William. "Militarization Has Become Our National Religion." *Nation*, Aug. 13, 2019, https://www.thenation.com/article/archive/militarization-national-religion/.

Attali, Jacques. *Noise: The Political Economy of Music.* U of Minnesota P, 2006.

Auvil, Shannon. "In Defense of Birthright Citizenship." *DePaul Journal for Social Justice*, vol. 10, no. 1, 2017, https://via.library.depaul.edu/jsj/vol10/iss1/3/.

Bacevitch, Andrew. J. *The New American Militarism: How Americans Are Seduced by War.* Oxford UP, 2005.

Baines, Gary. "SADF Soldiers' Silences: Institutional, Consensual and Strategic." *Acta Academica*, vol. 47, no. 1, 2015, pp. 78–97.

Bajak, Aleszu. "Philip Caputo: What I've Learned." Esquire.com, May 23, 2015, https://www.esquire.com/news-politics/interviews/a35119/philip-caputo-wil-interview/.

Barreto, Matt A., and David L. Leal. "Latinos, Military Service, and Support for Bush and Kerry in 2004." *American Politics Research*, vol. 35, no. 2, Mar. 2007, pp. 224–51.

Barry, Jan, and W. D. Ehrhart, editors. *Demilitarized Zones: Veterans after Vietnam.* East River Anthology, 1976.

Barthes, Roland. *The Responsibility of Forms.* Translated by Richard Howard, Hill and Wang, 1984.

Batalova, Jeanne. "Immigrants in the U.S. Armed Forces in 2008." Migration Policy Institute, May 15, 2008, https://www.migrationpolicy.org/article/immigrants-us-armed-forces-2008#13.

Bates, Milton J. *The Wars We Took to Vietnam: Cultural Conflict and Storytelling.* U of California P, 1996.

Batson, C. Daniel. *Altruism in Humans.* Oxford UP, 2011.

Baumeister, Roy F., Laura Smart, and Joseph Boden. "Relation of Threatened Egotism to Violence and Aggression: The Dark Side of High Self-Esteem." *Psychological Review,* vol. 103, no. 1, 1996, pp. 5–33.

Beard, David. "A Broader Understanding of the Ethics of Listening: Philosophy, Cultural Studies, Media Studies and the Ethical Listening Subject." *International Journal of Listening,* vol. 23, 2009, pp. 7–20.

Beck, Kristin, and Anne Speckhard. *Warrior Princess: A U.S. Navy Seal's Journey to Coming out Transgender.* Advances, 2013.

Beckett, Samuel. *The Unnamable.* Grove Press, 1970.

Belew, Kathleen. *Bring the War Home: The White Power Movement and Paramilitary America.* Harvard UP, 2018.

Benavidez, Roy. *Medal of Honor: A Vietnam Warrior's Story.* Brassey's, 1995.

Benjamin, Walter. "The Storyteller: Reflections on the Work of Nicolai Leskov." *Illuminations: Essays and Reflections.* Translated by Harry Zohn, Schocken, 1969.

Bennett, Jill. *Empathic Vision: Affect, Trauma, and Contemporary Art.* Stanford UP, 2005.

Bergengruen, Vera. "The US Army Promised Immigrants a Fast Track for Citizenship. That Fast Track Is Gone." Buzzfeed News, Mar. 5, 2018, https://www.buzzfeednews.com/article/verabergengruen/more-bad-news-for-immigrantmilitary-recruits-who-were.

Berland, Jodi. "Contradicting Media: Toward a Political Phenomenology of Listening." *The Sound Studies Reader,* edited by Jonathan Sterne, Routledge, 2012.

Berman, Larry. *No Peace, No Honor.* Free Press, 2001.

Berry, Wendell. "How to Be a Poet." *Given: Poems.* Counterpoint, 2006.

———. *What Are People For? Essays by Wendell Berry.* Counterpoint, 2010.

Bersani, Leo. "Realism and the Fear of Desire." *A Future for Astyanax: Character and Desire in Literature.* Longman, 1992.

Bertrand, Natasha. "Here's What We Know about the 'Pro-White' Organizer of 'Unite the Right,' Who Was Chased Out of His Own Press Conference." *Business Insider,* Aug. 14, 2017, https://www.businessinsider.com/who-is-jason-kessler-unite-the-right-charlottesville-2017–18.

Beynon, Steve. "The Rise of Female Commanders in Combat Arms." Military.com, Aug. 17, 2020.

Bhagwati, Anuradha. *Unbecoming: A Memoir of Disobedience.* Simon & Schuster, 2019.

Bica, Camillo. "A Therapeutic Application of Philosophy." *International Journal of Applied Philosophy,* vol. 13, no. 1, Spring 1999, pp. 81–92.

Bieger, Laura. "Living in Translated Worlds—A Pragmatist Approach to Transnationalism." *Review of International American Studies,* vol. 2, no. 3, 2007, pp. 16–20.

Birkerts, Sven. *The Art of Time in Memoir: Then, Again.* Graywolf Press, 2007

Bishop, James Gleason. "'We Should Know These People We Bury in the Earth': Brian Turner's Radical Message." *War, Literature, and the Arts: An International Journal of the Humanities,* vol. 22, no. 1, 2010, pp. 299–306.

Black, Helen K. "Three Generations, Three Wars: African American Veterans." *Gerontologist,* vol. 56, no. 1, 2016, pp. 33–41, https://doi.org/10.1093/geront/gnv122.

Bleakney, Julia. *Revisiting Vietnam: Memoirs, Memorials, Museums.* Routledge, 2014.

Blight, James G., and Janet M. Lang. "Prologue." *The Fog of War: Lessons from the Life of Robert McNamara.* Rowman and Littlefield, 2005.

Boghani, Priyanka, Marcia Robiou, and Catherine Trautwein. "Three Murder Suspects Linked to Atomwaffen: Where Their Cases Stand." PBS Frontline, June 18, 2019. https://www.pbs.org/wgbh/frontline/article/three-murder-suspects-linked-to-atomwaffen-where-their-cases-stand/.

Bolzenius, Sandra M. *Glory in Their Spirit: How Four Black Women Took on the Army during World War II.* U of Illinois P, 2018.

Bonds, Eric. "Strategic Role Taking and Political Struggle: Bearing Witness to the Iraq War." *Symbolic Interaction*, vol. 32, no. 1, 2009, pp. 81–92.

Boswell, Thomas D., and James R. Curtis. *The Cuban-American Experience: Culture, Images, and Perspectives*. Rowman and Allanheld, 1984.

Brands, Hal, et al. "Credibility Matters: Strengthening American Deterrence in an Age of Geopolitical Turmoil." Center for Strategic and Budgetary Assessments (CSBA), May 8, 2018. https://www.csbaonline.org.

Brissenden, Robert F. *Virtue in Distress: Studies in the Novel of Sentiment from Richardson to Sade*. Macmillan, 1974.

Brody, Reed. "Contra Terror in Nicaragua, Report of a Fact-Finding Mission: September 1984 January 1985." South End Press Collective, 1985.

Bronfen, Elisabeth. *The Knotted Subject: Hysteria and Its Discontents*. Princeton UP, 1998.

Brook, Tom Vanden. "Black Troops as Much as Twice as Likely to Be Punished by Commanders, Courts." *USA Today*, June 7, 2017.

Brooks, Jennifer E. *Defining the Peace: World War II Veterans, Race, and the Remaking of Southern Political Tradition*. U of North Carolina P, 2004.

Brooks, Peter. *Reading for the Plot: Design and Intention in Narrative*. Oxford UP, 1984.

Brown, Bert. "Face Saving and Face Restoration in Negotiation." *Negotiations: Social Psychological Perspectives*, edited by D. Druckman, Sage, 1977.

Brown, Megan. *American Autobiography after 9/11*. U of Wisconsin P, 2017.

Browne, Ryan, et al. "There Are as Many National Guard Members Activated in the US as There Are Active Duty Troops in Iraq, Syria and Afghanistan." CNN, June 1, 2020.

Buchanan, David A. *Going Scapegoat: Post-9/11 War Literature, Language, and Culture*. McFarland, 2012.

Budiman, Abby, et al. "Naturalized Citizens Make Up Record One-in-Ten U.S. Eligible Voters in 2020." Pew Research Center, Hispanic Trends, Feb. 26, 2020, https://www.pewresearch.org/hispanic/2020/02/26/naturalized-citizens make-up-record-one-in-ten-u-s-eligible-voters-in-2020/.

Bulmer, Sarah, and M. Eichler. "Unmaking Militarized Masculinity: Veterans and the Project of Military-to-Civilian Transition." *Critical Military Studies*, vol. 3, no. 2, 2017, pp. 161–81.

Bulmer, Sarah, and Jackson David. "'You Do Not Live in My Skin': Embodiment, Voice, and the Veteran." *Critical Military Studies*, vol. 2, no. 1–2, 2016, pp. 25–40.

Bumiller, Elisabeth. "Trying to Bypass the Good-News Filter." *New York Times*, Oct. 20, 2003, Section A, p. 12.

———. "A Well-Written War, Told in the First Person." *New York Times*, Feb. 7, 2010, https://archive.nytimes.com/www.nytimes.com/2010/02/08/us/08military.html.

Burke, Cathy. "*American Sniper* Triggers New War: Conservatives vs. Liberals." *Newsmax*, Jan. 19, 2015.

Burke, Kenneth. *A Grammar of Motives*, 3rd ed., U of California P, 1969.

Busch, Frederick. "Deaths." *Writers on Writing: The Art of the Short Story*, edited by Maurice A. Lee. Praeger, 2015.

Bush, George H. W. "Remarks to the American Legislative Exchange Council." Mar. 1, 1991, *Public Papers of the Presidents of the United States, 1991*, book I, *January 1 to June 30, 1991*. Government Printing Office, 1992.

Bussel, Rachel Kramer. "Why War Books by Veterans Will Always Be Popular." Forbes. com, Nov. 12, 2018.

Butler, Judith. *Gender Trouble: Feminism and the Subversion of Identity*. Routledge, 1999.

Buttigieg, Pete. *Shortest Way Home: One Mayor's Challenge and a Model for America's Future*. Norton, 2019.

Buzzell, Colby. *My War: Killing Time in Iraq*. Berkley Caliber, 2007.

Cameron, David R. "Toward a Theory of Political Mobilization." *Journal of Politics*, vol. 36, no. 1, 1974, pp. 138–71.

Capps, Walter H. "Postscript." *Vietnam: A Reader*, edited by Walter Capps, Routledge, 1991.

——. *The Unfinished War: Vietnam and the American Conscience*, 2nd ed., Beacon, 1990.

Caputo, Philip. "Goodnight, Saigon." Invited lecture at the United States Air Force Academy, April 27, 2000. Reprinted in *War Literature and the Arts*, vol. 12, no. 1, Spring/Summer 2000, pp. 19–27.

——. *A Rumor of War*. Henry Holt, 1996.

Careja, R., and P. Emmenegger. "Making Democratic Citizens: The Effects of Migration Experience on Political Attitudes in Central and Eastern Europe." *Comparative Political Studies*, vol. 45, no. 7, 2012, pp. 875–902.

Carlsen, Erika. "Rape and War in the Democratic Republic of the Congo." *Peace Review*, vol. 21, no. 4, 2009, pp. 474–83.

Carpentier, Nico. *Culture, Trauma, and Conflict: Cultural Studies Perspectives on War*. 2nd ed., Cambridge Scholars, 2015.

Carr, Michael. "Chinese 'Face' in Japanese and English." *Review of Liberal Arts*, vol. 85, 1993, pp. 69–101.

Caruth, Cathy. *Unclaimed Experience: Trauma, Narrative, and History*. Johns Hopkins UP, 1996.

Carver, Ron, et al., editors. *Waging Peace in Vietnam: U.S. Soldiers and Veterans Who Opposed the War*. NYU P, 2019.

Castner, Brian. "Afghanistan: A Stage without a Play." *Los Angeles Review of Books*, Oct. 2, 2014.

Cetinic, Marija. "Sympathetic Conditions: Toward a New Ontology of Trauma." *Discourse: Journal for Theoretical Studies in Media & Culture*, vol. 32, no. 3, 2010, pp. 285–301.

Chambers, John W., II. "War: American Way of War." *Oxford Companion to American Military History*, edited by John Whiteclay Chambers II, Oxford UP, 1999.

Chapman, Raymond. *The Treatment of Sounds in Language and Literature*. Blackwell, 1984.

Chatterjee, Partha. *The Politics of the Governed: Reflections on Popular Politics in Most of the World*. Columbia UP, 2006.

Chavez, Joaquin M. "How Did the Civil War in El Salvador End?" *American Historical Review*, vol. 120, no. 5, Dec. 2015, pp. 1784–97, doi.org/10.1093/ahr/120.5.1784.

Chavez, Leo R. *The Latino Threat: Constructing Immigrants, Citizens, and the Nation*. Stanford UP, 2008.

Clements-Nolle, Kristen, et al. "Attempted Suicide among Transgender Persons: The Influence of Gender-Based Discrimination and Victimization." *Journal of Homosexuality*, vol. 51, no. 3, 2006, pp. 53–69.

Cliff, Michelle. "Notes on Speechlessness." *Mouths of Rain: An Anthology of Black Lesbian Thought*, edited by Briona Simone Jones. New Press, 2021.

Copp, Tara. "Immigrant Soldiers Now Denied US Citizenship at Higher Rate Than Civilians." *McClatchy News*, May 15, 2019, https://www.mcclatchydc.com/latestnews /article230269884.html.

——. "More Veterans' Requests for Help on Immigration Are Rejected Now, Data Shows." *Military Times*, July 5, 2018, https://www.militarytimes.com/news/2018/07/05 /more-veteran-requests-for-help-on-immigration-are-rejected-now-data-shows/.

Cortright, David. "Conscience and War." Review essay, *Peace and Change*, vol. 35, no. 3, July 2010, pp. 502–11.

——. "I Never Expected to Protest the Vietnam War while on Active Duty." At War Series, *New York Times Magazine*, Nov. 8, 2019.

Couser, G. Thomas. *Memoir: An Introduction*. Oxford UP, 2012.

Crawford, John. *The Last True Story I'll Ever Tell: An Accidental Soldier's Account of the War in Iraq*. Penguin, 2005.

Crump, James. "Marine Veteran Stands outside Utah Capitol in Support of Black Lives Matter for So Long His Shoes Reportedly Started to Melt." *Independent*, June 10, 2020.

Cusick, Suzanne G. "'You Are in a Place That Is out of the World': Music in the Detention Camps of the Global War on Terror." *Journal of the Society for American Music*, vol. 2, no. 1, 2008, pp. 1–26.

Dancygier, Barbara, and Eve Sweetser. *Figurative Language*. Cambridge UP, 2014.

Dansby, Mickey R., et al., editors. *Managing Diversity in the Military*. Transaction, 2001.

Darwall, Stephen. *The Second-Person Standpoint: Morality, Respect, and Accountability*. Harvard UP, 2005.

Daughtry, J. Martin. *Listening to War: Sound, Music, Trauma, and Survival in Wartime Iraq*. Oxford UP, 2015.

Davies, Wallace. E. "The Problem of Race Segregation in the Grand Army of the Republic." *Journal of Southern History*, vol. 13, no. 3, 1947, pp. 354–72.

Decker, Stephanie, and John Paul. "The Real Terrorist Was Me: An Analysis of Narratives Told by Iraq Veterans Against the War in an Effort to Rehumanize Iraqi Civilians and Soldiers." *Societies Without Borders*, vol. 8, no. 3, 2013, pp. 317–43.

Delgado, A. J. "Justice for Jesse: Ventura Was Right in His Lawsuit." *National Review.com*, July 30, 2014.

DeMarzo, Peter M., et al. "Persuasion Bias, Social Influence, and Unidimensional Opinions." *Quarterly Journal of Economics*, vol. 118, no. 3, 2003, pp. 909–68.

Demertzis, Nicolas, ed. *Emotions in Politics: The Affect Dimension in Political Tension*. Palgrave, 2013.

Dempsey, Jack K. *Our Army: Soldiers, Politics, and American Civil-Military Relations*. Princeton UP, 2010.

Denton-Borhaug, Kelly. "Beyond Iraq and Afghanistan: Religion and Politics in United States War-Culture." *Dialog: A Journal of Theology*, vol. 51, no. 2, 2012, pp. 125–34.

———. *US War-Culture, Sacrifice and Salvation*. Taylor & Francis, 2014.

Dickson, Keith D. "War in (Another) New Context: Postmodernism." *Journal of Conflict Studies*, vol. 24, no. 2, 2004.

Dickson, Paul, and Thomas Allen. *The Bonus Army: An American Epic*. Walker, 2004.

Dilevko, Juris, and Keren Dali. "The Self-Publishing Phenomenon and Libraries." *Library & Information Science Research*, vol. 28, no. 2, Summer 2006, pp. 208–34.

Dimock, Wai-Chee. Introduction. *American Literature in the World: An Anthology from Anne Bradstreet to Octavia Butler*. Columbia UP, 2017.

Dovere, Edward-Isaac. "We Have a Commander in Chief We Fundamentally Can't Trust." *Politico*, June 26, 2018. www.politico.com/magazine/story/2018/06/26/seth-moulton-interview-podcast-2020-campaign-218895.

Dovidio, John F., et al. "Understanding Bias toward Latinos: Discrimination, Dimensions of Difference, and Experience of Exclusion." *Journal of Social Issues*, vol. 66, no. 1, 2010, pp. 59–78.

Doyle, Don H. *The Cause of All Nations: An International History of the Civil War*. Basic, 2015.

Dreisbach, Tom, and Meg Anderson. "Nearly 1 In 5 Defendants in Capitol Riot Cases Served in the Military." NPR, "All Things Considered," Jan. 21, 2021.

Druckman, Daniel, editor. *Negotiations: Social-Psychological Perspectives*. Sage, 1977.

Dutcher, Mary. *Nicaragua, the Human Tragedy of the War, April–June, 1986: An Investigative Report*. Washington Office on Latin America, 1986.

Dyvik, Synne L., and Lauren Greenwood, editors. *Embodying Militarism: Exploring the Spaces and Bodies In-Between*. Routledge, 2018.

Earley, Charity Adams. *One Woman's Army: A Black Officer Remembers the WAC*. Texas A&M UP, 1996.

Ellis, Mark. *Race, War, and Surveillance: African Americans and the United States Government during World War I*. Indiana UP, 2001.

Ellis, Kate, and Stephen Smith. "Soldiers for Peace." American Public Radio Reports, Nov. 7, 2019, https://features.apmreports.org/soldiers-for-peace/.

Ellul, Jacques. *The New Demons*. Seabury, 1975.

Emerson, Ralph Waldo. "Ralph Waldo Emerson," edited by Richard Poirier, Oxford UP, 1990.

Ender, Morton G. *American Soldiers in Iraq: McSoldiers or Innovative Professionals?* Routledge, 2013.

Ender, Morten G., et al. "Intersecting Identities: Race, Military Affiliation, and Youth Attitudes toward War." *War & Society*, vol. 34, no. 3, 2015, pp. 230–46.

Engelhardt, Tom. *The End of Victory Culture: Cold War America and the Disillusioning of a Generation.* Basic Books, 1995.

Enloe, Cynthia. *Ethnic Soldiers: State Security in Divided Societies.* U of Georgia P, 1980.

Erikson, Kai. *Everything in Its Path.* Simon & Schuster, 1976.

Erikson, Robert S., and Laura Stoker. "Caught in the Draft: The Effects of Vietnam Draft Lottery Status on Political Attitudes." *American Political Science Review*, vol. 105, no. 2, 2011, pp. 221–37.

Erll, Astrid, and Ansgar Nünning, editors. *A Companion to Cultural Memory Studies.* Walter de Gruyter, 2010.

Eschbach, Karl, and Maggie Rivas-Rodriguez. "Navigating Bureaucratic Imprecision in the Search for an Accurate Count of Latino/a Military Service in World War II." *Latina/os and World War II: Mobility, Agency, and Ideology,* edited by Maggie Rivas-Rodriguez and B. V. Olguin, U of Texas P, 2014.

Espiritu, Yen Le. *Body Counts: The Vietnam War and Militarized Refugees.* U of California P, 2014.

Esposito, John. *The Islamic Threat.* Oxford UP, 1992.

Fabiny, Tibor. "The Ear as a Metaphor: Aural Imagery in Shakespeare's Great Tragedies." *Hungarian Journal of English and American Studies*, vol. 11, no. 1, 2005, pp. 189–201.

Fallows, James. "The Tragedy of the American Military." *Atlantic*, Jan./Feb., 2015, https://www.theatlantic.com/magazine/archive/2015/01/the-tragedy-of-the-american-military/383516/.

Fantina, Robert. *Desertion and the American Soldier: 1776–2006.* Algora, 2006.

Farrell, Mary Cronk. *Standing Up against Hate: How Black Women in the Army Helped Change the Course of World War II.* Harry N. Abrams, 2019.

Farris, Emily M., and Heather Silber Mohamed. "Picturing Immigration: How the Media Criminalizes Immigrants." *Politics, Groups, and Identities*, vol. 6, no. 4, 2018, pp. 814–24.

Farsetta, Diane. "Fake TV News: Widespread and Undisclosed." *PR Watch*, Mar. 16, 2006, https://www.prwatch.org/fakenews/execsummary.

Felman, Shoshana, and Dori Laub, editors. *Testimony: Crises of Witnessing in Literature, Psychoanalysis, and History.* Routledge, 1992.

Ferguson, Kennan. "Silence: A Politics." *Contemporary Political Theory*, vol. 2, no. 1, 2003, pp. 49–65.

Figueroa-Caballero, Andrea, and Dana Mastro. "Does Watching This Make Me Feel Ashamed or Angry? An Examination of Latino Americans' Responses to Immigration Coverage." *Journal of Cross-Cultural Psychology*, vol. 50, no. 8, 2019, pp. 937–54.

Finer, Jonathan. "Soldier Surrenders after Abandoning Iraq Unit." *Washington Post*, March 16, 2004, https://www.washingtonpost.com/archive/politics/2004/03/16/soldier-surrenders-after-abandoning-iraq-unit/adcb00e7-9c70-416c-8a81-54df2d00f558/.

Finifter, A. W., and B. Finifter. "Party Identification and Political Adaptation of American Migrants in Australia." *Journal of Politics*, vol. 51, 1989, pp. 599–630.

Fish, Stanley E. "Interpreting the Variorum." *Critical Inquiry*, vol. 2, no. 3, 1976, pp. 465–85.

Flores, David. "Politicization beyond Politics: Narratives and Mechanisms of Iraq War Veterans' Activism." *Armed Forces & Society*, vol. 43, no. 1, 2017, pp. 164–82.

Flores, John. "The Ballad of Freddy Gonzalez. The Navy Names a Battleship for a Hispanic Marine 28 Years after His Death in Vietnam." *Hispanic Magazine*, 1996.

Foley, Michael S. *Confronting the War Machine: Draft Resistance during the Vietnam War.* U of Carolina P, 2003.

Ford, Gerald R. "An Agenda for America's Third Century." Speech delivered at Tulane University, Apr. 23, 1975. *Public Papers of the Presidents: Gerald R. Ford, 1975,* book 1, 1977. https://history.state.gov/historicaldocuments/frus1969-76v38p1/d57.

Franklin, Marsha. "Dialogue: Author Tim O'Brien." Idaho Public Television, episode 18, Nov. 13, 2015. https://video.idahoptv.org/video/dialogue-author-tim-obrien/.

Franqui-Rivera, Harry. "National Mythologies: U.S. Citizenship for the People of Puerto Rico and Military Service." *Memorias: Revista Digital de Historia y Arqueología,* vol. 21, 2013, https://www.scielo.org.co/pdf/memor/n21/n21a04.pdf.

Franklin, Nancy. "Rethinking the Public Sphere: A Contribution to the Critique of Actually Existing Democracy." *Habermas and the Public Sphere,* edited by Craig J. Calhoun, MIT P, 1992.

Frevert, Ute. *Men of Honour: A Social and Cultural History of the Duel.* Translated by Anthony Williams, Polity, 1995.

Frijda, Nico H., et al., editors. *Emotions and Beliefs: How Feelings Influence Thoughts.* Cambridge UP, 2000.

Fussell, Paul. *Wartime: Understanding and Behavior in the Second World War.* Oxford UP, 1989.

Gallacher, John D., et al. "Junk News on Military Affairs and National Security: Social Media Disinformation Campaigns against US Military Personnel Veterans." Computational Propaganda Research Project, Oct. 9, 2017, https://comprop.oii.ox.ac.uk/research/vetops/.

Gallagher, Matt. "A Father's Impossible Promise." *New York Times,* Apr. 18, 2020, https://www.nytimes.com/2020/04/18/opinion/coronavirus-parenting-war.html.

———. *Kaboom: Enduring the Suck in a Savage Little War.* De Capo, 2010.

Gannon, Barbara A. *The Won Cause: Black and White Comradeship in the Grand Army of the Republic.* U of North Carolina P, 2011.

Gehrke, Pat J. "Introduction to Listening, Ethics, and Dialogue: Between the Ear and the Eye: A Synaesthetic Introduction to Listening Ethics." *International Journal of Listening,* vol. 23, 2009, pp. 1–6.

Gergen, David. "A Surge in Political Activism by America's Veterans." CNN political op-ed., May 7, 2018, https://www.cnn.com/2018/05/07/opinions/the-year-of-the-veteran-elections-opinion-gergen/index.html.

Gibson, James William. *The Perfect War: Technowar in Vietnam.* Atlantic Monthly, 1986.

Gilbert, Pail. "Evolution, Social Roles, and the Differences in Shame and Guilt." *Social Research,* vol. 70, no. 3, 2003, pp. 1205–30.

Gilbert, P., and M. McGuire. "Shame, Social Roles and Status: The Psychobiological Continuum from Monkey to Human." *Shame: Interpersonal Behavior, Psychopathology, and Culture,* edited by P. Gilbert and B. Andrews, Oxford UP, 1998.

Gilligan, James. *Violence: Reflections on a National Epidemic.* Vintage, 1997.

Gillman, Todd J. "That Harley Didn't Take MJ Hegar to the Senate." *Dallas News Online,* Dec. 1, 2020, https://www.dallasnews.com/news/politics/2020/12/01/that-harley-didnt-take-mj-hegar-to-the-senate-now-shes-selling-it-on-ebay/.

Gilmour, Peter. *The Wisdom of Memoir: Reading and Writing Life's Sacred Texts.* Saint Mary's, 1997.

Glantz, James. "Saving Face and How to Say Farewell." *New York Times,* Nov. 27, 2005.

Glenn, Cheryl. *Unspoken: A Rhetoric of Silence.* Southern Illinois UP, 2004.

Goddman, Erving. *Stigman: Notes on the Management of Spoiled Identity.* Simon & Schuster, 1963.

Goldberg, Jeffrey. "James Mattis Denounces President Trump, Describes Him as a Threat to the Constitution." *Atlantic,* June 3, 2020.

Goodwin, Gerald F. "Black and White in Vietnam." *New York Times,* July 18, 2017.

Goodwin, Jeff, et al. "Why Emotions Matter." *Passionate Politics: Emotions and Social Movements,* edited by Jeff Goodwin, James M. Jasper, and Francesca Polletta, U of Chicago P, 2001.

Goring, Darlene C. "In Service to America: Naturalization of Undocumented Alien Veterans." *Seton Hall Law Review,* vol. 31, 2000, pp. 400–478.

Gornick, Vivian. *The Situation and the Story.* Farrar, Straus and Giroux, 2002.

Gould, Deborah B. "Passionate Political Processes: Bringing Emotions Back into the Study of Social Movements." *Rethinking Social Movements: Structure, Meaning, and Emotion,* edited by Jeff Goodwin and James M. Jasper, Rowman and Littlefield, 2004.

Graham, Herman. *The Brothers' Vietnam War: Black Power, Manhood, and the Military Experience.* UP of Florida, 2003.

Grandin, Greg. *Empire's Workshop.* Henry Holt, 2006.

Gray, Chris Hables. *Postmodern War: The New Politics of Conflict.* Guilford, 1997.

Greene, John Robert. *America in the '6os.* Syracuse UP, 2010.

Grove, Gene. "The Army and the Negro." *New York Times Magazine,* July 24, 1966, https://www.nytimes.com/1966/07/24/archives/the-army-and-the-negro-the-army-and-the-negro-the-army-gave-the.html.

Gutierrez, Dave. *Patriots from the Barrio: The Story of Company E, 141st Infantry: The Only All Mexican American Army Unit in World War II.* Westholme, 2018.

Gzesh, Susan. "Central Americans and Asylum Policy in the Reagan Era." Migration Policy Institute, Apr. 1, 2006, https://www.migrationpolicy.org/article/central-americans-and-asylum-policy-reagan-era.

Halberstam, David. *The Best and Brightest.* Viking, 1973.

Hall, Stuart. "The Rediscovery of 'Ideology': Return of the Repressed in Media Study." *Culture, Society, and the Media,* edited by Michael Gurevitch et al. Methuen, 1982.

Harari, Yuval Noah. *Renaissance Military Memoirs: War, History, and Identity, 1450–1600.* Boydell, 2004.

Harvey, Frank, and John Mitten. "Fighting for Credibility: U.S. Reputation Building in Asymmetric Conflicts from the Gulf War to Syria." *Canadian Journal of Political Science,* vol. 48, no. 3., 2015, pp. 503–30.

Hattiangadi, Anita U., et al. "Non-Citizens in Today's Military: Final." CAN, Apr. 2005, pp. 1–129.

Hawk, Robert. *Florida's Army: Militia, State Troops, National Guard, 1565–1985.* Pineapple, 1987.

Hayden, Tom. *Hell No: The Forgotten Power of the Vietnam Peace Movement.* Yale UP, 2017.

Haynes, Chris, et al. *Framing Immigrants: News Coverage, Public Opinion, and Policy.* Russell Sage Foundation, 2016.

Heale, Michael. *The United States in the Long Twentieth Century: Politics and Society since 1900.* Bloomsbury, 2015.

Hegar, Mary Jennings. *Shoot Like a Girl: One Woman's Dramatic Fight in Afghanistan and on the Home Front.* Penguin Random House, 2017.

Helms, Monica F. *More Than Just a Flag,* edited by Laurence Watts. MB Books, 2019.

Hensler, Charles Peter. *There It Is . . . It Don't Mean Nothin': A Vietnam War Memoir.* Independently published, 2018.

Herlihy-Mera, Jeffrey. "Prefixes and the Limits of Rhetorical Distanciation." *After American Studies Rethinking the Legacies of Transnational Exceptionalism.* Routledge, 2018.

Herrera, Ricardo. *For Liberty and the Republic: The American Citizen as Soldier, 1775–1861.* NYU P, 2017.

Herring, George C. Foreword. *Binding Their Wounds: America's Assault on It Veterans,* edited by Robert J. Topmiller and T. Kerby Neill. Paradigm, 2011.

Herzog, Tobey C. *Vietnam War Stories: Innocence Lost.* Routledge, 1992.

———. Conversation with Tim O'Brien. *Writing Vietnam, Writing Life: Caputo, Heinemann, O'Brien, Butler.* U of Iowa P, 2008.

Hunt, Andrew E. *The Turning: A History of Vietnam Veterans against the War.* New York UP, 1999.

Huyssen, Andreas. *After the Great Divide: Modernism, Mass Culture, Postmodernism.* Indiana UP, 1986. Boydell, 2004.

Hybel, Alex R. *Power over Rationality: The Bush Administration and the Gulf Crisis.* State U of New York P, 1993.

Hynes, Samuel. *The Soldier's Tale: Bearing Witness to Modern War.* Penguin, 1997.

"Interview with Michael Anthony, Author of *Mass Casualties*." As the Pages Turn, weblog, Dec. 1, 2009, https://asthepagesturn.wordpress.com/2009/12/01/interview-with -michael-anthony-author-of-mass-casualties/.

Iraq Veterans Against the War (IVAW). "Winter Soldier Hearings: Iraq and Afghanistan. Testimony: Racism and War the Dehumanization of the Enemy," Mar. 13, 2008, https://www.ivaw.org/racism-and-war-dehumanizationenemy/mike-prysner.

Irving, Nicholas, and Gary Brozek. *The Reaper: Autobiography of One of the Deadliest Special Ops Snipers*. St. Martin's, 2015.

———. *Way of the Reaper: My Greatest Untold Missions and the Art of Being a Sniper*. St. Martin's, 2016.

Jackson, Derrick Z. "The Westmoreland Mind-Set." *New York Times*, Opinion, July 22, 2005. www.nytimes.com/2005/07/22/opinion/derrick-z-jackson-the-westmoreland -mindset.html.

Jackson, Sarah M. *The Devil Dealt the Cards: One Female Soldier's Account of Combined Action in Afghanistan*. Xlibris, 2014.

Jameson, Frederic. *Postmodernism, or, The Cultural Logic of Late Capitalism*. Duke UP, 1984.

Jeffords, Susan. "Commentary: Culture and National Identity in U.S. Foreign Policy." *Diplomatic History*, vol. 18, no. 1, 1994, pp. 91–96.

Jeffrey, James. "Memorial Day: America's Strained Salute to Its Black Veterans." BBC News, May 27, 2019.

Jelin, Elizabeth. *State Repression and the Labors of Memory*. U of Minnesota P, 2003.

Johnson, Daryl. *Right-Wing Resurgence: How a Domestic Terrorist Threat Is Being Ignored*. Rowman & Littlefield, 2012.

Johnson, Dave. "Behind the Front: The Creation of Vets for Freedom." Huffington Post, May 25, 2001, https://www.huffingtonpost.com/dave-johnson/behind-the-front-the-crea_b_27333.html.

Johnson, Lyndon B. "Remarks in the Capitol Rotunda at the Signing of the Voting Rights Act." Aug. 6, 1965. *Public Papers of the Presidents of the United States: Lyndon B. Johnson, 1965*, book 2, GPO, 1966.

Johnson, Samuel. *Taxation No Tyranny: An Answer to the Resolutions and Address of the American Congress*. Printed for T. Cadell, 1775.

Johnson, Thomas A. "G.I.'s in Germany: Black Is Bitter." *New York Times*, Nov. 23, 1970, pp. 1, 26.

———. "The U.S. Negro in Vietnam." *New York Times*, Apr. 29, 1968.

Jones, Sara. "Trump Wanted to Send in the Troops. Now Some Are Ready to Quit." *New York Magazine*, June 10, 2020, nymag.com/intelligencer/2020/06/after-pro-tests-some-soldiers-reconsider-their-service.html.

Kaiser, David. *American Tragedy: Kennedy, Johnson, and the Origins of the Vietnam War*. Belknap, 2002.

Kaplan, Robert D. "The Real Story of Fallujah: Why Isn't the Administration Getting It Out?" *Wall Street Journal*, May 27, 2004.

Karnow, Stanley. *Vietnam, a History: The First Complete Account of Vietnam at War*. Viking, 1983.

Kaufman, Gershen. *Shame: The Power of Caring*. Schenkman, 1999.

Keller, Jared. "Second Marine Veteran Identified as Charlottesville White Nationalist Leader." *Task and Purpose*, Aug. 16, 2017, https://taskandpurpose.com/news/nathan-damigo-charlottesville-marine.

Kellett, Anthony. "Combat Motivation." *Contemporary Studies in Combat Psychiatry*, edited by Gregory Belenky, Greenwood, 1987.

Kellner, Douglas. "Lying in Politics: The Case of George W. Bush and Iraq." *Cultural Studies ↔ Critical Methodologies*, vol. 7, no. 2, 2007, pp. 132–44. doi:10.1177/1532708606295649.

———. "Media Propaganda and Spectacle in the War on Iraq: A Critique of US Broadcasting Networks." *Cultural Studies ↔ Critical Methodologies*, vol. 4, no. 3, 2004, pp. 329–38.

Key, V. O. *Public Opinion and American Democracy.* Knopf, 1961.

Kilborne, Benjamin. "Superego Dilemmas." *Psychoanalytic Inquiry,* vol. 24, no. 2, 2004, pp. 175–82.

Kindell, Alexandra. "Bonus Army." *Encyclopedia of Populism in America: A Historical Encyclopedia,* edited by Alexandra Kindell and Elizabeth S. Demers, vol. 1, ABC-CLIO, 2014.

Kirbow, James. "The Problem of Face-Saving and Posturing in the Israeli-Palestinian Conflict." Examiner.com, Mar. 20, 2013, https://www.examiner.com/article/the-problem-of-face-saving-and-posturing-the-israeli-palestinian-conflict.

Kitromilides, Paschalis M. "Autobiography as Political Theory." *Il Pensiero Politico: Rivista de Storia Delle Idee Politiche e Sociali,* vol. 43, no. 1, 2010, pp. 81–86.

Klay, Phil. "The Citizen-Soldier: Moral Risk and the Modern Military." May 24, 2016, Brookings Institution, https://csweb.brookings.edu/content/research/essays/2016/the-citizen-soldier.html.

———. "Psychological Operations." *Redeployment.* Penguin, 2014.

———. "The Warrior at the Mall." *New York Times,* Opinion, Apr. 14, 2018.

Kleinreesink, Esmeralda. *On Military Memoirs: A Quantitative Comparison of International Afghanistan War Autobiographies, 2001–2010.* Egodocuments and History Series, vol. 10, Brill, 2017.

Knauer, Christine. *Let Us Fight as Free Men.* U of Pennsylvania P, 2014.

Kovic, Ron. *Born on the Fourth of July.* Pocket, 1976.

Kowalewski, Laurence R. "Tim O'Brien's *The Things They Carried:* Postmodern Fiction for a Postmodern War." *Inquiries Journal/Student Pulse,* vol. 3, no. 8, 2011, http://www.inquiriesjournal.com/a?id=568.

Krause, Kristina, and Katharina Schramm. "Thinking through Political Subjectivity." *African Diaspora,* vol. 4, 2011, pp. 115–34.

Krebs, Ronald R. "The Citizen-Soldier Tradition in the United States: Has Its Demise Been Greatly Exaggerated?" *Armed Forces & Society,* vol. 36, no. 1, Oct. 2009, pp. 153–74.

Krueger, James S., and Francisco I. Pedraza. "Missing Voices: War Attitudes among Military Service-Connected Civilians." *Armed Forces & Society,* vol. 38, 2012, pp. 391–412.

Krugler, David F. *1919, the Year of Racial Violence: How African Americans Fought Back.* Cambridge UP, 2015.

Lacquement, Richard A., Jr. "Maintaining the Professional Core of the Army." *Army,* vol. 47, 1997.

Ladd, Jonathan. *Why Americans Hate the News Media and How It Matters.* Princeton UP, 2012.

Lang, Brent. "'American Sniper' Stuns with $105.3 Million MLK Weekend." *Variety,* Jan. 19, 2015.

Laraña, Enrique, Hank Johnston, and Joseph R. Gusfield, editors. "Identities, Grievances, and New Social Movements." *New Social Movements: From Ideology to Identity,* edited by Enrique Laraña, Hank Johnston, and Joseph R. Gusfield. Temple UP, 1994.

Larson, Thomas. "The Age of Memoir." *Revie Americana,* vol. 2, no. 1, 2007, https://www.thomaslarson.com/publications/essays-and-memoirs/76-the-age-of-memoir.html.

———. *The Memoir and the Memoirist: Reading and Writing Personal Narrative.* Ohio UP, 2007.

Larson, Theresa, and Alan Eisenstock. *Warrior: True Strength Isn't Always What It Looks Like.* Harper, 2016.

Lawrence, Quil. "Soldiers Turned Authors Want You to Know: Our Books Don't Speak for All Vets." SDPD Radio, Aug. 8, 2016, audio, https://listen.sdpb.org/post/veteran-authors-look-reclaim-story-war.

Leal, David L., and Jeremy M. Teigen. "Military Service and Political Participation in the United States: Institutional Experience and the Vote." *Electoral Studies,* vol. 53, June 2018, pp.99–110.

Lee, Lieutenant Colonel Peter J. S. *This Man's Military: Masculine Culture's Role in Sexual Violence.* Drew Paper no. 26, Maxwell Air Force Base, Air UP Air Force Research Institute, 2016, https://lccn.loc.gov/2016022010.

Leicht, Robert. "Only by Facing the Past Can We Be Free." *Forever in the Shadow of Hitler? The Dispute about the Germans' Understanding of History, Original Documents of the Historikerstreit, the Controversy Concerning the Singularity of the Holocaust.* Translated by James Knowlton and Truett Cates, Humanities Press International, 1993.

Lembke, Jerry. *The Spitting Image: Myth, Memory, and the Legacy of Vietnam.* NYU P, 1998.

Lemer, Bronson. *The Last Deployment: How a Gay, Hammer-Swinging Twentysomething Survived a Year in Iraq.* U of Wisconsin P, 2011.

Levinas, Emmanuel, and Richard Kearney. "Dialogue with Emmanuel Levinas." *Face to Face with Levinas,* edited by Richard A. Cohen, State U of New York P, 1986.

Levinson, Nan. "Breaking the Code of Silence." *In These Times,* Nov. 30, 2004.

Li, Zunshuai. "A Comparative Survey of Vision Metaphors Base on the Corpus in English and Chinese." *Theory and Practice in Language Studies,* vol. 3, no. 7, 2013, pp. 1232–42.

Lifton, Robert Jay. *Home from the War: Learning from Vietnam Veterans.* Other Press, 2005.

Lind, Michael. *Vietnam: The Necessary War.* Free Press, 2002.

Linehan, Adam. "Leader of Charlottesville White Nationalist Group Was a Marine Corps Recruiter." Task and Purpose, Aug. 15, 2017, https://taskandpurpose.com/news/leader-of-charlottesville-white-nationalist-group-was-a-marine-corps-recruiter.

Litz, Brett T., et al. "Moral Injury and Moral Repair in War Veterans: A Preliminary Model and Intervention Strategy." *Clinical Psychology Review,* vol. 29, 2009, pp. 695–706.

Lodge, David. *Consciousness and the Novel: Connected Essays.* Harvard UP, 2002.

Logevall, Fredrik. *Choosing War: The Lost Chance for Peace and the Escalation of War in Vietnam.* U of California P, 1999.

Lomperis, Timothy J. *"Reading the Wind": The Literature of Vietnam War: An Interpretive Critique.* Duke UP, 1987.

Lovato, Roberto. "Latinos in the Age of National (In)Security." *NACLA, Report on the Americas,* vol. 39, no. 3, 2005, pp. 26–29. doi:10.1080/10714839.2005.11725321.

Love, Robert. "Before Jon Stewart." *Columbia Journalism Review,* Mar./Apr. 2007. https://archives.cjr.org/feature/before_jon_stewart.php.

Lucks, Daniel S. *Selma to Saigon: The Civil Rights Movement and the Vietnam War.* UP of Kentucky, 2014.

Luttrell, Marcus, and Patrick Robinson. *Lone Survivor: The Eyewitness Account of Operation Redwing and the Lost Heroes of SEAL Team 10.* Sphere, 2014.

Lyons, Paul. "Toward a Revised Story of the Homecoming of Vietnam Veterans." *Peace & Change,* vol. 23, 1998, pp. 193–200.

Maher, John. "New Lee and Low Survey Shows No Progress on Diversity in Publishing." *Publishers Weekly,* Jan. 29, 2020.

Marchi, Regina. "With Facebook, Blogs, and Fake News, Teens Reject Journalistic 'Objectivity.'" *Journal of Communication Inquiry,* vol. 36, July 2012, pp. 246–62.

Marcus, George E. "The Psychology of Emotion and Politics." *Oxford Handbook of Political Psychology,* edited by David Sears, Leonie Huddy, and Richard Jervis, Oxford UP, 2003.

———. *The Sentimental Citizen: Emotion in Democratic Politics.* Pennsylvania State UP, 2002.

Marcus, Laura. *Auto/biographical Discourses: Theory, Criticism, Practice.* Manchester UP, 1994.

Margolin, Uri. "Russian Formalism." In *Johns Hopkins Guide to Literary Theory and Criticism,* edited by Michael Groden, Martin Kreiswirth, and Imre Szeman. Johns Hopkins UP, 2005.

Margolis, Diane. *The Fabric of Self: A Theory of Ethics and Emotions.* Yale UP, 1998.

Mariscal, George. *Aztlán and Viet Nam: Chicano and Chicana Experiences of the War.* U of California P, 1999.

Matthews, Miriam, et al. "Needs of Male Sexual Assault Victims in the U.S. Armed Forces." RAND Corporation, 2018, https://www.rand.org/pubs/research_reports/RR2167.html.

McClintock, Michael. *The American Connection*, vol. 2, *State Terror and Popular Resistance in El Salvador*. Zed, 1985.

McDaniel, Nicole. "'Remaking the World' One Story at a Time in 'The Fifth Book of Peace' and 'Veterans of War, Veterans of Peace.'" *MELUS*, vol. 36, no. 1, 2011, pp. 61–81.

McDermott, Rose. "The Feeling of Rationality: The Meaning of Neuroscientific Advances for Political Science." *Rationality*, vol. 2, no. 4, Dec. 2004, pp. 691–706.

McFadden, Daniel. "A First Amendment Analysis of Military Regulations Restricting the Wearing of Military Uniforms by Members of the Individual Ready Reserve Who Participate in Politically Themed Theatrical Productions." *Boston College Law Rev.*, vol. 49, no. 4, 2008, pp. 1131–73.

McIntosh, Brock. "Veteran on *American Sniper*: The Lies Chris Kyle Told Are Less Dangerous Than the Lies He Believed." *In These Times*, Feb. 24, 2015, https://inthesetimes.com/article/17597/american_sniper_veterans.

McIntosh, Molly F., et al. "Non-Citizens in the Enlisted U.S. Military." Center for Naval Analyses Report, CAN Research Memorandum D0025768.A2/Final, Nov. 2011, https://www.cna.org/cna_files/pdf/D0025768.A2.pdf.

McIntyre, Lee. *Post-Truth*. Massachusetts Institute of Technology, 2018.

McKee, Oliver. "The Political March of the Veterans." *Commonweal*, Nov. 12, 1930, pp. 40–42.

McMahon, Robert J. "Credibility and World Power: Exploring the Psychological Dimension in Postwar American Diplomacy." *Diplomatic History*, vol. 15, no. 4, 1991, pp. 455–71.

McSorley, Kevin. *War and the Body: Militarization, Practice, and Experience*. Routledge, 2013.

Mejía, Camilo. *Road from ar Ramadi*. Haymarket, 2008.

Melling, Philip H. *Vietnam in American Literature*. Twayne, 1990.

Mencia, Robert. *From Here to Insanity: An Immigrant Boy Becomes a Citizen by Way of the Vietnam Draft*. Published by the author, 2019.

Mendelsohn, Daniel. "But Enough about Me: What Does the Popularity of Memoirs Tell Us about Ourselves?" *New Yorker*, Jan. 25, 2010, https://www.newyorker.com/magazine/2010/01/25/but-enough-about-me-2.

Menjívar, Cecilia, and Andrea Gómez Cervantes. "El Salvador: Civil War, Natural Disasters, and Gang Violence Drive Migration." Migration Policy Institute, Washington, DC, Aug. 29, 2018, https://www.migrationpolicy.org/article/el-salvador-civil-war-natural-disasters-and-gang-violence-drive-migration.

Mershon, Sherie, and Steven Schlossman. *Foxholes and Colorlines: Desegregating the U.S. Armed Forces*. Johns Hopkins UP, 1998.

Mettzler, Suzanne. *Soldiers to Citizens: The G.I. Bill and the Making of the Greatest Generation*. Oxford UP, 2005.

Miller, Nancy K. *But Enough about Me: Why We Read Each Other's Lives*. Columbia UP, 2002.

Miller, Patrick R. "The Emotional Citizen: Emotion as a Function of Political Sophistication." *Political Psychology*, vol. 32, no. 4, 2011, pp. 575–600.

Miller, Toby. *The Well-Tempered Self: Citizenship, Culture, and the Postmodern Subject*. Johns Hopkins UP, 1993.

Miller, William Ian. *Humiliation and Other Essays on Honor, Social Discomfort, and Violence*. Cornell UP, 1995.

———. *The Mystery of Courage*. Harvard UP, 2000.

Mooney, Michael J. "The Legend of Chris Kyle: The Deadliest Sniper in U.S. History Performed Near Miracles on the Battlefield. Then He Had to Come Home." *D Magazine*, April 2013, https://www.dmagazine.com/publications/d-magazine/2013/april/the-legend-of-chris-kyle-01/.

———. *The Life and Legend of Chris Kyle: American Sniper, Navy SEAL*. Back Bay, 2015.

Moore, Emma. "Women in Combat: Five-Year Status Update." Center for a New American Security, Mar. 31, 2020, https://www.cnas.org/publications/commentary/women-in-combat-five-year-status-update.

Mor, Ben D. "Using Force to Save Face: The Performative Side of War." *Peace and Change,* vol. 37, no. 1, 2012, pp. 95–121.

Morris, Aldon. *The Origins of the Civil Rights Movement: Black Communities Organizing for Change.* Free Press, 1984.

Morton, Brennan. *Dying for Strangers: Memoirs of a Special Ops Operator in Iraq.* Gatekeeper, 2015.

Moskos, Charles C., Jr. "The Marketplace All-Volunteer Force: A Critique." *The All-Volunteer Force after a Decade: Retrospect and Prospect,* edited by William Bowman, Roger Little, and G. Thomas Sicilia, Pergamon-Brassey, 1986.

Mullen, Mike. "I Cannot Remain Silent: Our Fellow Citizens Are Not the Enemy, and Must Never Become So," *Atlantic,* June 2, 2020.

Nasa, Rahima. "Marines Move to Tackle Racial Extremists in the Corps." *Frontline,* Aug. 30, 2018, https://www.pbs.org/wgbh/frontline/article/marines-move-to-tackle-racial-extremists-in-the-corps/.

Neilson, Jim. *Warring Fictions: American Literary Culture and the Vietnam War Narrative.* UP of Mississippi, 1998.

Nelsen, Aaron. "Hector Barajas Served in the American Military. He Was Deported Just the Same." Vice.com, Sept. 11, 2019, https://www.vice.com/en/article/qvgdn7/hector-barajas-served-in-the-american-military-he-was-deported-just-the-same-v26n3.

Neumann, Birgit. "Fictions of Memory." *Erinnerung–Identität–Narration: Gattungstypologie und Funktionen Kanadischer.* Gruyter, 2005.

Newport, Frank. "Imiigration Jumps as Top Problem, Still Trails Government." News, Gallop.com, Feb. 15, 2018, https://news.gallup.com/poll/227021/immigration-jumps-top-problem-trails-government.aspx.

Newton, Adam Zachary. *Narrative Ethics.* Harvard UP, 1995.

Ngai, Mae N. *Impossible Subjects: Illegal Aliens and the Making of Modern America.* Princeton UP, 2004.

Nicosia, Gerald. *Home to War: A History of the Vietnam Veterans' Movement.* Crown, 2001.

Nieto-Phillips, John. "Citizenship and Empire: Race, Language, and Self-Government in New México and Puetro Rico, 1898, 1917." *Centro Journal,* vol. 11, no. 1, 1999, pp. 70–105.

Nixon, Richard M. *The Memoirs of Richard Nixon.* Simon & Schuster, 1990.

———. *No More Vietnams.* Arbor House, 1985.

———. "Republican National Convention Acceptance Address." July 28, 1960, International Amphitheatre, Chicago, IL. American Rhetoric Online Speech Project, https://www.americanrhetoric.com/speeches/richardnixon1960rnc.htm.

———. "Speech on Cambodia." Apr. 30, 1970. Public Papers of the Presidents of the United States: Richard Nixon, 1970, 405–9, https://www.govinfo.gov/app/details/PPP-1970-book1.

Nordstrom, Carolyn. "Rape: Politics and Theory in War and Peace." *Australian Feminist Studies,* vol. 11, no. 23, 1996, pp. 147–62. doi:10.1080/08164649.1996.9994811.

Nye, Joseph. "No, President Trump: You've Weakened America's Soft Power." *New York Times,* Opinion, Feb. 25, 2020, https://www.nytimes.com/2020/02/25/opinion/trump-soft-power.html.

———. "Soft Power and Leadership." *Compass: A Journal of Leadership,* Center for Public Leadership, John F. Kennedy School of Government, Harvard University, Spring 2004, https://hbswk.hbs.edu/archive/the-benefits-of-soft-power.

———. *Soft Power: The Means to Success in World Politics.* Public Affairs, 2005.

Nyhan, Brenda, et al. "Taking Fact-Checks Literally but Not Seriously? The Effects of Journalitic Fact-Checking on Factual Beliefs and Candidate Favorability." *Political Behavior,* Jan. 2019, pp. 1–22.

Nyhan, Brenda, and Jason Reifler. "When Corrections Fail: The Persistence of Political Misperceptions." *Political Behavior,* vol. 32, no. 2, 2010, pp. 303–30.

O'Brien, Tim. "Good Form." *The Things They Carried.* Mariner, 2009.

——. "How to Tell a True War Story." *The Things They Carried.* Houghton Mifflin Harcourt, 1990.

——. *If I Die in a Combat Zone, Box Me Up and Ship Me Home.* Broadway, 1999.

——. "On the Rainy River." *The Things They Carried,* Houghton Mifflin Harcourt, 1990.

——. "President's Lecture." Brown University, Apr. 21, 1999, https://cds.library.brown.edu /projects/WritingVietnam/obrien.html.

——. *The Things They Carried.* Broadway, 1990.

——. "The Vietnam in Me." *New York Times,* Oct. 2, 1994.

O'Connor, Flannery. *Mystery and Manners: Occasional Prose.* Farrar, Straus and Giroux, 1970.

Oglesby, Carl. "Vietnamism Has Failed . . . The Revolution Can Only Be Mauled, Not Defeated." *Commonweal,* v. 90, 1969.

Oliver, Kelly. "Witnessing and Testimony." *Parallax,* vol. 10, no. 1, 2004, pp.78–87.

Oropeza, Lorena. "Fighting on Two Fronts: Latinos in the Military." *American Latinos and the Making of the United States: A Theme Study.* National Park System Advisory Board, 2013, https://www.nps.gov/heritageinitiatives/latino/latinothemestudy/pdfs /Military_web_final.pdf.

——. *¡Raza Si! ¡Guerra No! Chicano Protest and Patriotism during the Viet Nam War.* U of California P, 2005.

Ortiz, Stephen R. *Beyond the Bonus March and GI Bill: How Veteran Politics Shaped the New Deal Era.* NYU P, 2010.

Orwell, George. "Benefit of Clergy: Some Notes on Salvador Dali." The Orwell Foundation. https://www.orwellfoundation.com/the-orwell-foundation/orwell /essays-and-other-works/benefit-of-clergy-some-notes-on-salvador-dali/.

——. *Why I Write.* Penguin, 2005.

Parent, Geneviève. "Identifying Factors Promoting or Obstructing Healing and Reconciliation: Observations from an Exploratory Research Field in Ex. Yugoslavia." *International Journal of Peace Studies,* vol. 17, no. 1, 2012, pp.25–45.

Parker, Christopher S. *Fighting for Democracy: Black Veterans and the Struggle against White Supremacy in the Postwar South.* Princeton UP, 2009.

Pasquarella, Jennie. "The Impact of Current Immigration Policies on Service Members and Veterans." ACLU Report, submitted to US House Committee on the Judiciary Subcommittee on Immigration and Citizenship, Oct. 29, 2019, https://docs.house.gov /meetings/JU/JU01/20191029/110150/HHRG-116-JU01-WstatePasquarellaJ-20191029.pdf.

Patterson, Stephanie. "By an Iraqi Countryside in a Time of Violence: Brian Turner's Memoir, *My Life as a Foreign Country.*" *California English,* vol. 20, no. 3, 2015, pp. 21–23.

Paulson, Ronald. *The Fictions of Satire.* Johns Hopkins P, 1967.

Peebles, Stacey. *Welcome to the Suck: Narrating the American Soldier's Experience in Iraq.* Cornell UP, 2011.

Penn, Nathaniel. "Son, Men Don't Get Raped." *GQ Magazine,* Sept. 2, 2014, https://www .gq.com/story/male-rape-in-the-military.

Perez, Janet. "Functions of the Rhetoric of Silence in Contemporary Spanish Literature." *South Central Review,* vol. 1–2, Spring–Summer 1984, pp. 108–30.

Perry, Sam. "President Trump and Charlottesville: Uncivil Mourning and White Supremacy." *Journal of Contemporary Rhetoric,* vol. 8, no 1/2, 2018, pp. 57–71.

Pew Research Center. *Social and Demographic Trends.* Chapter 5, "The Public and the Military," Oct. 5, 2011, https://www.pewsocialtrends.org/2011/10/05/chapter-5-the -public-and-the-military/.

Phillips, Kimberley L. *War! What Is It Good For? Black Freedom Struggles in the US Military from World War II to Iraq.* U of North Carolina P, 2014.

Pierce, Todd E. "The Long Reach of Vietnam War Deceptions." *Vietnam Consortium News*, vol. 26, no. 108, Apr. 6, 2014, https://consortiumnews.com/2014/08/06/the-long-reach-of-vietnam-war-deceptions/.

Plummer, Ken. *Documents of Life 1: An Invitation to a Critical Humanism.* Sage, 2001.

Potter, W. James. "Perceived Reality in Television Effects Research." *Journal of Broadcasting & Electronic Media*, vol. 32, no. 1, 2009, pp. 23–41.

Powers, Kevin. *The Yellow Birds.* Back Bay, 2013.

Prados, John. "Essay: 40th Anniversary of the Gulf of Tonkin Incident." National Security Archive, Aug. 4, 2004.

Press, Daryl. *Calculating Credibility: How Leaders Assess Military Threats.* Cornel UP, 2005.

Proctor, Peter. *Containment and Credibility: The Ideology and Deception That Plunged America into the Vietnam War.* Carrel, 2016.

Prozorov, Sergei. "Why Is There Turth? Foucault in the Age of Post-Truth Politics." *Constellations: An International Journal of Critical and Democratic Theory*, vol. 26, no. 1, 2019, pp. 18–30. *Wiley Online Library*, doi:10.1111/1467–8675.12396.

Quinby, Lee. "The Subject of Memoirs: The Woman Warrior's Technology of Ideographic Selfhood." *De-Colonizing the Subject: The Politics of Gender in Women's Autobiography*, edited by Julia Watson and Sidonie Smith, U Minnesota P, 1992.

Rak, Julie. *Boom! Manufacturing Memoir for the Popular Market.* Wilfrid Laurier UP, 2013.

Ramsey, Neil. *The Military Memoir and Romantic Literary Cultures, 1780–1835.* Ashgate, 2011.

Ratcliffe, Krista. *Rhetorical Listening: Identification, Gender, Whiteness.* Southern Illinois UP, 2005.

Raymond, Jack. "Negro Death Ratio in Vietnam Exceeds Whites." *New York Times*, March 10, 1966, p. 4.

Ramos-Zayas, Ana. "Delinquent Citizenship, National Performances: Racialization, Surveillance, and the Politics of 'Worthiness' in Puerto Rican Chicago." *Latino Studies*, vol. 12, 2004, pp. 26–44.

Reagan, Ronald. "Address before a Joint Session of the Congress on the State of the Union." Jan. 25, 1984, The American Presidency Project, https://www.presidency.ucsb.edu/ws/?pid=40205.

———. "Remarks and a Question-and-Answer Session with Regional Editors and Broadcasters." Apr. 18, 1985, https://www.reaganlibrary.gov/archives/speech/remarks-and-question-and-answer-session-regional-editors-and-broadcasters-1.

Rein, Lisa. "VA Official Kept from Condemning Rally." Business Insights: Essentials, *Washington Post*, Dec. 5, 2018.

Reitman, Janet. "U.S. Law Enforcement Failed to See the Threat of White Nationalism. Now They Don't Know How to Stop It." *New York Times Magazine*, Nov. 3, 2018.

Ricks, Thomas E. "The Widening Gap between the Military and Society." *Atlantic Monthly*, July 1997.

Rísquez, Cristina Alsina. "Dissent as Therapy: The Case of the Veterans of the American War in Vietnam." *ATLANTIS Journal of the Spanish Association of Anglo-American Studies*, vol. 37, no. 2, 2015, pp. 99–117.

Roach, Ronald. "From Combat to Campus." *Black Issues in Higher Ed*, vol. 14, no. 2, 1997, pp. 26–29.

Robertson, James Oliver. *American Myth, American Reality.* Hill & Wang, 1980.

Robin, Corey. *Fear: The History of a Political Idea.* Oxford UP, 2004.

Rocco, Raymond. "Transforming Citizenship: Membership, Strategies of Containment, and the Public Sphere in Latino Communities." *Latino Studies*, vol. 2, 2004, pp. 4–25.

Rodewig, Cheryl. "Social Media Misuse Punishable under UCMJ." Army.mil.com, Feb. 9, 2012, https://www.army.mil/article/73367/social_media_misuse_punishable_under_ucmj.

Rohall, David E., et al. "The Effects of Military Affiliation, Gender, and Political Ideology on Attitudes toward the Wars in Afghanistan and Iraq." *Armed Forces & Society*, vol. 33, no. 1, 2006, pp. 59–77.

Roosevelt, Franklin D. "War Message to Congress, Dec. 8, 1941." *Great Issues in American History: From Reconstruction to the Present Day, 1864–1981*, edited by Richard Hofstadter and Beatrice K. Hofstadter. Revised ed., Vintage, 1982.

Rorty, Richard. "Human Rights, Rationality, and Sentimentality." *On Human Rights: The Oxford Amnesty Lectures*, edited by Stephen Shute and Susan Hurley, Basic, 1993.

Rosales, Steven. *Soldados Razos at War: Chicano Politics, Identity, and Masculinity in the U.S. Military from World War II to Vietnam.* U of Arizona P, 2017.

Rukavishnikov, Vladimir O., and Michael Pugh. "Civil-Military Relations." *Guiseppe Caforio, Handbook of the Sociology of the Military.* Kluwer Academic, 2003.

Ryan, Hugh. "The Postmodern Memoir." *Association of Writers & Writing Programs Magazine*, Mar./Apr. 2012, https://www.awpwriter.org/magazine_media/writers_chronicle_view/1887.

Sanders, Larry. *INCOMING! Memories of a Combat Medic: Growing Up Poor, Getting Drafted to Vietnam, Coming Home and Coming Out.* Independently published, 2019.

Sartre, Jean Paul. *Being and Nothingness.* Translated by Hazel E. Barnes, Washington Square, 1956.

Sassoon, Siegfried. "Dreamers." *Counter-Attack: And Other Poems (1918).* Kessinger, 2010.

Saville-Troike, Muriel. "The Place of Silence in an Integrated Theory of Communication." *Perspectives on Silence*, edited by Deborah Tannen and Muriel Saville-Troike, Ablex, 1985.

Scarry, Elaine. *The Body in Pain: The Making and Unmaking of Consciousness.* Oxford UP, 1985.

Schaeffer-Duffy, Claire. "Catholic Becomes First to Refuse Return to Iraq War." *Journal of the Catholic Peace Fellowship*, vol. 3, no. 2, Summer 2004, pp. 4–6.

Schallhorn, Kaitlyn. "Trump's Nicknames for Rivals, from 'Rocket Man' to 'Crooked ABC.'" *Fox News*, Oct. 21, 2017.

Scheer, Robert. "Bush Is Serving Up the Cold War Warmed Over." *Nation*, July, 18, 2005.

Scheff, Thomas. *Bloody Revenge: Emotions, Nationalism, and War.* Westview, 1994.

Scheff, Thomas, and Suzanne M. Retzinger. *Emotions and Violence: Shame and Rage in Destructive Conflicts.* Lexington, 1991.

Schelling, Thomas C. *Arms and Influence.* Yale UP, 1966.

Schildkraut, Deborah J. "Review Essay." *Perspectives on Politics*, vol. 2, no. 4, 2004, pp. 807–19.

Schmitt, Eric. "Iraq-Bound Troops Confront Rumsfeld over Lack of Armor." *New York Times*, Dec. 8, 2004.

Schrader, Benjamin. "The Affect of Veteran Activism." *Critical Military Studies*, vol. 5, no. 1, 2019, pp. 63–77.

Schwalbe, Michael. "Micro Militarism." *Counter Punch*, Nov. 26, 2012, https://www.counterpunch.org/2012/11/26/mico-militarism/.

Schwartz, Saul. "The Relative Earnings of Vietnam and Korean-Era Veterans." *Industrial and Labor Relations Review*, vol. 39, no. 4, July 1986, pp. 564–72.

Schweighauser, Philipp. *The Noises of American Literature, 1890–1985: Toward a History of Literary Acoustics.* UP of Florida, 2006.

Scranton, Roy. "Choosing War." *Dissent*, Winter 2016, https://www.dissentmagazine.org/article/choosing-war-nancy-sherman-afterwar-review.

———. "The Trauma Hero: From Wilfred Owen to 'Redeployment' and 'American Sniper.'" *Los Angeles Review of Books*, Jan. 25, 2015, https://lareviewofbooks.org/article/trauma-hero-wilfred-owen-redeployment-american-sniper.

Scranton, Roy, and Matt Gallagher, editors. Preface. *Fire and Forget: Short Stories from the Long War.* Da Capo Press, 2013.

Sedgwick, Eve. "Shame, Theatricality, and Queer Performativity: Henry James's *The Art of the Novel.*" *Gay Shame,* edited by David M. Halperin and Valerie Traub, U of Chicago P, 2009.

Shaheen, Jack. *Reel Bad Arabs: How Hollywood Vilifies a People.* Olive Branch Press, 2014.

Shane, Leo. "Signs of White Supremacy, Extremism up Again in Poll of Active-Duty Troops." *Military Times,* Feb. 6, 2020.

Shanker, Thom. "At West Point, a Focus on Trust." *New York Times,* May 22, 2011, Section A.

Shay, Jonathan. *Achilles in Vietnam: Combat Trauma and the Undoing of Character.* Atheneum, 1994.

Sheehan, Neil. *A Bright and Shining Lie: John Paul Vann and America in Vietnam.* Vintage, 1989.

Sherman, Ben. "You Posted What on Facebook?" *Fort Sill Cannoneer,* Aug. 6, 2012, https://www.army.mil/article/84850/you_posted_what_on_facebook.

Shields, David. *Reality Hunger: A Manifesto.* Knopf, 2010.

Shimko, Keith L. "Metaphors and Foreign Policy Decision Making." *Political Psychology,* vol. 15, no. 4, 1994, pp. 655–71. *JSTOR,* https://www.jstor.org/stable/3791625.

Shipler, David K. "Another View of Vietnam Veterans." *New Yorker,* May 2, 2015.

Sitkoff, Howard. "Racial Militancy and Interracial Violence in the Second World War." *Journal of American History,* vol. 58, no. 3, 1971, pp. 661–81.

Slater, Andrew. "As Far Inside as He Can Go: Iraq War Veteran and *The Yellow Birds* Author Kevin Power." *Poets & Writers Magazine,* vol. 42, no. 2, 2014, p. 46+.

Smith, Patricia. "Why the Vietnam War Still Matters 35 Years after It Ended." *New York Times Upfront,* vol. 142, Apr. 5, 2010, pp. 14–17.

Snyder, R. Claire. *Citizen-Soldiers and Manly Warriors: Military Service and Gender in the Civic Republican Tradition.* Rowman & Littlefield, 1999.

Soberon, Lennart. " 'The Old Wild West in the New Middle East': *American Sniper* (2014) and the Global Frontiers of the Western Genre." *European Journal of American Studies,* vol. 12, no. 2, Summer 2017. doi: https://doi.org/10.4000/cjas.12086.

Solomon, Robert C. "Justice v. Vengeance: On Law and the Satisfaction of Emotion." *The Passions of Law,* edited by Susan Bandes, NYU P, 1999.

———. *The Passions: Emotion and the Meaning of Life.* Hackett, 1993.

Sontag, Susan. "The Aesthetics of Silence." *A Susan Sontag Reader.* Farrar, Straus and Giroux, 1982.

Southall, Ashley. "A Changing of the Guard among Veterans in Congress." *Caucus Blog, New York Times,* Jan. 4, 2013, https://thecaucus.blogs.nytimes.com/2013/01/04/a-changing-of-the-guard-among-veterans-in-congress/.

Spears, Russell. "Group Identities: The Social Identity Perspective." *Handbook of Identity Theory and Research,* edited by S. J. Schwartz, K. Luyckx, and V. L. Vignoles, Springer, 2011.

Stahl, Pamela A. M. "The Legal Assistance Attorney's Guide to Immigration and Naturalization." *Military Law Review,* vol. 177, Fall 2003, pp. 1–48.

Stanley, Sharon. "Retreat from Politics: The Cynic in Modern Times." *Polity,* vol. 39, no. 3, 2007, pp. 384–407.

Steinberg, Blema S. *Shame and Humiliation: Presidential Decision Making on Vietnam.* McGill Queens UP, 1996.

Steinhauer, Jennifer. "In Battle at Capitol, Veterans Fought on Opposite Sides." *New York Times,* Feb. 10, 2021, Section A, p. 13.

Stillman, John. *Jumping from Helicopters: A Vietnam War Memoir.* Turtle Creek, 2018.

Stockdale, James Bond. *Courage under Fire: Testing Epictetus's Doctrines in a Laboratory of Human Behavior.* Stanford University, 1993.

Sturken, Marita. *Tangled Memories.* U of California P, 1997.

Suellentrop, Chris. "Polling the Troops in Iraq." *New York Times,* Mar. 2, 2006.

Sullivan, Tim. "Trump Tweet Intimating Military Will Fire on 'Looters' in Minnesota Sparks Another Warning from Twitter." *Military Times,* May 29, 2020.

Swiers, George. "'Demented Vets' and Other Myths. The Moral Obligation of Veterans." *Vietnam Reconsidered. Lessons from a War,* edited by Harrison Salisbury, Harper & Row, 1984.

Swofford, Anthony. *Jarhead.* Scribner, 2004.

Tal, Kali. *Words That Hurt: Reading the Literature of Trauma.* Cambridge, 1996.

Tangney, Juno Price, et al. "What's Moral about Self-Conscious Emotions?" *The Self-Conscious Emotions: Theory and Research,* edited by Jessica L. Tracy, Richard W. Robins, and Juno Price Tangney, Guilford Press, 2007.

Taylor, Paul, editor. "The Military-Civilian Gap: War and Sacrifice in the Pos t9/11 Era." 2011 Pew Research Center Report, https://www.pewresearch.org/wpcontent/uploads/sites/3/2011/10/veterans-report.pdf.

Teigen, Jeremy M. "Enduring Effects of the Uniform: Previous Military Experience and Voting Turnout." *Political Research Quarterly,* vol. 59, 2006, pp. 601–7.

Thompson, A. C. "Documenting Hate: New American Nazis." PBS Frontline, Nov. 20, 2018, https://www.pbs.org/wgbh/frontline/film/documenting-hate-new-american-nazis/.

Thompson, Simon, and Paul Hoggett, editors. *Politics and the Emotions: The Affective Turn in Contemporary Political Studies.* Continuum, 2012.

Tick, Edward. "Therapist in a Combat Zone." *A Perilous Calling: The Hazards of Psychotherapy Practice,* edited by Michael B. Sussman, John Wiley Press, 1995.

Toktas, Sule. "Nationalism, Militarism, and Gender; Women in the Military." *Minerva: Quarterly Report on Women and the Military,* vol. 20, no. 2, 2002, pp.29–44.

Tompkins, Paula S. "Rhetorical Listening and Moral Sensitivity." *International Journal of Listening,* vol. 23, 2009, pp. 60–79.

Topmiller, Robert J. *Red Clay on My Boots: Encounters with Khe Sanh, 1968 to 2005.* Kirk House, 2007.

Torgovnick, Marianna. "Rereading *The Iliad* in the Time of War." *PMLA,* vol .124, no. 5, 2009, pp. 1838–41.

"Transcript of General Dwight D. Eisenhower's Order of the Day (1944)." Supreme Headquarters Allied Expeditionary Force. US National Archives and Records Administration, https://www.ourdocuments.gov/doc.php?doc=75&page=transcript.

Trowbridge, Gordon. "Today's Millitary: Right, Republican, and Principled." *Marine Corps Times,* Jan. 5, 2004.

Truax, Barry. *Acoustic Communication.* Ablex, 2001.

Trujillo, Charley. *Soldados: Chicanos in Viet Nam.* Chusma House, 1990.

Turner, Brian. "Illumination Rounds." *Phantom Noise.* Alice James, 2010.

———. *My Life as a Foreign Country.* Norton, 2014.

Tuttle, Kate. "Army Medic Shares Tales from Dark Side in *Mass Casualties*." BostonGlobe.com, Dec. 22, 2016.

US Army/Marine Corps. *Counterinsurgency Field Manual.* FM 3–24, 2007, https://www.fas.org/irp/doddir/army/fm3-24.pdf.

US Citizenship and Immigration Services (USCIS). "Military Naturalization Statistics: Statistics through Fiscal Year 2018." https://www.uscis.gov/military/military-naturalization-statistics.

US Department of Defense (DoD). "2017 Demographics: Profile of the Military Community." 2017, https://download.militaryonesource.mil/12038/MOS/Reports/2017-demographics-report.pdf.

Vakili, Bardis, et al. "Discharged Then Discarded: How US Veterans Are Banished by the Country They Swore to Protect." ACLU Report, July 2016, https://www.aclusandiego.org/wp-content/uploads/2017/07/DischargedThenDiscarded-ACLUofCA.pdf.

Vandello, J. A., et al. "Precarious Manhood." *Journal of Personality and Social Psychology,* vol. 95, 2008, pp. 1325–39.

Van Reet, Brian. "A Problematic Genre, the 'Kill Memoir.'" *New York Times,* July 16, 2013, https://atwar.blogs.nytimes.com/2013/07/16/a-problematic-genre-the-war-on-terror-kill-memoir/.

Vera, Hernan, and Andrew M. Gordon. *Screen Saviors: Hollywood Fictions of Whiteness.* Rowman & Littlefield, 2003.

Vernon, Alex. *Arms and the Self: War, the Military, and Autobiographical Writing.* Kent State UP, 2005.

———. "Submission and Resistance to the Self as Soldier: Tim O'Brien's Vietnam War Memoir." *A/B: Auto/Biography Studies,* vol. 17, no. 2, 2002, pp.161–79.

Voegelin, Salome. *Listening to Noise and Silence: Towards a Philosophy of Sound Art.* Continuum, 2010.

von Clausewitz, Carl. *On War.* Translated by J. J. Graham, Wordsworth Editions, 1997.

Voss, Tom. *Where War Ends: A Combat Veteran's 2,700-Mile Journey to Heal.* New World Library, 2019.

Waldinger, R., T. Soehl, and N. Lim. "Emigrants and the Body Politic Left Behind: Results from the Latino National Survey." *Journal of Ethnic and Migration Studies,* vol. 38, no. 5, 2012, pp. 711–36.

Walker, Rob B. J. "Gender and Critique in the Theory of International Relations." *Gendered States: Feminist (Re)Visions of International Relations Theory,* edited by V. Spike Peterson. Lynne Rienner, 1992.

Weber, Cynthia. *Imagining America at War: Morality, Politics, and Film.* Routledge, 2006.

Weigel, David. "*American Sniper,* the Official Oscar Nominee of the Culture Wars: Conservatives Embrace the New Clint Eastwood Film." *Bloomberg News,* Jan. 19, 2015.

Weisger, Alex, and Keren Yarchi-Milo. "Revisiting Reputation: How Past Actions Matter in International Politics." *International Organization,* vol. 69, no. 2, 2015, pp. 473–95.

Welke, Barbara Young. *Law and the Borders of Belonging in the Long Nineteenth Century United States.* Cambridge UP, 2010.

Wesley, Marilyn. "Truth and Fiction in Tim O'Brien's *If I Die in a Combat Zone* and *The Things They Carried.*" *College Literature,* vol. 29, no. 2, 2002, pp. 1–18.

West, L. "The Real American Sniper was a Hate-Filled Killer." *Guardian,* Jan. 6, 2015, https://www.theguardian.com/commentisfree/2015/jan/06/real-american-sniper-hatefilled-killer-why-patriots-calling-hero-chris-kyle.

Westen, Drew. *The Political Brain: The Role of Emotion in Deciding the Fate of Nations.* Public Affairs, 2007.

Westheider, James E. *The African American Experience in Vietnam: Brothers in Arms.* Rowman & Littlefield, 2008.

Williams, Chad L. *Torchbearers of Democracy: African American Soldiers in World War I.* U of North Carolina P, 2013.

Williams, Kayla, and Lindsey Church. "The Deafening Silence of Veteran Service Organizations on Black Lives Matter." *Task & Purpose,* June 9, 2020.

Williams, R. "Department of Defense Salutes African-American Korean War Veterans." *Department of Defense News,* July 2001.

Winter, Jay. "Thinking about Silence." *Shadows of War: A Social History of Silence in the Twentieth Century,* edited by Efrat Ben-Ze'ev, Ruth Ginio, and Jay Winter, Cambridge UP, 2010.

Woehrle, L. M., et al. *Contesting Patriotism: Culture, Power, and Strategy in the Peace Movement.* Rowman & Littlefield, 2008.

Wolfe, Christopher Paul. "Sir, I Never Thought I'd See the Day I'd Be Working for a Colored Officer." *New York Times Magazine,* Feb. 7, 2019, https://www.nytimes.com/2019/02/07/magazine/army-racism-west-point.html.

Wong, Leonard, et al. *Why They Fight: Combat Motivation and the Iraq War.* Strategic Studies Institute, Army War College, 2003.

Wood, John. *Veteran Narratives and the Collective Memory of the Vietnam War.* Ohio UP, 2016.

Woodward, Rachel, and K. Neil Jenkings. "'This Place Isn't Worth the Left Boot of One of Our Boys': Geopolitics, Militarism and Memoirs of the Afghanistan War." *Political Geography,* vol. 31, no. 8, 2012, pp. 495–508.

Wolfe, Tobias. "Interview." *Believer,* May 2005, https://www.believermag.com/issues/200505/?read=interview_wolff.

———. *In Pharaoh's Army: Memories of a Lost War.* Vintage, 1995.

Wright, Evan. *Generation Kill.* Berkley Caliber, 2008.

Wyatt-Brown, Bertram. *Honor and Violence in the Old South.* Oxford UP, 1986.

Yagoda, Ben. *Memoir: A History.* Riverhead, 2009.

Yglesias, Jose. *One German Dead.* Eremite Press, 1988.

Young, John K. *Black Writers, White Publishers: Marketplace Poltics in Twentieth-Century African American Literature.* U of Mississippi P, 2006.

———. "The Textual 'Truth' behind Tim O'Brien's *The Things They Carried.*" U of Texas Austin Harry Ransom Center: *Ransom Center Magazine,* June 20, 2017, https://sites.utexas.edu/ransomcentermagazine/2017/06/20/the-textual-truth-behind-tim-obriens-the-things-they-carried/.

Zaller, John R. *The Nature and Origins of Mass Opinion.* Cambridge UP, 1992.

Zepeda-Millán, C. *Latino Mass Mobilization: Imiigration, Racialization, and Activism.* Cambridge UP, 2017.

Zimbardo, Phillip. *The Lucifer Effect: Understanding How Good People Turn Evil.* Random House, 2008.

Zong, Jie, and Jeanne Batalova. "Immigrant Veterans in the United States." Migration Policy Institute, May 16, 2019, https://www.migrationpolicy.org/article/immigrant-veterans-united-states-2018.

INDEX

MYRA MENDIBLE was born in Cuba and grew up in Miami, where she earned a PhD in English from the University of Miami. She was a National Hispanic Scholar, an American Association of University Women fellow, a National Endowment for the Arts grant recipient, and a founding faculty member of Florida Gulf Coast University in Fort Myers, Florida, earning the university's "Top 20" excellence award for her contributions. Myra has published widely in national and international journals and anthologies, and is editor of three books, From *Bananas to Buttocks: The Latina Body in Popular Film and Culture* (2007), *Race 2008: Critical Reflections on an Historic Campaign* (2010), and *American Shame: Stigma and the Body Politic* (2016). She teaches for the English and Integrated Studies programs at FGCU and is a fellow for the university's Center for Critical Race and Ethnicity Studies. Myra lives with her hubby, two cats, and a ninety-five-pound baby, her Dogo Argentino, Billy.